# WOMEN

## A GRASSROOTS GUIDE

# FOR A

## TO ACTIVISM

# CHANGE

## AND POLITICS

**Thalia Zepatos**
**and**
**Elizabeth Kaufman**

☑®
Facts On File, Inc.
AN INFOBASE HOLDINGS COMPANY

**Women for a Change: A Grassroots Guide to Activism and Politics**

Facts On File, Inc.
11 Penn Plaza
New York NY 10001

**Library of Congress Cataloging-in-Publication Data**
Zepatos, Thalia, 1955–
    Women for a change : a grassroots guide to activism and politics /
by Thalia Zepatos and Elizabeth Kaufman.
        p.   cm.
    Includes bibliographical references and index.
    ISBN 0-8160-3032-4 (hb)
    ISBN 0-8160-3492-3 (pbk)
    1. Women political activists—Training of—United States.
    2. Politics, Practical—United States.   3. Women in politics—United
    States.   4. Political participation—United States.   I. Kaufman,
    Elizabeth.   II. Title.
    HQ1391.U5Z47   1995
    324'.023'73—dc20                                           94-42402

Facts On File books are available at special discounts when purchased in bulk quantities for businesses, associations, institutions, or sales promotions. Please call our Special Sales Department in New York at 212/967-8800 or 800/322-8755.

MP VC   10   9   8   7   6   5   4   3   2

This book is printed on acid-free paper.
Printed in the United States of America

For Our Nieces . . .
Martha Kaufman, Rachel Philofsky,
Alexis Zepatos, and Jacqueline Zepatos
. . . And Their Nieces.

# Contents

# Acknowledgments

We are indebted to our agent, Susan Schulman, who inspired this project, and to our editor, Caroline Sutton, who enthusiastically supported our vision.

For energetic and committed research assistance, we gratefully acknowledge Sydne Didier, Holly Pruett, and Sheryl Sackman. Our thanks go to Carolyn Alcoke, Andrea Carlisle, Linda Ginenthal, Eleanor Haas, Sheryl Sackman, and the Tuesday Night Writers for reading and commenting on the manuscript.

Our appreciation to The Center for the American Woman and Politics at Rutgers University, and the Oregon State University Library in Corvallis for invaluable assistance.

We extend our loving appreciation to the many friends, family, and colleagues who cheered us on and helped us along the way, including Gabe Eisenstein, Ann Filloramo, Karen Hart, Ruth Kaufman, Tony Lafrenz, Tom Norton, Suzanne Pharr, Beverly Stein, and Ken Walker.

Finally, we would like to thank and acknowledge the many political women we've interviewed, talked with, organized with, strategized with, campaigned and run for office with. Long may you run!

# Introduction

▬▬▬▬▭▭▭▭

We'll be the first to admit . . . we think women can and should change the world. We're hoping that you will jump in to become part of that change.

Frankly, we're not out to promote a bunch of "good ol' boys" in skirts. As Gloria Steinem says, "Having someone who looks like us but thinks like them is worse than having no one at all." We believe that women can redefine leadership and open the political process to address the real social and economic needs of our people.

In promoting this new kind of leadership, we're looking for women who are bright, progressive, and committed to social change. Women who believe in justice and equality for all. Women who awake in the morning and go to sleep at night with strong convictions.

If you've ever thought about talking back to the TV, writing a letter to the editor, shaking your fist at city hall, or stepping forward to run for political office, you know that strong convictions have to be backed up by practical strategies.

*Women for a Change: A Grassroots Guide to Activism and Politics* is designed to give you the tools to build power. We'll share our definition of activist politics, and our ideas on how to jump the hurdles that may hold you back. We'll describe the realities of the political system, and regale you with stories of American women who've turned the system upside down.

This book tells you how to form a group to fight for power, and outlines the skills you need for leadership. We'll show you how you can get involved for as little as an hour per week, or broaden your commitment from volunteer to a whole new career. We'll explain how political campaigns work, and give you a timeline to prepare for your own run for office. And we'll provide ideas on how to raise the money you need to get the job done. Throughout the book, we'll suggest whom to call and what to read for further information.

Women's electoral involvement is a key component of political activism. In essence, while the 1992 elections were a milestone in the progress of women winning seats as elected officials, the 1994 elections brought us back to the realities of slow but steady progress in increasing our numbers in office. It is our intention to encourage many more women to go the distance.

In short, this book includes all our favorite organizing and campaign tips to help you get started as an activist or candidate. And we've interviewed dozens of activist women from coast to coast, from small towns and big cities, to learn the wisdom and lessons of their lives. Excerpts from our conversations, which are not formally footnoted, appear throughout the book, including a section at the end of each chapter entitled "Women Who Dare." We hope you are as dazzled and motivated by these ordinary women who've accomplished extraordinary results from activism as we are.

As former sharecropper Early Mae Wallace told us,

*"If you don't stand for something, you'll fall for anything."*

We invite you to take a stand.

                                        ELIZABETH KAUFMAN AND THALIA ZEPATOS
                                        PORTLAND, OREGON

# Why Politics?

Welcome to the world of politics! Whether you're turned on by the idea of getting involved in issues, or frustrated with what's going on in your community, the political arena has room for you.

Politics can be a woman-friendly, accessible, scintillating aspect of our busy lifes. In fact, politics should help provide a break from ordinary daily routines, and perk up the adventurous, strategic, and righteously responsible in us. While we sometimes feel disappointed with the way politics works, perhaps that's because we've allowed it to be defined by the "old boys," a small group of power-mongers, who keep power out of our reach and personify the dark side of public life. We invite you to explore the multitude of opportunities, avenues, and techniques available to women for success in the political arena.

## WHAT IS POLITICS?

More and more women are stepping into the place and practice of politics. They've jumped in, turned on the lights, and galvanized others to join them. In smaller corners of their lives or on center stages, women are changing the black hole of politics to what it should be: the methods, maneuvers, principles, and practices of public affairs.

Increasingly, women are realizing that politics is *involvement* in the way our common lives are run, cared for, and supported. Politics is governing bodies from block clubs and elementary school councils, to groups pursuing animal rights or acting on incidents of workplace discrimination. It embraces student councils and activist attention to the safety of children's toys.

Further, politics is the action of vying for power. It is access to the guarantee of fairness and justice in our lives and those of our neighbors, coworkers, fellow and sister students. Politics is a stimulating challenge, an opportunity, and our contribution to society. And no matter what issue really influences us, politics is the effort we expend to achieve power and, in turn, derive a change, a policy, or a result that is in our self-interest.

*I always felt that if there is something wrong, you can't just sit back and watch it happen, you have to do something about it. That's why I'm a constant letter writer—I call, anything, that's how I am.*
            —GENEVIEVE RICHARDS–WRIGHT
            1993 BLACK EDUCATOR'S TEACHER OF THE YEAR

## HOW WOMEN CAN STEP FORWARD AND GET INVOLVED

*I have a sense that people before me have made certain things possible, opened up certain avenues that weren't there before. And so I draw some inspiration from them and then try to pass some of that on. It's kind of an historical highway that's out there. And I really encourage people to figure out how they can feel a part of that.*
            —LISA JO BROWN
            WASHINGTON STATE REPRESENTATIVE

A broader definition of politics calls for an expansion of the roster of players. In fact, politics involves many more people and portions of society than just government. *Politics includes everyone who has power:* both those who claim power and those who display potential power. From giant, multi-national corporations to the corner Christmas tree vendors, from the PTA group to the women's association at work, from the neighborhood newsletter to the largest television network—all are players in the universe of politics.

A wide angle lens on the political landscape reveals that women are not only seeking and gaining a presence in every aspect of political life but are increasingly present on the horizon of leadership roles. Ten years ago, there were just two women serving in the United States Senate out of the fifteen *ever* elected to that body in the 185 years of our country's history. Now, seven women are serving, for a total of 22. In 1992, we finally elected the first African-American woman United States senator.

## In 1994, Women Held Public Office in Greater Numbers Than Ever Before:

- The number of women mayors, of cities with populations over 30,000, is 172 of 973, a tenfold increase over the past 20 years. Among the 100 largest United States cities, 18 have women mayors.
- 1,517 out of 7,424 state legislators are women, of which 13.5%, or 205 are women of color.
- 48 women from 27 states serve in the United States House of Representatives and there are 7 women United States senators; In 1990, the numbers were 28 representatives and 2 senators.[1]
- 14 members of Congress are women of color.
- Four women are state governors, 11 are lieutenant governors.

## Other Political Strides We've Made:

- Women now comprise 41% of all managers in the United States.
- For the first time, in 1993, women-owned small businesses employed more Americans than all the Fortune 500 companies combined.
- Women comprise fully 37% of the membership of the nation's trade unions.[2]
- Women hold 40% of the news and editorial staff jobs at American newspapers, according to the Newspaper Association of America. The majority of television and radio news shows now include a woman anchor.

Further, women lead activist, issue-oriented organizations that vie directly for power in our society—from women's concerns and environmental groups to labor unions to senior citizen organizations. When people think of women and activism, they typically conjure up the

names of national women's organizations. Often we overlook the huge
number of community and issue-based organizations that are run by
women, who strive not only to achieve pay equity with men and outlaw
sexual harassment and exploitation, but also to lower defense spending
in favor of programs for children and families, increase gun control,
and create economic development opportunities in rural areas.

Women organize to improve conditions for low income, single mothers, immigrants, the disabled, and the mentally ill. They work to gain
more attention and resources for elderly shut-ins. They lead groups
that provide and advocate for low-cost medical care to the indigent.
Women head organizations that train successful marketers, independent travelers, and workers in traditional male trades. These groups
accomplish real victories for people in our society; providing tangible
services and sounding a voice for the underrepresented. Women demand attention to needs and concerns that aren't often the priority of
government, business communities, or news media.

From the volunteer to the paid organizer, to the prominent leader,
to the reporter, a growing number of women want to get in and "do"
politics. This increasing number of women activists can walk the road
paved by a small number of preceeding women who stepped forward to
win their place in the public arena.

## WHY WE NEED STILL MORE

■ For years, Susan Hadley played tennis four times a week and
drove her children to numerous activities. Her life changed the day
she dropped her son off at church and stopped in downstairs to ask
about their battered women's crisis line.

■ Bernice Kaczynski didn't know she was an activist, until her city
and a large corporation decided to try to tear down her home and her
community.

■ In the 12 years since Candy Lightner's daughter was killed, she
spearheaded and inspired the formation of Mothers Against Drunk
Driving (MADD), the group largely responsible for getting 1,200 new
laws passed nationwide.

A great many more women must get involved because:

**1.** Women are more likely to advocate and activate others around
issues that *benefit people*, illustrated by the percentage of organizations

devoted to human interest issues, whose leaders and members are largely females. As activists, as officeholders, and as public interest workers, our priority issues are education, health care, housing, jobs, and environmental protection. The more leaders with these priorities, the more we can look forward to progress made in each area. We're not in it for money or acclaim; we really want to make the world a better place.

**2.** Women are the best force to agitate for equal rights, for respect, and the effective use of our abilities in the world. As evidenced over and over, from the defeat of the Equal Rights Amendment, to the 125 year struggle to win the right to vote, it is clear that the "powers-that-be" will not simply *hand over* equality to women. We cannot be absent during the debates concerning women's issues and rights. It is incumbent upon *us* to organize, promote women leaders, and win equal status.

**3.** Women know what it is like to be on the outside.

*Whether you're a Republican or Democrat, if you're a woman you understand what it means to be an outsider. You understand what it means to be powerless . . . The absence of women in any elective body means that the concerns of over half the population in that city, town, or state will not be addressed.*

—IRENE NATIVIDAD
NATIONAL COMMISSION ON WORKING WOMEN

Until the percentage of women in leadership positions reflects our percentage of the population, we will remain outsiders. As outsiders, we sacrifice the opportunity to provide input on critical issues directly affecting our lives:

- Should we continue to depend on energy from nuclear power plants?
- Should our country step in to help end atrocities like those experienced in Bosnia and Rwanda?
- Should women hold at least half of the elected and appointed public offices in our country?
- Should we welcome the diversity of other languages into our schools and communities, or should we require that everyone speak English in public institutions?
- Should we deny equal rights to gay men and lesbians?
- Should women continue to work in situations in which others are allowed to harass you, pay you less, and be promoted over you?

When women are not involved sufficiently in answering these questions (and working toward their reconciliation), we allow others to make the decisions for us, decisions we may not agree with. It's that simple. When we get involved, our voices are heard, and our power is taken seriously. When we tune out, remain uninformed, or refuse to participate, we hand the future to others. When we stand up, speak out, organize, and fight for our position, we encourage others to do the same, empower the less powerful, and sometimes win positive change.

**4.** Finally, it takes a *lot* of people continually involved and working for change in order to win on our issues. The number of critical issues facing us is not getting any smaller. Nor are the institutions we must confront to make change—the government, the churches, the corporations, the media—are not getting smaller. It's no longer possible to sit back and expect our elected officials and community leaders to solve complicated problems. Rather, *we have to back them up with our own activism.* The process is not only absolutely necessary, it's fun, exciting, and even addicting.

With the plethora of critical issues developing every day, there are innumerable access points where women can jump in to make a difference. Whether you have an hour a week, or would like a job as a full-time activist, there's a place and a serious need for you. The more individual women are involved, the more women have power, and the more women have power, the more we will affect decision-making processes. Not only will we increase the number of activists and leaders, we'll adjust the issue priorities, and bring a change in the style of taking action and leadership that will benefit everyone.

## Women Lead Differently—the Secret's Out

Simple observation, backed up by numerous formal studies, indicates a marked difference in the way women, as opposed to men, lead others. Three areas in particular, clearly manifest these differences:

### *Power* with, *not power over*

*Access to decision-making is critical if people are to own and be excited about decisions made in their name. Leadership becomes not the ability to make decisions for people, but the ability to excite, persuade and energize people about making certain choices and moving in a certain direction.*[3]

Women leaders include more employees and constituents participation in decision-making. Women value others' contributions. They exercise power through inclusion rather than commanding and using "titles." They use consensus building instead of hierarchical decision-making. Many women leaders take their constituents into account at every step in the process of governing and managing. A study from the *Harvard Business Review* summarizes women leaders as *"more likely to encourage participation, share power and information, enhance other people's self-worth and get others excited about their work."*[4]

In 1974, Clara Dunn, the first Roman Catholic nun elected to a state house seat, described the reason many believe women tend to share power: "The decision-making of women will be shaped by different values. I believe women have learned something from having been excluded from power so long. They have suffered. Suffering teaches you something about the use of both power and money."[5]

Often as a result of former exclusion, women leaders and office-holders actively change the way government works, by bringing more citizens into the process. They conduct legislative business in public view instead of behind closed doors, and provide greater access for the economically disadvantaged to the legislative process. Indeed, these changes are why more people are likely to vote for a woman candidate.

### Women have significant and distinctive perspectives on issues

*If we really believe, as I've heard over and over during the last three years, that our political leaders don't have a clue about real life, look for a woman. I've rarely met a woman who didn't know more about the supermarket, the bus stop, and the prevailing winds than her male counterparts. Not to mention about child care, human rights, abortion, the minimum wage, and sexual harassment.*[6]

—ANNA QUINDLEN

## Women Activists and Officeholders Are More Likely Than Men to Prioritize Pressing Issues of Concern to Women, Children, and Families, as Indicated by a Wide Variety of Studies and Polls.

- After the economy and jobs, health care is women's biggest concern.
- Women are more likely to favor measures to protect the environment, and to check the growth of nuclear power.
- Women are more supportive of efforts to achieve racial equality than men.
- Women are less militaristic on issues of war and peace.
- 80% of women and 62% of men favor a national family medical leave law.

- 70% of women favor laws making it harder to buy firearms; 50% of men do.
- 66% of women consider unequal pay a very serious problem for women in the workplace; 50% of men agree.
- Women public officials are more likely to give priority to public policies related to their traditional roles as caregivers in family and society, issues concerning children, health, aging, education, environment, and housing.
- Women officials are more likely to give top priority to women's rights policies.[7]

Women are more likely to consider the specific effects of a potential policy on women and children. For example, in seeking to encourage more use of public transportation, the New Jersey Department of Transportation listened to women serving on the committee working to augment the state's park-and-ride facilities. Women suggested recruiting useful commercial services—dry-cleaners and convenience stores—to locate at the park-and-ride sites, allowing commuters to complete their errands more easily. Men realize that their needs are also served by this approach.[8]

### "No simple solutions to complex problems"

Multnomah County, Oregon, Chair Beverly Stein issued this warning recently to a group of prospective women candidates. From her experience, Stein believes that women enter public office largely for different reasons from men. Men are more likely to enter political office because they seek a leadership title and believe they can be elected. Once in office, men accept that part of their job is to address issues. Most women, on the other hand, have very recently realized they are electable, and are more likely to undertake political efforts because women want to confront and solve our society's most obstinate problems. They are skilled in making important connections between previously isolated issues, and address them more comprehensively.

It follows that when issues are taken seriously, there are no simple solutions to complex problems. One example is crime. Many women activists understand that decreasing the incidence of crime requires attacking it from a number of angles—job creation, adequate wages, gun control, punishing domestic violence, pre-natal and children's health care, and facilitating the means for the have-nots to contribute to the community. This strategy involves a lengthy timeline for addressing the issue by providing comprehensive family support systems to replace criminal behavior. It does not treat crime as a sickness that can be expeditiously cured with a simple answer or solution.

## JUST DO IT!

Three typical women explain why they got involved in politics:[9]

Susan Hadley led a solid middle class life which, she felt, needed something more:

Even though I grew up in an upper middle class family, I knew that women were not treated fairly in this culture, and that made me angry. I've seen the injustice and I picked one facet of that injustice to work on.

I started volunteering at a crisis line for battered women while I was doing my graduate work in public health. And I thought, "What happens to a battered woman when she enters an emergency room?" I did some research on what was available around the country, and found that only one woman at Yale New Haven Hospital was trying to get them to identify battered women who walked in. This woman was the pioneer because no one else was doing this work.

In 1986, I went to a local hospital, Fairview Medical, and talked with some people about identifying and helping battered women who came to the hospital. Not long after, I set up a nonprofit organization called WomanKind, Inc., to provide this service.

We train emergency room staff. First we cover "Domestic Violence 101"—how to identify battered women and understand the myths relating to domestic abuse. Then we discuss intervention—what to say to her. Then we train them on the role WomanKind plays, which is to connect battered women with the appropriate community service—from shelters to job training programs. This makes the health care provider's jobs easier. I knew if it wasn't in their best interest to use me, I wouldn't be called in.

In the beginning stages, I was on 24-hour call, and I had several volunteers who took calls with me when abused women were identified in the emergency room. I slowly built a corps of volunteers over the years—one has been with us since 1986. The job of the volunteer advocates is to acknowledge the battered woman's experiences—listen to her, believe her, and supporting her—then lay out her options and support her choices, no matter what. They may not be the changes we want her to make. The goal is to respect her process and timetable.

What we accomplished at this Minneapolis-area hospital is a fundamental change in the health care system. Offering services for battered women through health care has now become acceptable and accepted. As of mid-1994, we have served over 7,000 clients.

There's no violence or abuse in my family. I did it because I felt there was a problem that truly needed to be remedied. Probably the reason I turned my whole life over to WomanKind is that I needed the professional and personal growth.

When life dealt her a supreme tragedy, Candy Lightner became political. After her daughter was killed by a drunk driver, Lightner jumped in to help prevent that fate for others. She worked for five years to build Mothers Against Drunk Driving (MADD) into an impressively successful activist organization.

MADD became the force behind tougher laws to prevent accidents involving drunk drivers. Among the statutes passed with the help of MADD are those that raised the drinking age from 18 to 21 in many states. Today, MADD includes more than 400 chapters in 48 states and a membership of 2.8 million people.[10]

Lightner has moved on to new work, including a book on grieving for the death of a loved one and another book on MADD. She promoted Arab-American culture (she is of Lebanese descent) and recently lobbied at the federal level. Her life circumstances led her to political activism. Now Candy Lightner can't turn back.

Bernice Kaczynski was a housewife who lived all her life in Hamtramack, a largely Polish neighborhood known as Poletown in Detroit, Michigan. Taking on the world's largest corporation, General Motors, was not going to be easy. Yet Kaczynski, and thousands of other homeowners, business owners, pastors, and community leaders had no choice; either confront this giant or lose their entire community to a new Cadillac assembly plant.

The neighborhood was a rich mix of ethnicities, half of whom were older people, 80% had incomes under $10,000 a year, and most owned the homes they had lived in most of their lives, as had their parents. General Motors maneuvered an agreement from the mayor of Detroit, Coleman Young, and the city council to raze the neighborhood, displacing all 3,500 residents for the new car factory. General Motors would pay only $8 million of the $200 million cost. Taxpayers picked up the balance.

Kaczynski and a dedicated group of neighborhood residents organized valiantly to protest this injustice. With little or no prior experience, they confronted the corporation with a variety of tactics. They "flyered" the neighborhood to inform the public, organized protest rallies and marches, held community meetings, wrote to politicians, went to court, sought out the media, and physically tried to block demolitions.

While they lost the fight, Kaczynski and the activists of Poletown revealed to the larger Detroit community that General Moters was neither the responsible neighbor nor the boost to the area's dying economy that it claimed to be. Kaczynski's organizing exposed the truth of the situation. General Motors had promised thousands of jobs from the new plant, that number dwindled to 6,000, then to 3,000, and then to 3,000 replacement jobs for those who had lost jobs when two other General Motors plants were closed. A majority of the 150 small businesses in Poletown closed, costing the jobs of thousands. About that many jobs of General Motors workers were saved.

What was clear to Kaczynski during the fight was the substantial contribution of women in the neighborhood:

> Just about every day we had meetings trying to figure out what to do. Women played a more important role than men did . . . I think we find it more natural to go out and fight for what we think is right . . . The women went through all the stages everyone else went through—the same shock, and denial, and depression. But they were astute; they never lost sight of the fact that their rights were being violated . . . They were angry, and they channeled that anger in a constructive way. The women put themselves out front. They were the conscience of what was going on . . . Whether it's a lost cause or not, you still have to go to the bitter end.[11]

When women get involved in social change, they provide forceful role models for other women. If we see women organize, fight, run for office, win, and hold leadership positions in the community, government and business, then they believe other women can do so too. And if we don't have local women speaking and organizing, leading, and contending for power, then other women are likely to be more hesitant about trying it.

Fortunately, more and more women are stepping forward and providing models and motivation for us to do it ourselves.

- In the tradition of Eleanor Roosevelt, Hillary Rodham Clinton is helping to change forever the lack of consideration by many Americans for the first lady's intelligence.
- Ann Richards, former governor of Texas, put hard-driving chutzpah and enthusiasm at the helm of power.

- Mary Robinson won the presidency of Ireland on a platform supporting the right of women to choose an abortion, in a country where merely discussing the topic has been illegal.
- Hanan Ashrawi of the Palestine Liberation Organization has exponentially raised the level of intelligent debate around the Mideast peace negotiations.
- Jocelyn Elders, the former surgeon general of the United States, brought unique dignity, courage, and outspokenness to a prominent public position.
- Florence Graves of the *Washington Post* persists in breaking controversial news stories, such as the sexual harassment charges against Senator Bob Packwood.
- Dorothy Lee Bolden organized the National Domestic Workers Union, which improved the wages and working conditions of domestic workers, first in the South, and later, nationally.
- Martha Wollstein earned admittance as the first woman member of the American College of Pediatrics in 1930, a time when it was difficult for women to gain the right to become doctors.
- Jackie Barrett, the first female African-American sheriff in the nation, oversees a $28 million budget and 900 deputies and civilian employees in the Atlanta, Georgia area.

Now it's your turn to get involved, for your daughters, sisters, grandchildren, neighbors, and potential activists everywhere.

*"It's time to imagine a change . . . Step through the looking glass and there (will be) 47 female governors, 45 state attorneys general, 499 Fortune 500 CEO's, countless college presidents, labor leaders, Army generals, network heads."* [12]

The question is not whether there's work to do, it's what to do, and how to do it.

**Notes**

[1] John Harwood and Geraldine Brooks, "Ms. President: Other Nations Elect Women to Lead Them, So Why Doesn't U.S.?, *Wall Street Journal*, December 14, 1993, p. A1.

[2] Median weekly earnings for women union members were 35% higher than median weekly earning for non-union women employees. See *United Auto Workers Research Bulletin*, prepared by the Research Department, UAW, Detroit, Michigan, May 1994, p. 9.

[3] Nancy Sylvester, "Women and Public Office: Creating Alternative Approaches," *The Catholic World, vol. 234, no. 1404,* November-December 1991, p. 268.

[4] Study commissioned by the International Women's Forum, in Judy B. Rosener, "Ways Women Lead," *Harvard Business Review,* November-December 1990, p. 120.

[5] Nancy Sylvester, "Women and Public Office: Creating Alternative Approaches," *The Catholic World,* vol. 234, no. 1404, November-December, 1991, p. 266.

[6] Anna Quindlen, "Little Big Women," *New York Times,* February 2, 1992, p. E17.

[7] Recent study by the Center for the American Woman and Politics and poll from *Life* of 1,222 Americans-a representative cross-section of the population (614 women and 608 men, ages 18 and older)—to find out what women want. Lisa Grunwald. "If Women Ran America," *Life,* June 1992, pp. 36–46.

[8] Susan J. Carroll, "Taking the Lead," *The Journal of State Governments,* vol. 64, no. 2, April-June 1991, p. 43. (Ms. Carroll is a senior researcher at the Center for the American Woman and Politics, Rutgers University, New Brunswick, New Jersey.)

[9] Dorothy W. Cantor and Toni Bernay, *Women in Power: The Secrets of Leadership,* (New York: Houghton Mifflin Company, 1992), pp. 240–244.

[10] Margaret Rankin, "Diary of a MADD Housewife: Candy Lightner, Then and Now," *Washington Times,* October 10, 1990, p. E1.

[11] Anne Witte Garland, *Women Activists: Challenging the Abuse of Power* (New York: Feminist Press, 1988), pp. 17–36.

[12] Lisa Grunwald, "If Women Ran America," (*Life,* June 1992), p. 40.

# 2

# Removing Barriers to Activism

Women taking on new roles must often overcome discouragement, lack of experience, and sexism. A successful activist is able to demystify politics and gain confidence in her ability to learn, organize her time, and to succeed. Clear your own path toward involvement by examining some of the most common hurdles for women who want to become political activists.

## HURDLE 1:

### The Government Will Take Care of That Problem for Us. That's Their Job.

Many feel it is the job of government to stick up for us, and solve the problems we face in our communities. Unfortunately, it doesn't always work out that way. In many instances, the government will not naturally put citizen's interests first.

In Lorri L. Jean's case, this meant the loss of the life she and her family knew for decades:

In 1971, during the Nixon administration, our family lost our farm. We were the largest pork producing operation west of the Mississippi, with 5,000 head. An exciting thing was about to happen to us, my Dad was flown to Texas to meet with Jimmie Dean who had this idea for doing sausage. Dad was discussing the possibility of being a partner, as a supplier of the pork.

In the meantime, I remember when the load of hogs came in that had the cholera although we didn't know it at the time. Not much later, the animals began getting sick, and I remember helping Dad do vaccinations for pneumonia. The situation wasn't improving. Ultimately we discovered they had cholera. Cholera is a respiratory illness; it doesn't affect meat at all. Dad said of course we had to vaccinate those hogs not yet exposed, and cure those who had it. That's when the door was slammed in our face.

The government had just enacted a policy making it illegal to vaccinate pigs with certain diseases. The theory was, kill the infected animals to eradicate the disease and split the cost of paying the farmer for the herd with the home state. But the state of Arizona would not pay their half because our herd was so large. Dad said, "Well heck, if you're not going to pay us for the animals, we're not going to kill them. They're our livelihood, They're all we've got." I remember we went into town and hired 10–12 guys right off the street, and we vaccinated 24 hours a day. It was a family crisis. We mobilized to save the herd; we were going to make it.

The straw that broke the camel's back occurred when the government finally gave us permission to vaccinate but told us we could not sell the meat out of state. We had been the biggest supplier for the biggest meat packing house in the West. But there was only one place to sell it *in* state, and they offered only one-half of market price—take it or leave it. We couldn't even make our money back at half-price. A law suit was filed, but it never went anywhere. The herd dwindled and we were prohibited from replacing it. From there we lost our home, we lost our ranch and our cars were repossessed in the middle of the night. It was a traumatic experience.

It was so unfair. The government had rules and laws that were supposed to help us. It felt like it was us against the world. I decided then to become a lawyer and get involved in politics and change the way things worked. Nobody else should have to go through what my family had to go through.

Stories abound of the "little" people being stepped on by the government. Loss of farms, illegal police searches and seizures, the inability of women providing child care to get licenses, lack of attention to low-income housing issues, inaction on behalf of workers being exploited—the list goes on. While we should get more from public agencies that are supposed to serve the common good, in reality it is necessary for citizens to stand up and get involved to make sure the government and other power players operate on our behalf.

## Jumping the Hurdle

### Citizen's organizations to the rescue

Only with an organized citizen effort can we overcome the inadequacies and inequalities of government action. The rise and prominence of organized voices around citizen's concerns have led to greater accountability of government and other powerful institutions. Citizen's groups are critical to watchdogging, whistleblowing, and pressuring power holders to do the right thing—prioritizing the concerns of ordinary people, their families, and communities. Activist groups need energetic, resourceful, reliable members to galvanize the type of strategy and pressure that will win action on their behalf. Our job is to find the groups most relevant to our concerns and get involved in their activities. Here are just a few ideas:

- **United Seniors of Colorado** uses community organizing to win change that improves the quality of life for Colorado's elders. Recent work includes defeating a utility company's rate increase request and lowering the cost of a local health care plan for seniors.
- **League of Rural Voters** in Minnesota and Nebraska coordinates voter education and get-out-the-vote (GOTV) drives in an effort to strengthen the impact of rural voters.
- **9 to 5, The National Association of Working Women** is a membership organization for office workers, working for higher pay and better workplace conditions. Offices are located in Cleveland, Atlanta, Milwaukee, and Los Angeles, and on Long Island, New York.

## HURDLE 2:
---
### Women Can't Be Successful In Politics; That's Really a Man's World.

### Is the cup half-empty or is it half-full?

Women remain only 10.1% of the members of United States Congress (55 of 535 voting members). At this point, women in many leadership bodies only fill token slots; and they are often the sole female member on corporate boards of directors, in the top ranks of many labor organizations, and on editorial boards of newspapers. Women are still paid less, only 70.6 cents for every dollar earned by men. In the state of Utah, women were prohibited from wearing pants on the floor of that state legislature until 1994. While nations around the world are choosing women leaders, a significant number of American voters— between 12 and 32%—still say they would never vote for a woman for president, even if they felt she was qualified.[1]

On the other hand, recent progress made in both the private and public sector results from women becoming involved and standing up as activists—pushing for results on issues, for power in the decision-making process, and for equality for all women. Discover for yourself the arenas in which women have made political gains, and participate as equal partners in the political process. Check out your local community's leadership. Are women present? Are there more women leaders in public office, in business, in community organizations, and in the media, than there were ten years ago?

In fact, women leaders are ubiquitous, and the numbers are growing. Did you know that women are starting businesses at between three and five times the rate of men?[2] Or that women hold 23% of the statewide executive offices across the country? Did you know that a cluster of 11 mountain peaks are named after women leaders prominent in Canada's recent history? And did you know about women's impressive leadership preparation? In the past 10 years, more women than men earned bachelor's and master's degrees; in high school and college women's grades are higher, and more women than men continued with their education after the age of 30.[3]

## Jumping the Hurdle

### Women often win elected office due to the help of other women

Statistics prove that women are winning elected office in numbers never before achieved. The reasons behind this are manifold:

- Women have encouraged other women to run for office.
- Women have taken the risk and put together the plan, the people, and the money to run and win.
- Women have helped women campaign—as volunteers, staff, financial contributors, voters, house party hosts, pollsters, and political consultants.

- Women elected to entry-level offices have observed others take the risk for greater power, and that has galvanized them to follow their lead.
- Women winning higher office inspire others to run.

Martha Fuller Clark, a mother of three in Portsmouth, New Hampshire, ran for her state legislature in 1990 because other women convinced her to. Clark's prior activism, especially around environmental issues in her community, gave her many connections to tap for her campaign:

I really decided to run for office because of the encouragement and help of two women I respected a lot. One was a woman state senator who had to retire because she was dying of breast cancer; I really admired her and very much wanted to be able to follow in her footsteps. Another was the head of the New Hampshire Women's Lobby. Other women who had served in the legislature helped me with my campaign too, including a woman who was on the local school board. These were absolutely critical people to go to for advice when I got anxious about the campaign.

### Women have power as voters

Women voters have made the difference in many electoral and issue victories. We provided the difference in the elections of President Bill Clinton, several women United States senators, and others who have effectively appealed to women as a bloc of voters. In 1976, with the election of President Jimmy Carter, women first used the power of their numbers, and voted more frequently than men: 45.6 million women voted, compared with 41 million men. In 1988 the number was 55 million women and 48 million men. In the 1992 presidential election, 60.6 million women voted, compared with 53.3 million men.[4]

The difference the women's vote makes as a bloc (sometimes referred to as the gender gap) is a formidable power because it can swing an election. The national Republican Party has done a poor job in attracting the women's vote. At their national convention in 1992, the consistent theme portrayed positions of monumental importance to women, such as the right to choose an abortion and the ability for many women's gay sons and lesbian daughters to enjoy equal rights, as morally wrong and unacceptable.

This aspect of the Republican convention infuriated women of all stripes: "The in-depth polling shows that the great majority of the public didn't care for the gay-bashing, didn't care for the feminist-bashing, didn't care for the Hillary-bashing and thought the whole exercise was too negative. It was."[5] It also lost the Republicans the election.

The Clinton-Gore campaign was able to appeal to more women because they supported women's positions on several issues of the utmost importance. Beyond the social issues of abortion and gay and lesbian rights, the Clinton-Gore ticket lured more women to vote for Democrats than Republicans because of their public support for greater attention to child care, accommodating the needs of special schedules for working mothers, and the paramount urgency of providing universal health care. Future candidates can learn much from this model—court the vote of people who agree with you on specific issues.

### Women raise money for women candidates

Women have come together to build campaign chests for women candidates. In 1992, the so-called Year of the Woman (why do we get only one?), EMILY's list raised more than $6 million from women all over the country for 32 federal-level Democratic women candidates, 23 of whom won their seats. EMILY stands for Early Money Is Like Yeast, and is a national political action committee devoted to raising money for Democratic women candidates. Early money, or significant funds raised early in a political campaign, is a strong indication to prospective donors and supporters of a candidate's viability.

The United States Senate campaign of Barbara Boxer in California is one of the greatest examples of women giving money to women candidates. Boxer raised as much ($4.5 million) as her leading male Democratic primary opponent. Nearly two-thirds of her contributions (after the Anita Hill hearings) were from women. In total, Boxer raised money from over 52,000 individual donors with an average contribution of $28. In contrast, her opponent raised the same amount of money, but nearly 94% was from people that gave over $200 and only 6% gave contributions of less than $200.

### Women organize to bring public attention to unaddressed issues

In the arena of domestic and sexual violence, women have organized shelters, networks, and advocacy groups to put this issue on the map in most states by drawing increasing attention from law enforcement agencies, health care providers, the government, and the general public. Certainly we have some distance to go before ending the cycles which perpetuate abuse, but women are organizing every day to make that happen. According to the Family Violence Prevention Fund in San

Francisco, there are at least 1,600 organizations around the nation whose chief focus is confronting domestic violence.

Lois Gibbs was a housewife in upstate New York whose children were chronically ill. Gibbs believed they got sick from school, and her investigation confirmed that indeed the school building sat on top a hazardous waste site. The neighborhood movement she organized to clean up Love Canal (with absolutely no prior experience) and to compensate homeowners for their loss of property launched a wide-ranging citizen movement connecting environmental causes to neighborhood health problems. Through her efforts Lois Gibbs put hazardous wastes on the map in this country as an urgent issue which could not be ignored.

When elected to office, women leaders do the same for other concerns. In 1993 United States Senator Carol Moseley–Braun led the campaign to stop congressional funding of the Daughters of the American Revolution (DAR), because their public symbol is the Confederate flag and is viewed by many to be racist. Several women senators are currently leading the charge to win increased federal funding for research on women's diseases.

Current efforts to identify and punish stalkers, raise the minimum wage, achieve adequate school funding, advance birth control technology and availability, increase accessibility of financial aid for college students, establish stronger gun control laws, and decrease the country's defense budget are just some of the issues largely raised by, organized around, or resolved through the urgent efforts of women activists.

### Women win progress and victories on issues

Women are, and have been throughout history, the heart, soul, power, and fuel behind countless fights for a change.

The dedication and energy of Lillian Wald fundamentally and permanently changed our system of health care delivery. The early 1900s in New York City were years plagued by an epidemic of tuberculosis. Wald and a sister graduate of the Woman's Medical College opened a settlement house in New York, similar to Jane Addams' Hull House in Chicago. Wald, however, engaged in a unique form of outreach to families with an emphasis on nursing. The nurses worked particularly with immigrant women and families who sought a more healthy life. In 1895 six nurses were working out of the Henry Street house; by 1917 there were over a hundred nurses making almost 250,000 calls a year.

These women originated public health nursing in America. At that time, women were rarely allowed to become medical doctors with equal status as men. Instead, they chose to operate independently of doctors, as what eventually became the Visiting Nurse Service. Motivated by the need for better health care for children and families, Lillian Wald understood the connection between improved health care and better working conditions, for women.

The former Henry Street House, founded by Lillian Wald, still exists—as a community center in lower Manhattan, serving children, teenagers, and the elderly. Immigrants were the first clients of Henry Street, and in the tradition of honoring the diverse cultures of America, they remain an important focus of the center today.[6]

It is no accident that United States voters' views have reversed significantly on the issue of a woman's right to choose a safe, legal abortion. Shortly before the 1973 Supreme Court decision in *Roe v. Wade* that legalized abortion, polls showed that only about 40% of the population were pro-choice, the remaining 60% were either unsure, or anti-choice. Over the subsequent 20 years, a women's movement, led primarily by the National Abortion and Reproductive Rights Action League (NARAL), organized a national grassroots campaign to persuade people that women must be allowed the right to choose. Indeed, currently, 65% of American voters describe themselves as pro-choice and oppose overturning *Roe v. Wade.*

### Women activists learn many skills from the organizations they belong to

Impressive too, are the political positions and activities undertaken by organizations that represent primarily women members. Ninety-seven percent of nurses are women. A majority of the National Association of Social Workers (NASW), are women. On the national level, and in its state chapters, NASW has stepped forward to become involved in several political areas. From opposing discriminatory ballot measures, to lobbying in the legislatures, to working to elect friendly officeholders, NASW and its members are active and involved.

Teachers' Unions and Nurses' Associations, representing largely female professions, are major contributors to political campaigns. State chapters are often skilled in involving the group's members in the election campaigns and lobbying, as well as encouraging members to run for office. A record number of nurses served as political party representatives at the Democratic and Republican national conventions in 1992. The American Nurses Association Political Action Committee

(ANA-PAC) estimated that 76% of the candidates it endorsed were elected. Equally important, Texas elected the first registered nurse (RN) to the United States Congress—Eddie Bernice Johnson. Now the ANA has launched a Federal Appointment Project by which they promote RNs for health-related government appointments.

### Women activists take on some of the most difficult, entrenched institutions in order to gain equality and fair treatment

*"The master's tools will not dismantle the master's house."*

—AUDRE LORDE

Many women activists instinctively heed this advice. We cannot rely on change coming from inside the system, by the power holders in that "house." Instead, we must stand up and take action to insure that powerholders act in our interests.

■ *Catholics for a Free Choice:* Perhaps one of the most difficult institutions in which to effect lasting social change is the church, and particularly the Roman Catholic Church. Catholics for a Free Choice (CFC) is engaged in lobbying and public education, supporting the right to legal abortion and family planning. The CFC's work directly challenges the church's position on abortion. The Church has responded by threatening or leveling excommunication against those who advocate for laws allowing abortion.[7] Yet the women of CFC continue their work because they know they represent the views of numerous women. In fact, according to a CFC poll, more than half of Catholics believe abortion should be legal in many or all circumstances. Many Catholic churches in the United States foster an environment where parishioners on both sides of the issues can communicate comfortably.

Historically run by men, even the Catholic Church has had to face the growing voices of women who want equality and power. Recently, the Pope asserted his approval of naming "altar girls" in parish churches. Further, while refusing to ordain women priests, the Catholic Church in America has assigned leadership roles to growing numbers of nuns in parishes where the number of available priests has dwindled. The Anglican Church of England (Episcopalian) went one step further, voting to allow the ordination of women priests. Perhaps it's just a matter of time before we earn the titles along with the jobs.

■ *Mothers Against Police Harassment (MAPH)* have their work cut out for them. After Harriet Walden's teenage sons and two friends were pulled over by a police car (that immediately called for an 11-car backup squad), she and her neighbors founded this organization in Seattle, Washington. MAPH is a membership group whose activists stand up to police harassment of minority youth. One of the objectives is to establish a board of citizens to review charges of local police harassment. They set up a 24-hour hotline to take complaints about questionable police conduct. They receive two to three dozen calls each month from people who are usually afraid to file formal complaints. The group tries to track the number of complaints against particular officers, and take action when there is none by the police department. MAPH organizes workshops where youth can learn what their rights are when faced with police searches and questioning.[8]

One would have had to hide in a cave shortly after the Anita Hill–Clarence Thomas hearings in 1991, to have missed the impact that debacle had on the lives of men and women in America. Vindication through a defeat of Thomas would have been a more overt victory for Hill and the droves of women dealing with sexual harassment across this country. But the disrespect and ineptitude of the all-male Senate committee leading the inquiry on national television provided the same impact: Since that disappointing episode in 1991, sexual harassment has gone public, as have the perpetrators, as has date rape, and new policies and sensitivities to encourage respect for women. Perhaps, most importantly, a new crop of women activists have sprung up across America to demand and gain justice, respect, and the right to be heard.

Our daughters now grow up thinking that they can get a job as either an executive or a lineworker for the telephone company because others have done so. Today, girls believe they can one day succeed at a business venture of national scope or at sportswriting because women have done so. And the reason the girls of the future will know that they can run a corporation, get higher pay for serving as a child caregiver, serve as a priest, or win the presidency is that women will have done all those things too.

## HURDLE 3:

### I Believe That Women Should Be Equal, But I Don't Want to Be Called a "Feminist"

*I myself have never known what feminism is. I only know that people call me a feminist when I express sentiments that differentiate me from a doormat*
—REBECCA WEST,
THE CLARION, 1913

Linda Ellerbee says that feminism means the belief in equal rights for women.

According to *Webster's Dictionary,* feminism is the principle that men and women should be equal on social, political, and economic levels. It's time to take back the "F-word!" Feminism defines the basic way we view the two sexes. It is the lens we use to view the world. It is not a goal, it is a perspective, a perspective with which many women and men agree. **Feminism—the desire for equal rights—should be what we have in common with other women, *not* that which divides us from one another.**

Unfortunately, those intolerant of equality have successfully created a negative connotation around this word. The dispute surrounding the word "feminist" serves to keep women marginalized; a means by which our detractors can label, and often dismiss us. Worst of all, the controversy around the world helps to keep us polarized from our own cohorts in the women's movement. Since many view the word suspiciously, they tend to stay out of a movement which claims to be feminist. We cannot allow misinformation to keep us from participating in our own liberation movement.

## Jumping the Hurdle

### *Don't fall for it!*

Throughout this country's history women have been ridiculed for attempting to gain simple equal rights. When women wanted to own property, they were accused of stepping out of line. When women wanted the right to be educated, to attend college, or become licensed doctors, they were accused of being anti-family. When women worked for the right to vote, they were accused of being man-haters. These attacks allowed our adversaries to dismiss us. This tactic continues to keep women who fear the name-calling out of politics and activism.

### *Stand up for your rights . . . Cecilia Kirkman did:*

I grew up in Georgia. Many of my friends married straight out of high school. My school was all white. I did not consider myself a feminist. The community college I went to in the late 1970s had a fraternity and I used to dress up for it as a Playboy bunny because that's what our goals were, and I thought that was really neat. That is the traditional world view I came from. I really expected to get married at an early age and have kids. College was something I was doing because I wasn't doing anything else. I had no career plans.

After three years at a community college in Georgia, I transferred to an elite university in Boston. A couple of months later there was a series of four rapes in two months on campus, and these were just the ones that were known about.

At the same time something sexist was printed in the school newspaper, and a woman named Leah challenged it in the student court. The student court ordered the paper to retract what they had said before. And the newspaper did that, but at the same time they ran a cartoon set at the site of the last rape. It portrayed a man from the knees down, with her kneeling down in front of him. And it said, "OK Leah, you wanted it and you got it."

I had never been politically active, but I was really upset. The first thing I thought was, "Oh my god! What about the woman who was raped? She's probably still on campus and is reading this!" So I put a little sign on one of the school doors, that said if anyone else is upset about this cartoon please meet me at the student lounge. Over 100 people showed up. And I didn't know what to do, I had never been to a political meeting in my life and everybody sort of turned to me to lead the meeting. And that is what really turned me into an activist. Because women shouldn't be treated like that.

Statistics show that while only 40% of women consider themselves feminists, a whopping 98% support greater equality on social, political, and economic levels. An average of 70% of women like groups that are working for women's equality or women's rights.[9] Indeed, while women activists for equal rights may keep the traditionalists uncomfortable for a while, the majority of women are behind us. Our task is to motivate their participation on the basis of issues about which they feel strongly.

## Three ways to overcome your fear of feminism

**1. Read About It** Through historical biographies, magazine stories of women who have made a difference, or books focused on the debate of "feminism," you can find out more about the term, and how it defines women's struggles. Three recent helpful books on the topic include *Backlash: The Undeclared War Against American Women* by Susan Faludi; *The Morning After: Sex, Fear, and Feminism on Campus* by Katie Roiphe; and *Fire with Fire* by Naomi Wolf.

**2. Get Inspired** Many women who fear the label of "feminist," are able to ignore this undercutting tactic by watching activist women in action. Go to public debates, public hearings, or lectures involving women who are standing up and getting something done about an issue of importance. Call an inspirational women leader in your community and interview her. Ask her how she got involved, and how she copes with ongoing efforts to label and ignore her.

**3. Keep Your Eyes on the Prize** The process of reclaiming the word "feminist" can easily be incorporated into the process of being an activist. Women who are activists provide necessary role-models for other women and girls. That is the effect of standing up and being counted as a "feminist." Our articulation of equal rights in specific demands and changes, makes our opponents nervous and defensive, but also motivates our allies to join with us. Individually we are more vulnerable to name-calling and marginalization. Together with like-minded crusaders for equal rights, we are powerful enough to stave off the nay-sayers and win change through activism.

---

## HURDLE 4:

### I Don't Have Time:
### You Can Either Be a Political Leader
### OR Have a Life

We've all heard it before: if you become a political activist, the other parts of your life—your family, your work, your leisure—all suffer.

How important is it to you that a man not be promoted over you, simply because he's a man? How important is it that more women are elected to public office? How urgent is it that a new stoplight or street sign is put in at that busy intersection around the corner? Is it a priority that women who are battered have a shelter to go to with their children, and from which they can start a new life? How vital is clean drinking water to you, especially in light of the toxic pollutants coming from a nearby factory, or the oil spill never cleaned up by that multinational oil company? And exactly how significant is it that most of the family wage jobs in this country are being shipped overseas to third world countries?

Sometimes women are discouraged to step forward, define the agenda, and fight for justice, either by our own families or other women. There is sometimes a concern that activist women are cheating their families out of the time they deserve, are not performing up to expectation on their paid jobs, are unfeminine, can never find themselves a husband, and are jeopardizing the role of women who choose to spend their time as family caregivers.

## Jumping the Hurdle

### *An activist in any other clothing . . .*

We sense a damaging, insidious double standard in these claims. In fact, for centuries men have taken on multiple roles in their lives. Men have been honored, cared for, and deferred to, while donning their many hats. Most men who serve in public office are accommodated on the job, not fired, but helped to fit in. Most who serve as leaders of boards and organizations are accommodated both on the job and in their families. In general, men who organize to effect change as members of unions, community groups, or business lobby organizations are respected as activists, not denounced for deserting their families, or for falling down on the job. Women deserve the same treatment. Nothing more, nothing less.

### Who benefits from women's activism anyway?

Ironically, it is to improve the conditions in which they work or raise their families that women become activists. Women should not be judged guilty of shortchanging the very institutions they are attempting to improve. If women do *not* assert themselves as activists, then the conditions of family life (child care facilities, schools, and neighborhoods), and of working life (wages, health, safety, and productivity), don't change and improve. Women are quite capable of making these kinds of connections between various facets of their lives because we already make similar connections in our daily lives. From the link between the lack of recreational facilities for kids and the increase of youth delinquency, to the relationship between environmental pollution and their family's health, to the ties between television and violence, women are trained problem-solvers in their own homes and communities.

In fact, women are often the best organizers. The skills women learn from their mothers and grandmothers, in managing a household, are applied repeatedly in all aspects of their lives. Glenda Straube of the Alaska Women's Lobby describes her role models this way, *"I don't have any one incredible person that serves as my role model. For me it's everyday women who are trying to struggle with children, trying to keep a job, manage to save a little money for their kids to go to college, and continue to live their feminist beliefs."*

Organizing a birthday party involves the same skills as organizing a fundraising banquet or a community meeting; all require a plan, leadership, turnout, an agenda, and roles for the participants. Each can be fun. Along with organizing skills, women have mastered time management skills. If women spent all their time on one thing (as sometimes claimed by detractors when we become activists), then wouldn't our families suffer from too many meals and not enough baths? From too many hand-knitted sweaters and not enough outdoor activities? It's ridiculous to assume that a woman is unaware of the many time demands upon her from life's many facets, or that she is unable to juggle them. Show us a woman who cannot cook, caregive, and manage details at the same time, and we'll show you a man.

Further, women are creative. Lisa Brown, a single mother from Spokane, Washington, was recently elected a state legislator, representing her district at the state capital in Olympia—clear on the other side of the state. Lisa is also an economics professor at Eastern Washington University. How does she juggle her work, family, and activism? First, many public employers are required to allow their employees to serve in public office by arranging their schedules accordingly. In some states that's the law. Check it out where you live. Second, instead of leaving her infant son at home, and only seeing him on weekends during the several month legislative session, Lisa was creative. When the session days turned into days and nights, she brought her son onto the floor of the legislature with her. Predictably, this raised the ire of many of the men with whom Lisa serves. In classic form, they claimed that the floor of the legislature was reserved for use by only elected legislators and their staff. Lisa laughed off their threats and made use of her ability to include her family in her activism.

There are countless examples of women who bring their families along with them to activist activities. Whether it's to a meeting where children are provided with child care, or at activist group offices where children are welcome and allowed a corner space to entertain themselves, women and feminist men have combined their activism with other aspects of their lives serving to enrich both. Children, husbands, sisters, cousins, partners, and aunts are resources and allies in the struggles women undertake as activists. The role model a woman activist or leader provides to these relatives, and to their children, is just another way in which she changes the world.

### A lot of time or almost no time, there's room for everyone

While polls show that, in general, women are satisfied with their families and jobs, many are greatly challenged to juggle all their life demands. Indeed, high on the list of priorities for women is alleviating some time constraints, through measures such as family leave legislation, flex time, and quality child care on the job.

Perhaps a run for the United States Congress is not possible for many women at this point in their lives. Fortunately there are small activist roles, discrete tasks women can undertake for the issue, organization, or campaign of their choice which will fit more reasonably into their busy schedules. *Women are not activists because they need one more thing to do.* Rather it is because they astutely see the connection between issues in their lives, and the local activist organizations that confront those issues.

Every woman who wants to be an activist can do something. Busy women are more likely to select an activist track that is closer to home or to their other life activities. For example, studies show that mothers are more likely to run for state legislature if they live near the state capital; those who don't get involved in local politics. We would wager that there are dozens of possibilities for you to explore within a short distance of your home, church, or workplace. Some organizations tap into the assistance activist women can give right from their own homes. See Chapter 8 for a complete set of suggestions.

## HURDLE 5:

### "I'm Not Sure How the System Works; I Wouldn't Even Know How to Get Involved Much Less Get Something Done!"

Many women read the daily paper and come across a situation or an issue that concerns them. Sometimes the issue is one affecting their own neighborhood, such as a proposed plan to cut down forest land to make room for a new housing development. It might be a concern on a larger level, such as a debate over the amount of health care benefits provided to public employees, or to the employees of a big high technology company. It may be a national problem, like the nomination of a Supreme Court justice who is against the right of women to choose a safe and legal abortion.

Who makes these decisions? Why is your neighborhood going to lose it's green space and common trails in order to build new houses? Where would you go to try to stop the project? And how can you sway the opinion of your senator so he or she will vote against the proposed Supreme Court justice?

Whose opinions do those decision-makers listen to? Many women allow their inexperience or lack of information to keep them from becoming activists. They may believe that in order to become active on an issue, they have to be an *expert* on all aspects of that issue, as well as the process by which that issue is debated and resolved. In fact, expertise on the complexities of the system is not a prerequisite for getting involved in matters that directly affect you or about which you have a strong opinion. *On the contrary, becoming an activist is the means to becoming more knowledgeable about the system.* Learning its manual of operations, so to speak, is one of the benefits of becoming a political activist.

## Jumping the Hurdle

If you want to become an activist, but feel somewhat uncertain about how the system works, or how to get involved at all, you have several options for proceeding:

*Join a public interest organization.* Many activist groups focus time and resources on training members in the workings of the political system and how to be effective activists in confronting the system. If you would like to participate in an issue-oriented organization that also focuses on the skill development of its members, interview a number of public interest groups in your area. Margarita Vargas, whose story appears at the end of Chapter 3, had never been involved in politics until she joined an organization through her church. Chapter 9 teaches activists how to select the right organization for their needs.

*Create your own "study group."* The collective intelligence of many women will produce a more knowledgeable and confident set of individuals. Gather your friends or contacts who are intrigued with politics or issues. List the areas of interest of each person, and map out a timeline in which to explore each. Assign each person one topic around which she will lead a future discussion. Use outside resources such as library materials, a newspaper reporter, or journalist, and other speakers to round out the curriculum.

*Get more active in the organization that already represents you.* Many women belong to organizations into which they don't put much time. Look into the union at your workplace, professional association, or neighborhood association. What programs and opportunities do each offer for first-time or returning activists?

Alex Brown is a jet engine machinist at the General Electric jet engine plant in Lynn, Massachusetts. Brown talks abut how she became active in her union and encouraged other women members to become more active:

I chaired the women's committee of my union. I think the most important job of the women's committee is to encourage women to get more involved with the union in a way that felt safe. Those union meetings are intimidating. Yet, the women's committee meetings involve sitting down with 15 other women and getting to see yourself as a leader, to speak out and start to get involved and learn what it means to be involved. Frequently, if you're a rank and file member you don't know much about how the union operates. Who is your steward, your executive board member, or the president? If you have an issue you want to bring to the union meeting, women especially don't know that you have to organize and go as a group.

We've really gone from a situation where women weren't really very visible in the union to having a number of women stewards. Women chair four of the most active union committees—legislative, activities, education, and the picket committee. We're more visible compared to our proportion which is about 9–10%.

We also participate in the women's institute for leadership development which is union women's training program, set up by Coalition of Labor Union Women (CLUW). The leadership development of women that goes on in this group is something you won't see anything like elsewhere in the labor movement, where leadership is almost exclusively male. The training speaks to a woman in terms of how is she a leader in your community, how is she already a leader, a leader in her home, especially if she's a single parent— that's the leadership that gets taken for granted. The training then goes on to explore what it means to put ourselves forward as a leader.

***Read this book!*** Many barriers provide us with excuses not to become activists or get involved with other activists. Indeed, these and other barriers have been the tools used by our opponents to keep us out of politics throughout history. Don't allow blockades in the road— and that's exactly what they are—to keep you from taking action around those issues and campaigns that motivate you. We recommend you take the first step, which is to view politics as accessible. The numerous avenues to joining in and making a difference will become clearer as you go along.

*When you stand behind a barrier, it looks very forbidding; it can look indestructible. But you find so often that once you jump that hurdle, the next hurdle and the rest of them don't seem as forbidding. And, in fact, the magic is that they can kind of disappear.*

—RUTH MANDEL, EXECUTIVE DIRECTOR
THE CENTER FOR WOMEN IN AMERICAN POLITICS

## ■■■■ WOMEN WHO DARE 🔲

## Doreen DelBianco

I grew up in Waterbury, Connecticut. When I was 21 years old and newly married, we opened a small luncheonette. We were struggling to survive with the business, and I was unhappy about the amount the electric company required for a deposit. An organizer from the Connecticut Citizen Action Group (CCAG) came to my restaurant and told me that if I didn't like the electric rates, I could protest them.

I was a Waterbury housewife and I didn't have a clue about activism. Although I was registered, I'd only voted a couple of times based on the person's looks, or whatever. I was surprised to hear that if I didn't like something, I could actually do something about it, that it was possible to win. I went to a meeting in a church basement, and people stood up and talked and so did I.

Then I went to the public hearing and I wore a sticker on my lapel for the first time in my life. The organizer assured me that I didn't have to talk very fancy, so I stood up and talked briefly about my high rates. It was fun, I met some nice people and people actually listened to me, so I wanted to do it some more. I got hooked.

I started to go to more meetings, and also started to run meetings, and eventually the utility company only got one-third or two-thirds of the rate increase that they wanted. Then came a city property tax re-evaluation, and I became a leader on that issue, and an expert on property taxes. We held a meeting at the local school and 1300 angry citizens showed up. While we were on stage running the meeting, the mayor came and people booed. We very skillfully held the meeting together.

We realized we couldn't just work on the local level, we needed to address these kinds of issues on state level. In working to change the way property taxes were assessed, I got my first taste of the state capitol, and I learned how the legislative session worked. My state representative did not support the CCAG bill—she lived in a wealthier part of town and was tied in with businesses who were assessed at a lower rate than the residential property owners. I remember lobbying her and thinking how it was not too nice the way she was talking to us.

Three, four, five nights a week I went to hearings, meetings. I was at the state capitol and also got involved on the national level. Looking back, I credit CCAG with a lot of things. One thing my experience taught me is that I wasn't stupid, that I wasn't wrong to question things, or to want to be involved. I grew up in a town that was working class and very prejudiced; we had backward notions about people's color and work ethic. CCAG really changed that for me, and I started to look at people differently, not to blame the victims. I worked with and got to know different people, and thought, 'this person is a good person and is just like me. How could I have thought that skin color matters?

Also, I was in a very traditional marriage—cook, cleaner, a subservient, ethnic Italian. As I became more involved I got more sure of myself. That was not something my husband was comfortable with, and we got divorced. My life was turned around.

As time went on, our network of activists came to the conclusion that we were doing a great job targeting people and getting things passed, but that we were fighting the fights with one hand tied behind our backs. Even though we were organizing, we were not using the ballot box. So a number of groups decided to pursue a two-pronged strategy—continue organizing and also look at running people for office. In a way, I became the guinea pig—I was going to be the person that would show that we could defeat someone who was not good on our issues.

We decided to go after the woman who had not been good on the property tax issue, and that I was going to run against her. We decided—a number of activists and their groups who had formed an electoral coalition. We would run one of our own instead of waiting for someone good to come along.

I started doorknocking in February for the November election. During that first race, we broke lots of records for how much money we raised, and we sent five or six pieces of literature to the voters, which no one had ever heard of before. At the time I was working in a state hospital for the mentally retarded, and I got fired from my job for being too controversial. But my activist peers raised the money so I could live for the last three months of the campaign.

All the political pundits said I couldn't win. But local people remembered me from the property tax fight, and the utility rate increase fight. They knew I was someone who had been there and who would speak out.

It took me four years, two full terms, to find my niche and even then I think I never quite fit in. The legislative process is one in which you always have to negotiate with the devil, and I never in eight years got comfortable with that. I was automatically discounted for being a woman, and being working class and all the things that go with that, a lot of decorum was expected. I don't think I ever quite measured up, even dressed in a suit and pumps.

I did become an expert on mental health and hospital budgets—I created some innovative ways to fund programs, advocated for the mentally ill, and those with alcohol and drug abuse problems. The chair of appropriations committee, who hadn't wanted me on the committee, said in her retirement speech that my being on the committee was one of the best things that had ever happened—that I had turned a lot of their work around.

In the end I had a choice to make—Connecticut was in a fiscal crisis, and we had to choose between an income tax or increasing sales or property taxes.

I decided to support the income tax—it was not as good of a proposal as I wanted, but it was the most progressive. I worried about how I would sell it to people in the district, and I was scared because the pressure against it was incredible. At one point I had gotten 610 phone calls, and about 600 were against the tax. But there was no other choice, it was that income tax or none. I voted for it, and it passed by one vote.

That was a tumultuous summer, the voters' wrath was incredible. Two legislators lost their seats because of their support for the income tax and I was one of them. I lost by 100 votes.

But life goes on. I quit the job I held while serving as a legislator and now I'm managing the campaign of a woman running for state comptroller. I feel great about doing it because she's a terrific candidate and I had my turn to serve in office and now I'm excited about helping others get there! Once again, I'm a full-time activist and it's the right place to be. I'm back!

---

## Notes

[1] John Harwood and Geraldine Brooks, "Ms. President: Other Nations Elect Women to Lead Them, So Why Doesn't U.S.?" *Wall Street Journal*, December 14, 1993, p. A1.

[2] Katharine E. Hickey, et al., "Women as Donors: The Hidden Constituency," *Advancing Philanthropy*, Winter 1993, p. 27.

[3] Gene Korety, "America's Neglected Weapon: It's Educated Women," *Business Week*, January 27, 1992, p. 22.

[4] Center for the American Woman and Politics Fact Sheet, "Sex Differences in Voter Turnout," Eagleton Institute of Politics, Rutgers University.

[5] Molly Ivins, "Bush's People: Notes from Another Country," *The Nation*, September 14, 1992, p. 1.

[6] Annette T. Rubinstein, review of *Fire, Grace, and Sisterhood: Two Women Activists of the Early 20th Century*, *Science and Society*, Winter 1991–92, pp. 473–481.

Anne Robertson, "Generations Praise Center: Immigrants Change, Mission the Same," *Newsday*, October 6, 1993, p. 29.

[7] Charles M. Madigan, "Catholic Church Gets Tough over Abortion," *Chicago Tribune*, July 8, 1990, p. C1.

[8] George Howland, Jr., "Mothers Take on the Police," *The Progressive*, August 1993, p. 16.

[9] African American, 79%; Latina, 71%; Asian American, 68%; and Caucasian, 64%. A Polling Report of Women's Voices: A Joint Project of the Ms. Foundation for Women and the Center for Policy Alternatives, Washington, D.C., 1992.

# 3

# The Women's Political Primer: Part I

Perhaps you were lucky in high school and your civics teacher kept that cumbersome, dated textbook locked in a forgotten closet. Perhaps she or he had students spend class time scrutinizing current events as case studies of the larger political system. After all, what use is memorizing the three branches of government if you can't visualize how each affects people's lives?

The next two chapters examine the real world political system in the United States. In this chapter, we explore three of the four power players of our system: the government, the corporate sector, and the media. Each player is portrayed broadly, followed by a description of access points which activists can use to confront, unmask, or gain accountability. Chapter four depicts the fourth bastion of power in our political system: citizen activism. Many components of the citizen activist sector are illustrated, complete with advice on how women can get active in this ever-expanding domain.

# PLAYER ONE:

## Government—Three Variations on a Theme

Government exists, even in it's loosest form, in every group of people we encounter. A form of government operates within families, in bowling leagues, in offices, even within the way a dinner party is run. In each case, as in our formal legislative bodies, government is most broadly defined as, "Who is doing what to whom, and how." [1]

At a dinner party, we experience a type of benign *dictatorship:* The host governs with absolute power. The entire event is typically carried out without the attendees voting on who will be present, what will be served, on what table, in what room, and at what time. Most workplace bosses and high school sports coaches run similar systems. We don't elect them but they control the levers of power.

In large corporations we encounter two centers of power, one is the "figurehead" authority of the corporate board of directors and the stockholders, whose power actually coexists with the second body of power—the staff managers of the firm—who oversee the day-to-day operations of the company. That scenario corresponds to the form of government known as a *constitutional monarchy.* Governing is shared by both the figurehead or member of royalty (the board of directors and stockholders) and the elected parliament or equivalent (the managers, vice presidents) who carry out the daily business of the country (or firm).

In a *democracy,* the third common form of government, power is exercised by the people and free, accessible elections are held to determine either leadership or policy. Can you point to a successfully operating democracy in your life? Perhaps your neighborhood ball game would qualify. In that case, either everybody votes on each rule and element of the game and its organization, or players informally vote for team captains who serve as the decision-makers.

If the two teams don't elect captains, but in fact take a popular vote about each aspect and detail of the game, that would comprise a *direct democracy.* Our United States government is *not* a direct democracy. If it were, every person in the country would regularly participate in decision-making perhaps through a weekly Thursday night vote, by each person, on the coming week's issues.

However, if the two teams actually elect captains, who in turn make the decisions for their team, that would denote a *republican democracy.* Leaders are democratically elected by constituents to represent them in decision-making. It can work on the ball field, in the workplace, and in the election of leaders to represent you at your city or town council, and in your state legislature.

One of the natural tensions in a republican democracy is around how elected representatives vote in relation to the feelings of their constituents. Shall they confer with team members, or the voters, about *each* decision they make? Or shall they use the power entrusted to them by their electors and use their judgment in representing their team, their district? Which approach is used by your congressional representative, your United States senator, your state legislators or town councilors?

## Symphonic Performance: Our Democracy in Action

In the aggregate, Americans vote for over 500,000 people to represent them in public governing positions, from local water reclamation boards to the United States presidency. Comprising a virtual symphony of players, they represent a growing number of specific jurisdictions, or areas mapped out for representation:

Elected officials (or "electeds," as we call them) in your area include some or all of these:

**City or town level:**
—City or town councils:
  *Also known as*
  boards of aldermen, selectmen, and city supervisors
—Mayor: Plays the role of conductor, or overall coordinator, for city business.

**Regions within or around cities and towns:**
—School boards: elected either by district or by city-wide votes. Districts are either subsets of the town or include several small towns.
—Environmental land use bodies: such as soil conservation district, water board, cooperative energy board, or planning commission
—Zoning boards or commissions

**County-wide:**
—Forty-six states have elected county governments.

**State-wide:**
  —State legislatures: comprised of two houses (bicameral); the senate and house of representatives, or assembly is elected from districts drawn by population. Nebraska has the only unicameral legislature.
  —Executive officers of the state; governor, attorney general, secretary of state, state treasurer; elected by all voters
  —United States congressional representatives: elected according to the state's population (1 per 500,000 people)
  —United States senators: each state elects two

---

### Variations on a theme

There is a whole world of government beyond the elected positions. Boards and commissions, made up of appointed citizens, regulate everything from teachers and barbers, to surgeons and realtors. Interests concerning parks, art, and port facilities, for example, may be promoted. Many plan for the future by conducting studies of problems or proposed solutions and recommending a particular course of action.

Another galaxy of government's daily operations are the public agencies, alias "the bureaucracy." The bureaucracy implements the programs agreed to by either the elected officials or the people of the area. The police department is a government agency. So is the department of public works, which deals with the water and sewer system of a town. Many states have a government agency that runs the lottery. Another state agency probably deals with complaints workers have about job discrimination or unfair pay.

People are often cynical about the monster bureaucracy they encounter when trying to accomplish a simple task such as renewing a driver's license, or complying with rules regarding the lowering of the amount of pesticides used in farming. Some of these practices make more sense to us than others. Yet, it is our job as the electors of public officials to give feedback on how the system works so that it can be made more efficient and accessible.

In response to current public complaints of inefficient government, one new method of operation for government agencies gets rid of the slow, complex processes of the old days. The RESULTS model (Reaching Excellence Using Leadership and Team Strategies) helps government workers to perform their jobs better and to satisfy their customers with greater efficiency. The RESULTS campaign reorganizes the structure and work of government agencies so that managers act as barrier-busters, coaches, and leveragers of resources, instead of functioning as command-style bosses. Workers are encouraged, and better able, to focus on the quality of the service they provide, and emphasize efficiency and productivity. This is only one example of the changes that some levels of government and corresponding agencies are attempting to achieve. *Reinventing Government* by David Osborne and Ted Graebler is filled with numerous possibilities in this context.

### The chorus and refrain

The central job of government is to make policy that reflects and benefits the collective public will. On every level, elected officials must juggle at least two balls at once. First, the daily business of government requires great attention and fine tuning in providing Social Security payments, maintaining roads, organizing county fairs and other short-term duties. Second, and equally important, electeds continually create and implement their vision of how government can be permanently altered to address the needs of the people in the long run. Each elected official will bring a different perspective to this formidable task, and thus, we experience a variety of styles and priorities in government service based on who's running the show.

## Access Points: Citizen Composers Can Influence Government

### THROW THE BUMS OUT.

### DON'T BLAME ME, I VOTED FOR GOD.

### VOTE FOR "NONE OF THE ABOVE."

These bumper sticker slogans reflect the dismissal of politics by those who feel the system doesn't work. Fortunately, with 500,000 or more elected positions, both paid and volunteer, there are many access points by which citizens can get involved in the election and governing process. Still, if you're not in line to serve in office right now, getting through to those who are can often be a mystery. There is a place to start. Here are some suggested points of access we encourage women to explore.

### Start close to home: influence your local elected officials

Assume you are concerned with the fast pace of commercial development in your neighborhood, and you would like to see the area retain its residential character. Government oversees the planning of what structures will comprise a neighborhood, a process known as zoning. How would you go about making your opinion known to the government about the zoning in your neighborhood? Three steps will place you smack in the middle of the decision-making process known as "land use planning."

*1. Learn who does what; you've got a lot to choose from.* The issue of land development is the bailiwick of many government bodies. Begin by calling city hall, the newspaper, or the library and ask for a list of all the people and parts of government that deal locally with land use. Some of the possible players include the planning commission (usually an elected body), the department of land use (a local government agency), and any board or group dealing with historic preservation. The news department of the paper, a specific reporter, or the local library can be helpful in providing the history of how zoning and development issues have been addressed in the past.

*2. Your allies come in all sizes and shapes; some are very close to home.* Often, those disgruntled with the system immediately think of writing their United States senator, because he or she is the most well-known politician. The job of the United States Senator is to represent you in Washington, D.C. On the issue of land use, you probably want to begin at the most local level of government. Try some of the members of the local planning department or commission, the local city council, or even the president of your neighborhood association. Not only are the people in these positions closer to the problem of land use, they might have experience in confronting the issue of over-development. Most importantly, they might agree with your position and have ideas about how to proceed. Ideally, you want to locate one or more allies in elected positions and/or government agencies who agree with your position and are part of a body of policy-makers that can do something about it.

*3. Lobby and bring others along.* Influencing the decision-makers is a process called "lobbying." The word came from those who gathered in the lobby of the United States Congress to wait for, and meet with, their respective legislators. **Electeds don't know how you specifically feel about your concerns unless you tell them.**

Once you've determined who are the best electeds to approach with your concern about neighborhood development, identify some other residents who share your feelings and lobby together. The voice of one is never as persuasive as the voice of many. Even if you don't win the desired change immediately, you will have begun a process of organized citizen power which can be directed at other targets until a victory is achieved.

In my parish in East Los Angeles, which includes about 5,000 families, they were going to build a motel two blocks from church. Leaders at church talked to other people to determine if we wanted it in our community, which was very poor, very residential, and didn't have too many businesses. People in the neighborhood said they would love to have a store or a restaurant but they did not feel a motel would be good because it could become a crime-ridden place and it would attract outsiders. So we organized. And when the motel owners went before the board of supervisors, we went to speak against it. The place was packed with our people. We testified against the motel and we won. The owners argued that the motel would create jobs but we knew they would be the lowest of the low paying jobs—motel housekeepers. They also argued that the motel would give our relatives from out of town a place to stay, but in our culture, the Mexican culture, when relatives come, they stay at our homes. That's just the way it is. So the motel was of no use to our community.

—Rosalinda Lugo
United Neighborhoods Organization

## Get appointed!

Appointments to public boards and commissions can serve as entry level positions for those who want to become more active in the public decision-making process. Believe it or not, most government officials who make appointments are continually seeking volunteers to step forward to serve. Many women who consider running for public office gain experience in politics by serving on a public board or commission.

I had three little boys, and was very involved in their activities. I wasn't political as such. I couldn't have told you what a precinct person was. I was brought up in a Republican family, but I became a Democrat when I voted for Kennedy. I had never before been active in party politics.

When I went back to work as a secretary, I met a woman who ran a residential treatment center for adolescents. This center did excellent work. They took children who were abused, or identified by the courts as potentially troubled kids, and involved parents in the treatment. As a result, there was not much recidivism. The community of Ft. Lauderdale was behind it and by the time I left Florida, there were five centers like it.

My friend Barbara asked if I wanted to be on the Governor's Children's Rights Advocacy Commission, which oversaw her treatment center and others like it. I applied for the appointment and I got on it as a user, because I had a son who was in the juvenile justice system.

Our tasks included monitoring how residential treatment centers behaved. The most traumatic thing I remember were cases that came before us where a decision was made to put a child in a foster home. Frequently a parent would challenge that type of decision and it was our responsibility to determine to decide if the proposed action was appropriate.

From that experience and particularly the influence of two very powerful women on that commission, I became interested in politics. I learned how to get things done from them. I went once or twice with them to Tallahassee and watched them lobby for children. It was my first exposure to any kind of political structure. My world view changed as I became aware that there are things regular people can do. I found out that the government and people in power were willing to negotiate with regular people. I saw, first hand, that trade-off and compromise were what accomplished real change.

Six years later, Carol Auger is the executive director of a statewide Democratic Party organization.

In some areas, the number of women serving on boards and commissions has greatly increased. In Oregon about 53% percent of Governor Barbara Roberts' appointments were made to women. Almost half of Ann Richards' 970 gubernatorial appointments went to women.[2] States like Iowa and Montana made room for women to serve; in those states the law requires that 50% of all public appointments to boards and commissions go to women. Over the last year, how many public appointments in your state were given to women?

### It's a "bull market" for women candidates

*At best, a society governed by men alone is a society half governed. At worst, communities governed almost exclusively by one group over another are in danger of being exclusionary and oppressive by their very nature, of becoming more and more insulated and isolated, losing touch with the realities of daily life for most of the citizens, and remaining truly ignorant of the feelings, thoughts, needs and life conditions of the people being governed.*[3]

—RUTH MANDEL

Polls show that nearly three-quarters of women believe the country would be better off if women held half the elected offices. **So go for it!** Get elected yourself. Public service appeals to many different types of people; once elected they do not all believe in the same priorities. There are those who want to get laws passed, who want to change current laws, and who simply want to cut back on the exorbitant number of laws already passed on every level of government. Some are motivated primarily by a single issue, others want to change the entire system. There is room for many styles and approaches.

In these days of growing discontent with government, incumbents, and the so-called system in general, women enjoy a window of opportunity in which to run for office and win. Particularly on the local level, pollsters note that, "all else being equal, their gender now gives a woman a 10% boost in races for legislative seats, partly because they are less tainted by the negative feelings voters have about incumbents."[4]

Gloria Molina is one woman who took advantage of that mood. In February 1991 she became the first woman, and the first Hispanic in over 116 years, elected to the Los Angeles County Board of Supervisors: "Molina embodies a new brand of politicians who are critical of the wheel-and-deal political system and its players. At a time when voters are being turned off by politics, she is viewed by many as the only hope for getting laws passed that address the needs of Hispanics. Yet it is important to note that most other groups—women, youth, men, Anglos, Asians, blacks, Democrats, all except Republicans—chose her over her opponent"[5]

### Don't go alone

Even with the current pulse of voters encouraging women candidates, it won't do much good to be just one voice trying to get heard by the power structure. Women who run for office must have a broad base of organized supporters who will help elect like-minded women to office and continue to work with the newly elected women from outside the system to achieve change. Too often, we elect good candidates and well-intentioned legislators or leaders who simply cannot do the job alone. *Women electeds need a team of activists to bring attention to the issues from outside the system.* They need help to demand accountability from power players in the political system, including the media and corporations.

*It's important to consider running for and serving in office as merely one of the many tactics that activists can use to achieve concrete change.* Those who have served in office must rejoin the activist ranks, to pressure the system from without. Those who serve in the ranks need to take their turn as a leader, by running for and holding office. **We can improve the "system" not only by electing more women to positions of power, but also by supporting them once they're there.**

You can work for an issue either from inside the system, as an elected or appointed official, or from the outside as a member of an organized voice of citizens. In any capacity, it is helpful to explore the other groups operating in our democracy, because the power structure in America includes interactions between government and other major players: the corporate business sector, the media, and the world of citizen organizations.

## The Power of Money

This country's republican democracy does not operate in a vacuum. On a daily basis, it coexists with the system of money that our society has chosen to embrace. As a whole our country is a "capitalist democracy."

In America, *capitalism* means private ownership of the means of production. We do not all own all of the property where we live or work. Instead, private ownership in our country is in the hands of the few. That means, only a small minority of people in our country own the means of production—the companies, the factories, the banks, the corporations—and these owners have the legal right to use this property for private gain. The great majority of us serve as the workers within those privately owned businesses. In fact, much of the activism women have engaged in throughout our country's history has resulted from the desire to make the system of private ownership equitable. As we know, for a long time women were not permitted to own private property, or even to serve as income-earning workers within the system. The first property rights bill for women wasn't passed until 1848, and took another 12 years to be complete in its provisions. Even that legislation included only *married* women.[6]

Our combined system of capitalist democracy empowers both the government and the people who own large businesses (i.e. corporations), to govern most aspects of our lives. Together, the government and the economy are inextricably linked in the power they wield in our society. It is rarely possible in modern America to investigate an issue which involves only the government and not the corporate sector, or vice versa.

The defense budget of the United States is one example which illustrates the ongoing link between our government and the corporate sector. Many people think their tax dollars pay the government to create the weapons of defense that serve us in time of war. In fact, the United States government uses our tax dollars to pay private corporations to produce weapons and other defense-related supplies. It sounds like a good way to run the system: we pay the government to buy the best defense products available for the best price. The defense industry corporations manufacture products that protect us and provide jobs to workers to accomplish that task. Unfortunately, the picture is not so rosy.

## PLAYER TWO:

### Corporations:
### The good-image government bad guys

There was a chapter missing from our government textbooks in high school, perhaps it was missing from yours. The chapter on the power of the Seven Sisters (the seven largest oil companies), General Mills, the pharmaceutical companies, and their brethren. Most of us are taught that the blame for any and all of our country's problems lies almost exclusively with the government. At the same time, an on-slaught of slick advertisements teaches us that anything good or bene-ficial occurring in our country is due to huge, multi-national companies like American Express or Nestlé. In fact, both the institutions of gov-ernment and big business provide opportunity and protection for citi-zens and both can be greedy, self-aggrandizing, and unconcerned with the true needs of our people.

Consider the example of our national defense. The Pentagon is the center of the federal Department of Defense. During the 1980s the Pentagon was caught using our tax dollars to pay private corporations ridiculously huge amounts of money for defense materials.

Remember the toilet seat sold by a private corporation to the govern-ment for $600? Or the coffee pot that cost $4,500? In fact, the Penta-gon spends at least $50 billion in procurement and purchasing every year, often for equipment like this that doesn't seem particularly defense-oriented.[7] When this duo operates in a way that costs the tax-payers an unfair amount of money, who is to blame? Both the govern-ment and private corporations are in fact responsible for this virtual fiscal fraud.

*Representative [Barbara] Boxer, a Democrat, claims that the little metal ring she wears on a chain around her neck costs about $20. But when the Air Force buys the same ring as a spare part of a fighter plane, it pays $850.[8]*

Overcharging the government is a common practice. General Dynamics Corporation recently agreed to refund the government for overcharges to the tune of $23 million. This arrangement should cause us to think long and hard about the ways our public institutions, government, and private companies, serve the citizens' interests.

How do corporations work? How are they related to the small business sector, the backbone of many communities?

### Eight quick facts about the business world in the United States

How many facts from the list below are new to you?

*1. Small businesses—those who employ 100 people or less—create and provide most of the jobs in this country.* During the 1980s, companies employing fewer than 20 people created 10.7 million new jobs, while the Fortune 500 corporations eliminated two million jobs.[9] From 1988 to 1990, American businesses with fewer than 100 employees created four million new jobs, while those employing over 100 workers eliminated 1.2 million jobs. Within the transportation and communications job sector alone, small business created 26% of the new jobs in that two year period, while large business only created 5%.

Further, small businesses are also the neighborhood citizens who give back generously to their community by sponsoring local sports teams, donating to the schools, and providing students with afterschool jobs. They're not going to close shop and move to Singapore, especially if we continue to support them with our patronage.

Try to determine the number of people in your community employed by large businesses and how many work for small businesses.

*2. Big business, a.k.a. "multinational" or "global corporations," have no particular allegiance to the United States or its citizens.* Ford Motor Company, Pepsico, Nike, Exxon, IBM, and hundreds of others, create their wealth on a worldwide scale by both manufacturing their products and selling them abroad. Many earn over 50% of their profits outside of the United States. Multinational corporations often identify themselves as American businesses, but have no allegiance to the United States or any country; they will not use local labor, raw materials, or make decisions that keep American cities and towns financially healthy.

Unfortunately, our society does not hold corporate America to standards for their contributions to our people and communities, such as:

providing secure and living wage jobs, producing their goods in America, acting responsibly toward the environment, and contributing to the vitality of our communities. Corporations manufacture wherever labor is cheapest and environmental regulations and taxes are minimal. In turn, they sell their products wherever they can earn top profits. They often leave environmental disasters in their wake for United States taxpayers to clean up!

In many cases those companies lay off our friends, relatives, and neighbors, and then open a new facility in another country where wages and salaries are lower. For example, from 1990–1992, it is documented that 58 United States plants were closed and 12,000 United States workers left jobless by companies that opened plants in El Salvador, Guatemala, and Honduras. Since there is no central public source of information on companies closing plants and laying off American workers, it is nearly impossible to measure the total number of United States companies shutting plants and offices here, to open new ones abroad.

**3. Corporate profits don't usually end up in the pockets of the employees and their families.** Many people believe that corporate profits are used to pay higher worker salaries, hire new workers, pay dividends to stockholders, or are invested into the company for expansion, research, and product development. Over the last decade, the profits of corporations increasingly go to none of the above, and instead go to the following:

(a) *Pay raises for their top leaders, Chief Executive Officers (CEOs).* Over the last decade, CEO pay has increased by 212% while factory worker's pay increased by only 54%. Interestingly, CEOs at major American corporations earn 85 times what their average worker makes, while in Japan, the average CEO makes only 17 times the average worker, leaving more to support the workers.[10]

(b) *Acquiring other companies.* Among the companies the Sara Lee Corporation owns are Popsicle, Jimmy Dean meats, Kahn's wieners, Pay Day and Zero candies, Capri Sun fruit drinks, Hanes, L'eggs and Sheer Energy pantyhose, Isotoner gloves, Bali intimate apparel, Coach leatherware, Electrolux vacuum cleaners, Kiwi shoe polish, Champion sweat clothing, as well as restaurants and institutional food services.[11] This is only one example of an enormous corporation predominantly in the business of buying more and more small companies. Corporate buy-outs don't put more money into the economy; rather, they concentrate larger assets in the hands of the few.

**4. *Corporations wield great political power, using big money to lobby elected officials, and contribute to political candidates.*** Highly paid corporate lobbyists often work to promote large business interests at the expense of the interests of workers, citizens, and small businesses. For example, during the 1980s, the auto industry managed to kill a package of 34 air-pollution and safety regulations, including one for air bags. Chemical companies regularly defeat regulations proposed by the United States Environmental Protection Agency to protect citizens from toxic materials, such as those regulating the amount of industrial wastes dumped into public waters.

In addition, corporations make huge contributions to political candidates they feel will serve to protect their interests. For example, in the 1992 elections, AT&T contributed $1.4 million to candidates, and the national bankers' political organization gave $1.7 million. As a result of these financial contributions to lawmakers, United States laws favor large companies over small business in at least three ways:

- Taxes: Corporate taxes are regressive because larger companies pay a lower rate than small businesses, despite their ability to afford more.
- Availability of credit: Small businesses have a much more difficult time acquiring loans for start-up or expansion. Corporations have a relatively easy ride lining up loans to acquire other companies.
- Safety regulations: Financial connections with lawmakers may allow corporations to avoid regulations of their operations, including clean water and air, environmental regulations, and worker health and safety precautions.

**5. *Corporations spend money to create a positive public image which hides the full story.***

QUOTE: *"A company with a soul that recognizes the value of human beings."*
*—Philip Knight, NIKE CEO*
*on how he would like the world to view Nike.*

UNQUOTE: *The average wage of workers (mostly women) in the Indonesian production plant where Nike's shoes are made, subcontracted by Nike, is $1.30 a day.*[12]

What is the average price of a pair of Nike sneakers in your area? Who gets the rest after subtracting $1.30 from $50 or $75?

Corporations enjoy favored status in our eyes, and by government, because they convey an image of power, attractiveness, and infallibility. Behind the image of the cool looking smoker or beer drinker on billboards and in magazines, lie the statistics of millions of people addicted to harmful substances. Scenic Georgia-Pacific television commercials do not inform the public that this company is the largest importer of freshly cut rain forest timber. Behind visions of scintillating, new computers are the forced early retirements of workers who have served high-tech corporations for 20 years or more.

If people were informed about corporate America, would they question these practices? Would we require multi-national corporations take responsibility for unfair practices, admit to having made mistakes, and pledge their effort to mitigate the negative impact precipitated? What secrets are corporations in your area hiding from public view?

**6. *Some businesses, regardless of their size, try to get away with breaking the rules.*** Where did your newest pair of slacks come from? How about your new dress? Many people think the days of oppressive sweatshops with immigrant garment workers are long past. They are wrong. Behind those apparel discount prices are a huge number of thriving sweatshop factories across America. Now the immigrant workers are largely Asian, Hispanic, and Russian, instead of Jewish, Italian, and Polish in the early part of this century. But the working conditions are similar: fire exits are locked, pay is considerably below minimum wage, and children play along narrow hallways with flammable plastic bags. New York City has more than 3,000 apparel sweatshops employing more than 50,000 workers; sweatshops are also common in Los Angeles, El Paso, and Seattle.

Since many sweatshops are contracted with by large clothing manufacturing companies, the abusers are hard to track. Government officials note, "Government can and is doing much to resolve this problem, but clothing manufacturers also have a large role to play. They should hire investigators, audit books, check time cards, and make unannounced visits to contractor's plants to spot child-labor violations." Frances Perkins, secretary of labor under Franklin Roosevelt, knew how to spot the abuse of garment workers. "The red silk bargain dress in the shop window is a danger signal," she said. "It is a warning of the return of the sweatshop." [13]

What's behind that window display at your local department store?

### 7. Corporate power holders don't necessarily believe that they benefit from the increased presence and equality of women.

- Only a few women have reached the highest levels of power in United States corporations. Many refer to the "glass ceiling," an artificial barrier to women gaining top corporate management and leadership spots through which they can see men gain access. The majority of boards of directors of Fortune 500 companies have only a single "token" woman. The Department of Labor estimates that only 2% of senior executive management positions are held by women.
- Of the 4,000 highest-paid directors and officers in private companies, only about 750 (19%) were women.[14]
- While women comprise over 40% of the managers in this country, they earn only two-thirds of what men do in these jobs.
- Only 2% of all companies provide on-site day care, even though this is a number one priority workplace issue for women.[15]

### 8. One of the fastest growing and most successful components of the United States economy is small businesses owned by women.

*American women own 30% of all U.S. sole proprietorships and partnership businesses . . . In utter frustration, many women executives have left corporations and begun their own businesses.[16]*

The Small Business Administration predicts that women are expected to own one-half of all small businesses by the year 2000. Currently women are starting businesses at three times the rate men are.

Further, women are now moving into business arenas that were traditionally male-dominated, such as construction and manufacturing. When women own the businesses, studies show that they are more likely than male owners to employ females.[17]

The role of business, large and small, in our political system is substantial and entrenched. For those of us who want to gain access to, and be heard in this current arrangement we need to gain knowledge, pay attention, and organize to confront it.

# CITIZEN ACCESS POINTS:

## Taking On Big Money

As activists, we can take advantage of opportunities to confront unfair practices, as well as promote those who are doing the right thing. Here are three things to do:

## 1. Discover and Promote the Use of Socially Responsible Corporations

Some corporations are sensitive to the effects of their policies, production processes, and relations with workers, customers, and communities. With access to information on corporate social performance, we find that while profit is always the bottom line, some corporations are better than others in their degree of social responsibility. Our job is to find out who the more socially responsible companies are, and encourage others to patronize them.

Some of the criteria used to judge the level of a corporation's public responsibility include:

- Respect for the environment, complying with government regulations or voluntarily instituting programs, such as recycling, not required by law
- Support of workers' rights to a union
- Concern for on-the-job health and safety of workers
- Work environments that are free from discrimination and harassment
- Representation of women and minorities on boards of directors and within upper management levels of the company
- Participation in the peace economy
- Amount of charitable contributions
- Participation in and sponsorship of local community cultural activities
- Commitment to workforce skill development and education
- Family leave policies
- Political contributions

Examples of companies with stellar records of corporate responsibility include:

### *Environmentally responsible record:*

■ *Polaroid:* This company closely monitors the toxic materials it uses in product manufacturing, as well as the hazardous waste it generates. By maintaining extensive records of the 1,700 chemicals used in its manufacturing, the company achieves environmental protection goals. For example, Polaroid has eliminated its use of mercury in its film-pack batteries.

■ *Hyde Tools:* Small companies are equally responsible in this arena. This Massachusetts manufacturer, employing 300, has reduced its annual waste water from 29 million to 1 million gallons in just three years.[18]

### *Responsibility on family issues:*

■ *Stride Rite:* They manufacture products from toy trucks to trifocal glasses, as well as Keds sneakers and Sperry Top-Siders. Recipient of the 1993 Personnel Journal Optimas Award in the Quality of Life category, the Stride Rite corporation is a useful model for others to follow. In 1971 Stride Rite was the first American corporation to provide on-site day care for its employees and community children. They've now expanded to offer day care at more of its corporate facilities as well as elder care—another first for United States corporations. Where these services are not provided for Stride Rite workers, the company offers resources, and referral for easy access.

Together with day care, Stride Rite facilitates flexible work schedules and job-sharing for its employees. These are not simply token efforts. Stride Rite has created an environment where workers can move ahead and around in the company. Externally, Stride Rite is also an impressive, socially responsible citizen, contributing 5% of its pre-tax profits to a charitable foundation.[19]

### Books available on this topic include:

*Shopping for a Better World: A Quick and Easy Guide to Socially Responsible Supermarket Shopping* by the Council on Economic Priorities. New York: Ballantine Books, 1992.

*Rating America's Corporate Conscience: A Provocative Guide to the Companies Behind the Products You Buy Everyday,* by Steven Lidenberg, Alice Tepper Marlin, Sean O'Brien Strub, and the Council on Economic Priorities. Reading, Mass.: Addison-Wesley, 1986.

***The 100 Best Companies to Work for in America*** by Robert Levering. New York: Currency/Doubleday, 1993.

Who are the socially responsible corporate neighbors in your community?

## 2. Elevate the Voice of the Good Guys

In one state, multinational food and household product companies squashed the attempt by an environmental citizen's organization to require recyclable packaging on at least one-half of all products. While many individual small businesses neither agree with these attacks on the environment, nor those on workers or women or minorities, they are rarely organized with a lobbying presence in the halls of state and federal legislatures. Who represents small businesses and the more socially responsible companies in the halls of the legislature in your state?

When you're stuck with an unrepresentative voice advocating only for big business, we suggest you try other means to get the word out about the good guys. Plan a public relations campaign to highlight socially responsible people-oriented businesses. Educate the public, give out awards in front of the media and bring together like-minded interests to strengthen the message about socially responsible businesses.

## 3. Get the Most for Your Money

As outlined earlier, government contracts out some of its work and buys many of its supplies from private big businesses. How is this arrangement played out in your community and state? For example, does your city government patronize local companies for its office supplies? Do they do business with responsible corporate citizens? The relationship between government and big business is ongoing and long-term. It is largely ignored by the public, because it is not often found on front pages of newspapers. Yet, it is a relationship that can be affected and watched by organized citizens who concentrate on monitoring business behavior.

Some of the most active corporate watch-dog groups include:

**Essential Information**
P.O. Box 19405
Washington, DC 20036
202/387-8030
(Publishes a monthly journal, *Multinational Monitor*)

**Data Center**
464 19th Street
Oakland, CA 94612
510/835-4692

**Interfaith Center on Corporate Responsibility**
475 Riverside Drive, Room 566
New York, NY 10115

## PLAYER THREE:

### The Media—
### The Public's Eyes and Ears?

With the omnipresence of news in our daily lives, it is easy to assume that the media is a public service or agency that responds to the wants, needs, and interests of the people. In fact, television and radio stations, newspapers, and magazines are a nucleus of power run by private businesses whose purpose, in our capitalist democracy, is to make money. They earn income by providing information to the public.

The media's power is flexed in several fundamental ways: perspectives in delivering the news, control over the placement of news, the amount and type of news delivered, the timing of a story, and the choice of reporters.

## The Eyes of the News

The compilers, writers, and reporters of the news are regular people who come to the job with personal perceptions. Thus, for better or worse, the media is biased, at least in terms of the perspectives of the reporters and writers, and often in accord with business people who own and control media sources.

Newspapers are published by conservatives, liberals, or moderates. For example, one paper may blast the president on his policies and administration, while another will be complimentary. Would you rate your daily newspaper as liberal or conservative?

## Location, Location, Location

The news media display priorities with respect to the physical place-ment of the news. For example, if a group of 10,000 citizens gathered together in the city center during lunch one day to protest an an-nounced layoff of 5,000 workers at a local high-tech corporation, would you expect to see that report on the front page of the newspaper, or near the beginning of the evening television or radio news? In fact, some editors will put this news up front; others will bury it. Very few newspapers have a "labor" section, but don't just about all of them have a "business" section? That's where stories about working people end up.

## *Most* of the News That's Fit to Print

New providers will ignore or refuse to print certain news they deem unimportant or which they feel sheds a negative light on the owner's priorities. This practice can vary from paper to paper, television station to television station. Some legitimate news stories are minimized. For example:

- Much coverage is devoted to the "war on drugs," while little is devoted to one of the root causes of drug use—poverty.
- Election campaign news is almost completely focused on who's ahead, at the expense of exploring the huge corporate campaign contributions behind the candidates or the complex issues facing society.
- AIDS coverage was minimal until HIV-positive celebrities—Rock Hudson and Magic Johnson—came forward.[20]

As information gatekeepers in our society, the selection by the news media of what gets attention effectively serves to define what comprises the political debate in our country. In the 1980s more people were able to identify the name of the president's pet, than knew about the millions of dollars in illegal United States arms sales to Iran and the right-wing Nicaraguan "contras." Citizens were effectively cut off from major public policy decisions. As political leaders look to the media as the source of priority issues, we should care about, and be involved with, what they select to cover.

## Timing Is Everything

As readers and viewers, we prefer to get the news quickly. The scandal involving Oregon's Senator Bob Packwood, and the two dozen charges of sexual harassment against him, did not become public until a few weeks *after* he was re-elected to a fifth term in the United States Senate, an election that was very close. Many felt that his denial, and attempts to quiet the story before the election effectively swung the vote his way. At least one self-respecting paper, the *Washington Post*, had the courage to come forward with the story, while the primary daily Oregon paper, *The Oregonian*, had heard the story, failed to do adequate research, and dropped the issue.

When the news media reports that American arms were purchased by Iran, and illegally shipped to contra death squads in Nicaragua, people are informed, and have the opportunity to get involved in correcting any wrongdoing. On the other hand, if this news is kept from the public until years after the acts have been perpetrated, we are virtually removed from affecting the public policy process around this issue, simply because we didn't know about it.

## Centralized Power

The media is powerful and omniscient because, increasingly, it is owned and run by large companies. According to Ben Bagdikian, an author of media watchdog literature, the mass media—news, magazines, broadcasting, books, and movies—are rapidly moving in the direction of tight control by a handful of huge multi-national corporations.[21] For example:

- Only eleven companies own almost every one of the daily newspapers around the nation.[22]
- There are more than 3,000 publishers of books in the United States but five produce most of the revenue.[23]
- The number of daily newspapers has diminished from 2,000 in 1900 to 1,676 today: during the same period, the number of urban areas increased from 1,737 to 8,765.[24]

The mega-multinational corporations that own most media outlets are careful to insure that the type and perspective of the news is consistent with the company's values: General Electric, owner of the NBC television and radio network, is the country's 10th largest corporation.

The network is extremely prudent about how topics of national defense and nuclear power are covered on those stations. Advertisers are another special interest that media owners strive to please. With more than $30 billion spent each year by advertisers, they've become the primary interest of for-profit media operations. Advertisements take a lion's share of time and space across the media. In 1940, hard news comprised 13% of the average newspaper, now it's about 7%.[25]

The media's job is not to challenge authority or speak up for the people as much as to protect their own financial interests. Who owns the paper in your town? In some large cities, such as Detroit, Michigan, two major daily papers survive to the present. Yet, while one is slightly more conservative and the other slightly more liberal, both are owned by the same company.

## Women in the News

One of the blatant deficiencies of the media in our society, and one which can be directly influenced by the raised voices of women demanding change, is the presence of women in the news media.

- Of the 22 people listed on the *New York Times* masthead, four— less than 20%—are women. The ranks of that paper's regular Op-ed columnists contain one woman.[26]
- Female opinion leaders are rarely viewed on television newscasts and seldom appear as spokespeople in business news articles. A four-month review of three daily papers—the *New York Times*, the *Wall Street Journal* and the *Fort Myers News-Press*—found that women accounted for about 12% of the references in business stories, despite the fact that about 40% of managers of private companies are women.[27]
- A recent 40-month survey of 865 broadcasts on *Nightline* found that 89% of the guest experts were men. Fairness and Accuracy in Reporting (FAIR), the national media watchdog group, found that in a six-month period 87% of the experts appearing on *The MacNeil-Lehrer News Hour* were men.

Look through your daily paper. How many women experts are quoted on government issues? On issues of business? In photos, graphics, and pictures in your daily newspaper, how many subjects are women?

Clearly there is no shortage of spokeswomen, experts, or analysts available for comment in the writing of news reports. Rather, there is a proclivity in the media to seek out its same old sources—typically, men. Because of the tendency to seek out spokesmen, women's issues are not covered with the same predictable priority as men's are. It is our job as activists to help them shape new media habits.

## CITIZEN ACTIVIST

### Access Points:
### Organizing an Ally in the Media

The media can select a number of different roles to play in the political arena. On the one hand, they can limit the amount, type, and timing of stories to benefit the interests of government or the corporate sector. On the other hand, the media can be activist in its tactics, by choosing to publicize with an in-depth approach, the issues faced by the less powerful in society. While we frequently hear one-time human interest news stories about individuals whose personal dilemmas can be, and are, resolved, the media can be a more effective tool for activists if we lead them to cover the collective issues, the plight of an entire group of people.

Sometimes it is the media attention to a class of people or a particular problem that, in fact, heightens public awareness to the level that will push the government or big business into making changes. The story of Watergate in the 1970s was brought to public attention by the exhaustive investigative reporting of Carl Bernstein and Bob Woodward of the *Washington Post*. Without the media, we might have never known about the Nixon administration's illegal acts.

The Community Reinvestment Act (CRA) requires banks to publish the number of loans granted and denied, neighborhood by neighborhood. Further, it obligates banks to grant a percentage of its loans to people in the community in which it is located. Citizen groups won passage of this regulation through persistent neighborhood organizing and skillful work with the media. These activists organized and persuaded the local media in many neighborhoods across this country, to reveal their research about the true lending behavior of banks, and their sometimes negligible community commitment. Preferring to avoid bad publicity, banks reformed their habits, in many cases, when the dual powers of citizen organizations and the media conveyed the truth about them.

The low-income elderly, laid-off workers from a particular company or industry, workers in hotels and restaurants who face daily mistreatment on the job, and mothers with no access to quality child care, these are just a few of the cohorts of people whose stories need to be told by the media, so that action will be taken on their behalf. Which groups of activists or under-represented groups deserve extensive media coverage in your area?

The media is most likely to provide extensive attention to a particular group or issue, when that group is sufficiently organized enough to demand media focus. In the case of AIDS, we would certainly not have such strong public attention, if it hadn't been for the tactics of well-organized AIDS funding advocacy organizations.

Groups have developed the following **media strategies:**

- Establish an ongoing relationship with individual reporters and columnists.
- Operate as a good source for media people.
- Create the circumstances, or media events, to draw attention to their issues and group.

*Media relations:* If you expect the press to come to you, you may grow moss between your toes, while waiting. Seek out local reporters at your daily and weekly newspapers, and at television and radio stations. Take along a small group active on your issue, or with your organization, and introduce yourselves. Brief the reporter on your group and its activities. Ask reporters about their style of writing. Engage them in conversation about issues, and determine their perspective and approach. Are these reporters well-informed about activists and issues? What are their primary areas of interest? Plan to follow-up with the reporter and conduct periodic check-ins to keep up your relationship. It takes a considerable amount of time to create an effective relationship with media people in your area. The time to start is now.

*Establishing your group as a good source for the media:* Reporters and columnists are faced with an enormous range of possibilities about which to write. Attract them to write about you because they know about your issue and activist organization. Send fact sheets, news advisories, and background briefings. Hold workshops for local press people about your group and its goals. Fill their files with background information. When it comes time for a story about your issue, they'll have the files to refer to, and it will likely contain exactly the type of information you've provided to them. The alternative is a hit or miss news piece that may not communicate to the public what you'd like them to know.

*Create newsworthy media events that make it easy for the press to cover your group.* Reporters are not typically assigned to cover activist movements. They cover events or announcements deemed newsworthy. Thus, as activists we compete for news coverage with other community events. The media—newspaper, television, or radio—have the power to determine what will be covered and how. While steps 1 and 2 alone will set you up for more accurate reporting from the perspective you'd prefer, only an event deemed newsworthy will actually get covered. Media events likely to draw attention include confrontations between activists and powerholders in the context of public forums or meetings; traditional direct-action tactics such as rallies, marches, demonstrations, pickets; non-traditional direct-action tactics such as arriving at the golf course of a corporate CEO, conducting a tour of housing conditions for a landlord or public officials, or a mass turnout at a public hearing. If the event does not get covered, deliver a written statement to the paper, television, or radio station.

Many resources exist for assisting active groups in developing media strategies. Read Chapter 7 for references to books and organizations that can assist you. In the meantime, don't forget to explore non-mainstream media outlets, from community newspapers to cable television. In this information age, people get their news from a variety of sources, and activists shouldn't limit their media strategies to just the most obvious players.

It is important to be assertive in seeking fair and helpful media coverage. Many have commented on the unattractive media coverage of the women's movement at its onset in the 1970s. "Women's libbers" were portrayed as hostile to men, and as aggressive, unreasonable crazies. Since isolated and arbitrary events are easier to cover than the changes in people's thoughts, the public received a rather narrow sense of exactly what was going on and the scope of movement. That lesson learned, use the steps outlined above to ease your relationship with the media, and get accurate, positive stories to the public.

All in all, the media is a power player to be reckoned with. We can use the media as a means to gather momentum and popular support around our issues, organizations, or movements, or as an activist strategy unto itself. Organized women have only power to gain by increasing our access to, and representation in, the media.

## WOMEN WHO DARE

### Margarita Vargas

I came to the United States when I was 21 years old. Like any Mexican woman, I thought my place was in the house, raising my family, and taking care of my husband. So I spent 20 years doing just that, and I raised 8 children. The only things I was involved with outside the house were school meetings and church.

We moved to Baldwin Park in the San Fernando Valley when I was expecting my seventh child. I remember walking down the street to register my kids for school—I was holding on to five kids, with one in the stroller, and I was pregnant. Everybody looked at me like I was from another world, and I felt really uncomfortable. And even though I didn't speak much English, I kept going because I had to get my kids into school.

As I got involved with school and church, I began to see things that I wanted to do. But I didn't feel that I had the tools or preparation to do them. At that time an Anglo lady invited me to join a new church-based community organization in Baldwin Park—the East Valley Organization (EVO). There were Anglos, Latinos, priests, professors, all different kinds of people, and I was a housewife. I was interested because they were trying to make a better community—it was really important to me to bring my kids up in a safe environment.

I went to some meetings, and then I went to an EVO training for its members. Before the training, I didn't know that I could make a difference. But I learned that the world is not just me in my little house. Even if my home is a safe place for my kids, when they go out it is not. So I decided to go out of my house and try to do something in the community. As a new activist, I went to school to learn to speak and read English, and I got my high school diploma.

Just a few years ago, we launched a people's campaign to raise the minimum wage in California. Through EVO, I had started speaking in public—I learned to speak in front of maybe 20 or 30 people in a meeting. Eventually, when we were trying to raise the minimum wage, I spoke at an assembly of 7,000 people—that was really a big step for me. Senator Ted Kennedy was there.

I told my story about coming from Mexico, about being an immigrant, how we had to fight to survive, for food, for a roof. And I told them that I wanted my kids to get a good education—that everybody had the right to a good education and a good future. We wanted to raise the minimum wage, but we knew that a lot of immigrants weren't even earning that much.

After I spoke, Kennedy came and congratulated me. Then my kids came to me and said, "We're really proud of you." What they said was more important to me than shaking Kennedy's hand. I was somebody important, at least for my children.

There was a commission of five appointed by the governor to vote on raising the minimum wage. Two members represented the workers, two represented the corporations, and the fifth was the deciding vote. So we went to see Muriel Moore, the woman who was the deciding vote. She lived in Pasadena and I went with other leaders to talk to her, to convince her to vote to raise the minimum wage.

We realized she would have voted with the corporations because they have the money and they would have to pay the minimum wage. First we took her to the garment district to show her the conditions of how people were working there. Then we took her to a tortilla factory and showed her women who were covered with burns and were making nothing. We took her to a house where people were living who worked two or three jobs, and still they could not make it. We took her all over the place, and by the end she was convinced that the minimum wage had to be raised.

A lot of people from LA went to San Francisco when the final vote by the commission was going to happen—we drove all night in buses, and got there in the morning. We filled up the place where the vote was going to happen. We had to be sure the fifth voted would come through. And it did.

In 1988 we organized another campaign, "Sign Up and Take Charge," to register people to vote during the election. We'd go to the swap meets to register them, we went door to door, we went out in their neighborhoods, to the markets, and to church. In Baldwin Park we registered 11,000 people to vote in a few months and we went further: In my precinct, for the first time, 90% of the people turned out to vote.

A lot of Hispanic women don't get involved in activism because their husbands won't let them. But my husband stayed with the kids at night. Sometimes we had discussions, especially when the food wasn't ready because I was at a meeting. But he understood that I wanted to do something with my life. He wanted me to be happy, and he understood that I was doing something to benefit our kids and other kids, in our community. The kids helped too; the older ones took care of the younger ones. They came to actions, and they loved it, especially if they got to be on TV.

When I started, I didn't know anything about politics—I didn't know who the mayor was, who my assemblyman was, anything. Now my son is the mayor of the city where I live—he was the youngest elected mayor in the United States.

Involvement with this organization has helped me to learn that one person can really make a difference—especially if you organize people together. After ten years as a leader, I could say let someone else do it, but I think a lot of people see me like a role model—if she can do it, I can do it.

---

## Notes

[1] Acknowledgment to our friend and the best high school social studies teacher ever, Carol Kilpatrick.

[2] Patricia Aburdend and John Naisbitt, *Megatrends for Women* (New York: Villard Books, 1992), p. 29.

[3] Ruth Mandel, executive director of the Center for Women in American Politics.

[4] John Harwood and Geraldine Brooks, "Ms. President: Other Nations Elect Women to Lead Them, So Why Doesn't the U.S.?" *Wall Street Journal*, December 14, 1993, p. A1.

[5] Beatriz Johnston Hernandez, "Shaking the House Down," *HISPANIC*, July 1991, pp. 12–15.

[6] Due largely to the efforts of Ernestine Rose, Paulina Wright, and Elizabeth Cady Stanton. See Edward T. James, ed., *"Notable American Women 1607–1950: A Biographical Dictionary*, vol. 3. (Cambridge, Mass.: The Belknap Press of Harvard University Press, 1971), pp. 195–196.

[7] "Reagan Appoints Defense Watchdog," from Reuters North European Service, June 17, 1985. Richard A. Stubbing and Richard A. Mendel, "How to Save $50 billion a Year," *Atlantic Monthly*, vol. 263, no. 6, June 1989, p. 53.

[8] Peter Jones, "The Debate over Defense Spending," *Scholastic Update*, vol. 117, September 21, 1984, p. 6.

[9] "Review and Outlook: A Tax on Dreams," *Wall Street Journal*, June 1, 1993, p. A12.

[10] Paul G. Wilhelm, "Application of Distributive Justice Theory to the CEO Pay Problem: Recommendations for Reform," *Journal of Business Ethics*, June 1993, pp. 469–481.

[11] Steven Lidenberg, et al, *Rating America's Corporate Conscience* (Reading, Mass: Addison-Wesley, 1986).

[12] "NAMING NAMES," *MS*. March–April 1993, p. 92.

[13] Karen Nussbaum and Maria Echaveste. "96 cents an Hour: The Sweatshop Is Reborn," *New York Times*, March 6, 1994, p. F13.

[14] Ellen Fagenson, et al, "The Status of Women Managers in the United States," *International Studies of Management and Organization*, June 22, 1993, p. 26.

[15] Ibid., p. 32.

[16] Ibid., p. 26.

[17] Patricia L. Smith, et al, "Female Business Owners in Industries Traditionally Dominated by Males," *Sex Roles*, vol. 26, nos. 11/12, 1992, pp. 485–496.

[18] Marc J. Epstein, "A Formal Plan for Environmental Costs," *New York Times*, April 3, 1994, p. F11.

[19] Jennifer J. Labbs, "Family Issues Are a Priority at Stride Rite," *Personnel Journal*, vol. 72. no. 7, July 1993, p. 48.

[20] Jeff Cohen and Norman Solomon, *Adventures in Medialand: Behind the News, Beyond the Pundits*, 4th ed. (Monroe, Maine: Common Courage Press, 1994).

[21] Ben Bagdikian, *The Media Monopoly*. 4th ed. (Boston: Beacon Press, 1992), p. 3.

[22] Ibid. p. ix.

[23] Ibid.

[24] Ibid., p. 220.

[25] Ibid., p. 136.

[26] Rebecca Haggerty, "Feminism as a Cudgel," *Z*, April 10, 1994, p. 10.

[27] "Women in the Press," *New York Times*, January 23, 1994, p. F7.

# 4

# The Women's Political Primer: Part II

*Do Not Wait to Be Motivated*
*Do Not Wait to Be Motivated*
*Do you understand that we cannot wait to be motivated?*
We Must Work Now.

—AUDRE LORDE

Historians and organizers alike point out that social change in this country comes largely as a result of tireless, persistent grassroots organizing by citizens across towns, cities, and rural communities. For example, people of color did not gain equal rights during the 1960s and 1970s because the white male elected majority in Washington, D.C. decided to hand them those rights. (At the time, the United States Congress was composed of 97% white men.) Rather, African-Americans organized church by church, and community by community, fighting hard for each and every victory. Women were not given the right to vote; they organized and demanded the right during 150 years of living as second-class citizens in this country. The women's rights movement in the last three decades gained acceptance *not* because elected officials or the corporate community decided it was time for women to enjoy more equal opportunity. We organized and won change through pooling our power and demanding it.

Corporate lobbyists, network television, and elected officials may think they represent the true interests of everyday people. Yet, given the number of times our concerns have been ignored, our opinions and positions have been acted against, and the virtual inability for individuals to affect government or business policy, it is incumbent upon us to hoist ourselves into the arenas of society's decision-making processes.

Citizen organizations come in as many varieties as types of bread. Some are focused on a single issue, such as school funding. Others involve multiple issues which are related to the membership interests. One example of a multi-issue organization is an environmental group which works on preserving endangered species and old growth trees. Another might consist largely of low-income community residents engaged in tenant's rights struggles or demanding equality with suburban neighborhood areas in receiving public monies for streets and lights. Some organizations are oriented toward working within the system; they work to influence the votes of elected officials, or gain better quality service. Others work from the outside to alter the system permanently through, for example, establishing commissions that monitor police brutality, or instituting campaign finance reform. There is no shortage of groups with which to get involved. Women should examine the range of possibilities on the menu of citizen organizations so they can make the best investment of their time.

## ANATOMY OF CITIZEN ORGANIZATIONS

### Species A:
### The "Traditional" Special Interest Groups

Many of the so-called special interest groups are really organizations to bring attention to the concerns and opinions of our unheard majority. Traditionally, the term *special interest groups* referred to working people's organizations—trade unions who maintain lobbyists in the halls of the United States Congress. Since most Americans consider themselves working people, it is hard to accept that label "special" for those that represent the interest of such a large component of society.[1]

Other organized groups who have traditionally represented specific citizen interests are farmers, physicians, firefighters, attorneys, and small businesses. Together with unions, these groups maintain lobbyists in the halls of Congress, both to defend against attacks on their self interests, and to promote legislation that benefits their constituencies. Often these groups hire lobbyists on the state level to represent their interests in state government.

If an elected official proposes that $100,000 of the state or city budget be allocated to social services for Hispanic citizens, and there is no one present from that community to speak on behalf of the proposal, chances are the money will not be allocated to that group. Instead funds will go to programs that benefit the constituencies who *are* represented in the budget hearings. Business lobbyists are permanently present at government decision-making sessions. *Citizens' interests often benefit from their lobbyists who speak up on their behalf.*

Political parties are the traditional manifestation of electoral activism. Historically, the United States has considered itself a two party system, referring to the Democratic and the Republican parties. Each has enjoyed a colorful and eventful history. Each has gone through periods of more conservative leadership and organizing, and then tipped its balance back to more liberal leanings.

In the past, political parties were more grassroots-based. Increasingly, they tend to be dominated by big-money, corporate interests on the east coast.

Activists around the country attempt to reinvigorate the parties with participation by local people. This is positive because it draws on a fresh wave of interested persons who would like to be involved. However, many eventually turn away, discouraged by their lack of power to affect the issue positions of the national level party.

Other activists have turned to forming alternative third parties which they hope will grow to contend with the two major parties. This is smart organizing because it takes advantage of the energy local people infuse by presenting new options of representation to the American people.

The rise of the United We Stand, America, movement, initiated around the presidential candidacy of H. Ross Perot, is a signal that people are both dissatisfied with the current structure and platform of the two traditional political parties and are ready to forge ahead with alternative solutions. Perhaps we are entering a time period in which organized voices in the form of new political parties can alter the existing system.

## Species B:
## The New Kids on the Block

Another version of so-called interest groups has emerged and entered the political arena to vie for power and progress on a variety of issues. Better known as activist groups, these organizations are involved in a wide range of political strategies, beyond lobbying electeds.

Activist groups are power oriented; they focus on building an organization of people that will be well-organized and poised to have impact on any issue at any time. *Their central mission is to use the power of organized people to confront the power of organized money.*

One excellent example of the newer breed of interest groups is the movement around protecting a woman's right to a safe and legal abortion. The effort has been organized by groups like NARAL, NOW, and Planned Parenthood. These groups have chapter organizations in most of the 50 states as well as national offices on the East Coast. They are focused exclusively either on the fight to maintain a woman's right to choose, or they work to organize on women's reproductive rights issues.

Groups like NARAL have organizational goals beyond just the specific issue of choice. They want to hold permanent political power, so that whatever happens on the issue of abortion rights or related reproductive issues, they are prepared to stand up for the interests of women. Thus, one of their organizational goals is to continually recruit new pro-choice women and men into their membership.

Other goals are development of members to take leadership positions, training, and organizational activities that are largely initiated and conducted by the members and leaders of the groups, not solely by the staff. These include public education in the form of outreach at events, speaker's bureaus, and neighborhood door-to-door or house party campaigns, as the groundwork and centerpiece of these efforts. Members are also involved in election campaigns of pro-choice candidates, and in citizen lobbying accountability of electeds. New individuals, with or without prior public interest experience, are welcomed to participate as activists.

Many women have formed organizations to promote their interests. Dental hygienists, a profession comprised primarily of women, have formed political action organizations in many states to pass legislation allowing them to operate as dental health providers independent of dentists. They have won the right to practice independently in New Mexico and have made limited gains toward this goal in the states of Washington and Colorado. Nurse-midwives, another largely female vocation, have organized political action groups to become licensed in some states so that clients can be reimbursed for the use of midwives by their insurance carriers.

There are organized women's lobbies in 26 states. These groups organize women to lobby the state legislature for issues benefiting women and against proposed bills that threaten women's rights and issues. One unique example of an effective, efficient, and resourceful women's lobby is in Alaska.

As an activist, I give the most time to the Alaska Women's Lobby. The organization is made up of seven steering committee members in three sites in the three largest towns of Alaska: Anchorage, Fairbanks, and Juneau. We usually meet once a year, just to discuss money matters and legislation. We only meet when we need to. We wanted one group where we had a very limited number meetings to attend. Our main goal is to lobby on women's issues which we describe as just about as everything. We do two things on the Steering Committee. We do a lot of fundraising to pay for our full-time lobbyist in Juneau and then we also spend time deciding the issues we're going to emphasize, pay attention to, fight hardest for, which legislation, where to put our energy and our money. We rarely work on local or federal legislation although if another organization wants our name tied to something, we will do that.

We have an annual budget of $29,000—which is not a lot of money. We consider ourselves very cost effective. We have very little administrative overhead. Our goal is for each of our active groups around the state to raise the same amount of funds for the budget, although it's difficult because there's more money in some areas than in others.

Right now with the conservatives in power in the Alaska legislature we spend most of our time defending against legislation harmful to women's interests. We have been able to stop as much as 90% of the legislation that we don't like. What's harder is getting legislation passed that we propose. If we have a friendly legislature, we do better. We work with other organizations to introduce pieces of legislation: the Alaska Women's Political Caucus, the Network on Domestic Violence and Sexual Assault, Business and Professional Women, Alaska NOW, the Association of Social Workers, and the Association of University Women. Primarily, the person who does the work is our lobbyist. And she is absolutely great. She is very well-respected in Juneau and she gets the job done. We've only had two lobbyists in our 15-year history.

—GLENDA STRAUBE

Another example of issue organizations initiated primarily by women activists include anti-violence groups such as those opposing guns and gangs. These groups attract many mothers, relatives of at-risk children, and victims of violence. Groups that want to end violence against women are excellent examples of grassroots efforts by women to bring public attention, and thus public resources, to an issue which has long been ignored.

Two of the fastest growing citizen issue movements in the United States are environmentalism and gay and lesbian rights. These activist groups are engaged in activities that both defend, as well as assert, the interests or rights of these constituencies. While working to maintain the environmental protections previously gained through citizen organizing and legislation, environmental groups are also busily at work to gain further protection for the earth. Organizations have formed to protect endangered species and wildlife habitats; oppose nuclear power; promote the use of alternative energy (such as solar and wind energy), prevent the devastation of old-growth and rain forests, protect green and open spaces, wetlands, drinking water supplies; encourage and/or require recycling; and halt the deadly pollution of our oceans.

Gay and lesbian organizations are equally varied in their focus. Groups agitate for equal rights for gays and lesbians, provide resources to AIDS patients, advocate for AIDS research funding, bring together local communities of lesbians or gay men, provide support for daughters or sons or friends who are gay or lesbian, and oppose anti-gay ballot measures in states around the country.

Sharon Rasof of Skokie, Illinois discovered her son's homosexuality 17 years ago while sneaking a look at his diary. After crying for six years, Rasof felt less devastated by attending Parents and Friends of Lesbians and Gays (PFLAG) meetings. PFLAG (pronounced P-FLAG), is a national organization with 350 local chapters across the country. Begun in 1981 as a support group, PFLAG is working to undo discrimination against lesbians and gays. As mothers, fathers, sisters, brothers, and lifelong friends, this group has powerful influence on attitudes. They work to help other parents and friends "come out" as relatives of gays and lesbians and to move them from shame to acceptance. PFLAG chapters organize speaker's bureaus to get out and tell the truth about their members' loved ones: "We love and affirm each child for the unique person he or she is. We can try to force our own fantasies and expectations on our kids, and risk alienating and losing them. Or we can experience the richness of unconditional love."[2]

What these groups have in common is their focus on winning positive change. In particular, they often involve their membership directly in confronting their issues. We call them activist organizations instead of special interest organizations because these groups are fueled by people who are motivated to stand up and be counted, to organize for and demand change; and to activate the numbers of people necessary to accomplish change.

All over the country, activist groups are organizing around countless issues. Even within the arena loosely known as women's issues, activist groups are ubiquitous. From groups who advocate equal pay for equal work, to those who contend for decriminalization of prostitution, to those working against sterility abuse, to others working to achieve equal treatment of girls in the classroom and for girls and women in sports, there is a horizon full of opportunity for involvement.

Which are the activist organizations in your community? What issues do they take on? What concrete changes have these groups won? How do these groups get new people involved?

### Activists and election campaigns

There are advantages and disadvantages for activist groups to become directly involved in political election campaigns. Those who favor electoral involvement feel its advantages outweigh its negatives. Electoral work is a way to promote the group's candidate of choice, as well as the means to oppose a candidate who is against the group's issues. If the group decides to run one of its own members, it is a means to achieve direct political power. Further, election campaign activities are a great way to recruit new volunteers into the organization.

Groups involved in electoral politics form a political action committee (PAC), a committee formally registered with the state or country's election division, allowing them to spend or collect money for election campaign purposes. Many issue organizations, as well as private businesses, have set up PACs in order to donate money to their favorite political candidates or to influence certain electeds' votes. Activist groups utilize their PAC funds to give both financial and volunteer resources to the candidates of their choice.

Many groups shun electoral politics for a variety of reasons: (1) campaigns are intense and can drain substantial energy and resources from the issue work of the organization; (2) it is difficult to hold elected officials accountable whether or not you worked for them during their campaign; and (3) selecting one particular candidate over another can discourage some members from joining, or remaining involved with, the organization.

Some citizen organizations who deal with a variety of neighborhood and community issues choose to be involved in electoral politics in a limited but effective way. These groups sponsor public forums prior to elections to which their members hear the positions of various political candidates. Although no candidates are formally endorsed by the organization, the members of these citizen groups are encouraged to vote

for those candidates they feel best represent the views of the organization, or who are most likely to help forward the issues of the group.

## FITTING THE PUZZLE PIECES TOGETHER

The political jigsaw puzzle is multi-dimensional with pieces fitting
together on many levels. In nearly all of today's issues, all four of the
major power players are involved and interact with one another. The
access points for activists are even more numerous when we view
the component parts of the system.

### Consider Attacking an Issue from All Dimensions

The view from the ground floor is that the problems we face are big,
the decision-makers can seem intimidating, and sometimes we don't
know where to start. For example, how would people go about cleaning
up a neighborhood site where toxic waste had been dumped?

First, find out which players have or do not have the power to do
something about this situation. Neighbors united around the cause can
confront a range of power holders who can address the situation:

*The government-elected officials representing the district:*
   Local: City councilors, environmental commission
   State: Legislators (house of representatives, senate); attorney
      general
   Appointed members of boards and commissions who watch-dog,
      or protect, environmental interests

*Government agencies responsible for the environment:*
   Public servants whose job is to:
   Identify the perpetrator
   Treat injured victims of the site
   Confront and charge the perpetrator
   Enforce correction of the problem
   Clean up the hazardous materials

*The guilty corporation:*
   The manager and owner of the plant that dumped the materials
   The board of directors—ultimately responsible for the company's
      behavior
   Stockholders with a strong financial interest in a responsible
      company

Government and public relations departments of the company

Lawyers for the company

The insurance company liable for damages

Banks providing credit to the company, who may be vulnerable to financial loss

### The media:

The news editor with potential interest in the story

The reporter assigned to the story

The editorial board who would write a piece supporting one side of the conflict

The publisher, who decides whether printing the story is in the financial interest of the corporate owners of the paper, television, or radio station

The number of interests and institutions involved in confronting a problem like cleaning up a toxic waste dump is formidable. Yet, women across the country have identified urgent environmental problems and organized to achieve their resolution.

Andrea Shear and a group of local citizens led an organizing drive in the Naugatuck Valley of Connecticut to address the problems of several hazardous waste sites created by local industry. The collective effort of many similar community efforts around Connecticut led to passage of the state's right-to-know law, requiring industries to provide citizen access to information about the toxics they use, and dispose of, in manufacturing. Once the public knew the ingredients of local industrial waste, they moved to initiate a state program that would help companies reduce the use of toxic materials at the front-end of the manufacturing process. These critical victories came out of intensive citizen pressure on the government, and by getting the manufacturing industries to agree that a problem existed. The citizen group's use of the local and statewide media outlets assisted to reinforce and repeat the message of danger to people. Once Connecticut's laws were on the books, citizen organizers in other states worked to achieve similar legislation.

## Effective Activists Use the Power of Numbers

It is not an uncommon story. Your neighbor feels very strongly about the frightening shortage of fish in our nation's rivers, lakes, and oceans, or about the lack of consequences for those delinquent in child support payments. She carefully composes a sincere, substantial letter to her representative in Congress, hoping that she and many others who have similarly communicated their points of view will sway their vote on a piece of legislation. Time passes. No reply is received from the representative. A vote on this very issue is taken, and your neighbor's point of view is not only defeated, but it is opposed by her representative. Finally, well after the congressional vote, your neighbor receives a reply to her letter—a form letter which has been sent to anyone who advocated that particular point of view.

Voters and constituencies feel cut off from their elected officials, because voters and constituencies are cut off from their elected officials. Accountability of an elected official is available *after* the vote is cast. Women in particular feel this way because our circumstances are still so different from those of men. We earn less money even in comparable jobs. Of the nation's 12 million women without health insurance three-quarters are employed but do not receive insurance at work.[3] Many women are still without financial security in case of divorce or widowhood. Females comprise a greater share of the poor and the elderly, and are more dependent upon government services. In addition, women are traditionally the unpaid and low paid caregivers—mothers, teachers, nurses. Lack of attention to these issues and this status has caused women to feel shut out of power and unable to gain access to their public officials.

**The organized power of many voices has a dramatic impact on the votes of elected officials. Our power is in our numbers.** Women are 51% of the population and 53% of the voters. In the above scenario a single women voiced her opinion to her congressperson. If 300 women had united to write to, visit, or confront the representative with their point of view, it would have been difficult to ignore and to put off. If 500 women come together to demand a piece of legislation that would counter another bad proposal, they would enjoy substantially more power than if a small handful undertook the task.

Low-income workers in southern California (primarily immigrants and women) wanted to raise the state's minimum wage. After a great deal of preparation, they kicked off the organizing drive with an assembly of 7,000 people.

Katie Christie, a high school student in Miami, Florida, brought together 100 kids from diverse and conflicting communities to produce a play about Miami's problems of violence and racial tension. While the cast seemed self-segregated at the start, the group soon mixed together and operated beautifully. They realized they had something in common, regardless of their ethnic background, and left the project knowing what they had to do to make a difference in their families, schools, and communities in order to bridge differences.

As the chapter chair of Amnesty International, college junior Kate Shunney organized 300 students to write letters to heads of state on behalf of political prisoners. The letters called for the release of individuals imprisoned because of race, religion, political orientation, or affiliation. The following spring, the group was informed that nearly a dozen prisoners had been released by the governments to which the activists had written.[4]

The key to the effective use of large numbers is organization. Our numbers, when well organized, can do a lot more than affect governmental policies. Our numbers can win changes in the behavior of large corporations so that child care is a priority, or recycled products are made available to consumers; win a decrease in noise pollution from a factory or an airport, win changes in the ways schools are run, win increased media coverage of women's lives and issues, and win election to public office.

The power of organized numbers of people to address an issue is to create a set of relationships and a mechanism which remains in place long after one problem is solved or one elected official retires. Organized groups are long-term structures that focus on a variety of issues and targets over a period of time. One reason women have gained more power in our society is that women's organizations have been built, continue to grow, and enjoy a common long-term goal of achieving increased attention to women's issues.

## Announce and Produce Your Expertise

Speaking of women's issues, our issues are *the* issues. Smack dab in the center of public attention are those issues once marginalized as "women's" jobs, education, and health care.[5] Because **women have been active on these issues for decades, we are the experts.**

These are topics of concern for women, because they so directly affect families, households, and communities. Women have chosen, or had access, to work as activists in each of these arenas for the same reasons. An interesting momentum is now building. Because women are now voting more often than men and making a difference in elections, political leaders have developed more interest in women's views and concerns. This interest causes more of us to become involved and vote, providing the power to have greater effect on elections.

### Education first

Approximately 1.7 million of the public school teachers in this country are women. Of the 97,000 elected and appointed school board members in 15,000 school districts across the country, women compose 40%.[6] Women volunteer in classrooms, participate in field trips, serve food in school cafeterias, drive school buses, counsel students, teach special education, and lobby for school funding as well as money for higher education. Women organize or provide child care before and after school for their children. Women leaders have identified many of the changes that the education system needs. Where the debate has already gone public, and the prime issues of education—curriculum, teacher qualifications and compensation, program funding, and accountability of schools—are identified, women are the workers, the service providers, the program directors, and the active parents who serve as informed sources about the system.

Because we've been integrally involved with education of our children, we have a major self-interest in these issues and largely untapped insight into how the system could work better. In other words, women as teachers, school board members, and mothers are central players in resolving the crisis in education. Genevieve Richards-Wright's story of an innovative approach to providing children with education is at the end of this chapter.

### Health care for all

Health care providers are largely female. We are 97% of nurses. Women are the primary caregivers in families for sick children, partners, or parents. Women are the majority of nursing home caregivers and alternative medicine providers—from naturopaths to chiropractors, the majority of social workers, physical therapists, and medical technicians. Further, more women than men are employed in unsafe and unhealthy working conditions. On average, women outlive men by seven years, thus they comprise a larger share of the elderly and utilize the health care system more often. Women have the greatest self-interest in achieving a system of health care delivery in this country that is affordable and accessible for themselves and their kin.

For all of these reasons, women are experts on health care and our voices, particularly if well organized, can lead the way to meaningful reform. It's no accident that Hillary Clinton stepped up to center stage to take on this formidable issue. Taking leadership on this central issue, Clinton symbolizes how the women of this country are directly motivated about health care. All of the power players in our political system have a self-interest and a role in the campaign for health care reform. What is really at stake are fundamental changes in the way we deliver and obtain health care services. The government, the corporations (as providers to their employees, and as direct care providers), the media, and the citizenry will battle to make their positions known, and work to win policies which reflect their interests.

Groups of organized, activist women have long taken advantage of the call to action around the multi-faceted issue of health care.

The use of pesticides on produce both before and after harvest, is a growing health concern. Nancy Ross, of the Maine Organic Farmers and Gardeners Association, works to inform consumers specifically of the post-harvest use of dangerous pesticides on imported produce. Their group publicizes which pesticides are used on produce and the country of origin.

Frances Moore Lappe boldly took on the issue of health and food in co-founding the Institute for Food Development Policy, which published *Food First* and related works. Moore is an expert on nutrition who advocates the alleviation of hunger by educating people on their food choices and restructuring economic systems so they assist malnourished and starving populations. Her books connect recipes with concepts of nutrition and the politics of how certain foods are promoted in society.

Senior citizens receive health care services largely through the government subsidy of Medicare. Medicare programs set limits on the amount they will pay for various health care services. Physicians are free to charge seniors more than this rate of Medicare assignment, but patients make up the difference from their own pockets. Seniors are organizing around the country to pressure physicians to accept Medicare assignment. Groups in Tennessee, for example, asked individual doctors to comply, and won cooperation in numerous cases. The Tennessee Valley Energy Coalition (TVEC), and similar groups in other states, have compiled local directories of physicians who accept Medicare assignment, and encourage the public to patronize these providers.

Jocelyn Elders is a courageous and inspirational role model as former United States surgeon general. In her role of disseminating information about widespread public health problems, Elders was refreshingly outspoken about controversial issues. "My number one priority during my tenure in Washington is to do something about the startling rate of unintended pregnancies," explained Elders.[7] She has spoken out about the need for family planning and the use of contraception, particularly condoms, whenever she has the chance. "We want to make condoms available to those who choose to be sexually active. I am not of the opinion that just because you have a condom, you are going to go out and have sex. There is not a person in this room that doesn't have car insurance, but you're not going to go out and have a wreck because of it."[8] As the second woman—and the first African American to hold this job, Elders made some people uncomfortable with her candor. In this age of frustration with the government's solutions, Elders brought an alternative approach that emphasized prevention of some of our most dogged health problems.

## Getting Paid

The Facts:

1. Women are 50% of the world's population. We do two-thirds of the world's work; earn one-tenth of the world's income; and own one one/hundredth of the world's land.[9]

2. Women and children are the majority of welfare recipients in this country.

3. In 1994 United States taxpayers will pay more for programs to aid corporations—$104.3 billion—than for programs designed to help the poor—$75.1 billion.[10]

4. Studies show that up to 70% of women on public assistance are off within two years; almost half never go back on.[11]

5. By the year 2005, it is estimated that nearly 62% of the workforce will be comprised of women.[12]

6. Women earn an average median income of $20,500; for men the median is $29,500.[13]

As one-half of the workforce and the majority of welfare recipients without jobs, women have a big stake in the availability of secure, meaningful jobs with a living wage. Contrary to public belief, no one really wants to survive for the long term on $300–$500 a month, the amount Aid to Families with Dependent Children (AFDC) recipients receive. Women are the experts on addressing the issues of poverty, because they have the greatest interest in overcoming low-income status. We have organized and won some state legislation providing poor women with concrete assistance such as job training, child care, tuition assistance, and transportation subsidies. Many are organizing around increasing women's income.

Nothing is as glaring an inequity as the lower level of pay women receive in the same or comparable jobs as men. Women in Minnesota and a handful of other states have taken this injustice on. Minnesota was the first state to pass a pay equity law in which women in public jobs are guaranteed an equal wage with men in the same or comparable jobs. Still, we have a way to go.

The Women's Economic Agenda Project (WEAP) in California brings poor women together for support and to protest some government actions. WEAP's Poor Women's Convention brought together activists from across the country to create a national issue agenda. Their goals include: *real* welfare reform in the form of higher benefits, better support for job pursuit, decreasing violence against women, and the creation of more affordable housing. Other groups organized to win power for poor women include the Welfare Warriors in Milwaukee, the Coalition for Human Needs in Boston, and the Coalition for Welfare Rights in New York City.[14]

*When the president had his economic summit, he invited all sorts of business people to sit around a big table. When Hillary Rodham Clinton was cooking up a health care plan, she put together a panel of people from the industry. And anyone who truly wants welfare reform has this responsibility: to get together a group of women who are in the system and ask them what keeps them there. The answers are complicated; the experts are poor.*[15]

—ANNA QUINDLEN

Our expertise as women, comes from a strong incentive to change the practices of our society. We motivate other women to get involved by bringing our issues to the forefront and standing up and being counted in speaking to these causes. Together with the power of our organized numbers, we can bring our issues into the limelight.

*Indeed, if there is one constant in all my years of observing politics, it is the single, shocking fact that the most far-reaching developments in my memory did not emanate from Washington or anywhere else in the elected structure of politics but came instead from obscure, unpredictable places where unanointed citizens found a way to express themselves.*

—WILLIAM GREIDER,
WHO WILL TELL THE PEOPLE?

## ■■■■■■■■■ WOMEN WHO DARE [▭▭▭▭▭▭▭]

## Genevieve Richards-Wright

I always wanted to be a teacher, from the age of five. I was born in St. Croix, Virgin Islands, and I started out teaching everyone else their prayers for first communion. We moved to Brooklyn, New York, and when our family became too large for the projects, we got a house in East New York. Then the city government decided to build the Charrett Education Complex in our neighborhood, and we were forced to move. They touted it as the greatest educational thing that would happen in East New York, but the complex never came about.

We were totally disillusioned, displaced, uprooted, and scattered to the five boroughs. Ours had been a beautiful neighborhood, you could walk up the street and buy sliced bread on Blake Avenue; it was just a wonderful community. And after that it was destroyed, left just like a wasteland. I think I am where I am now because of that incident. The school was not built there, but I ended up bringing the school to the neighborhood anyway.

I became an activist soon after Father Hinch, of East Brooklyn Congregations (EBC), a neighborhood citizens organization, had a meeting with me. In that first meeting, we found out where my anger was: people say they'll do things in the neighborhood and they never do them. From there I started working with EBC, where we always say, "People are the most important product."

The first project we did was to go into the local supermarkets and take stock of the quality of the food—the products, and how people were being treated. Many of the inner city neighborhoods were poorly served by the supermarkets in quality and quantity of food and service. Ten of us went into each store with clipboards, just like inspectors, and checked products and service. We told the owners that we'd be back, and things started getting better because until then we were just getting leftovers from other stores. Then we started thinking about creating a new school.

Two years ago, a group of people—teachers, parents, EBC members, and administrators—sat around a table and just dreamed. We sat there night after night and week after week. We drew a vision of a new school and put it onto a board. Now everything is coming off that board and becoming reality, it's so exciting.

Last February we got the lease for the new East New York school. I was appointed Project Director in July, and had two months to get the school ready. And we were pushing those construction workers to get it done. The school is in an old sewing warehouse, the entire first floor. When it opened on September 20th everyone came in the door just smiling at the brand new building, with central air conditioning and beautiful white walls and teal blue highlights—it was just gorgeous. That was challenging, hard work, and I feel like it's where I need to be.

It's called the High School for Public Service. Our theme is public service, community service. If the kids give back now through community service, they'll help build a better community while they are going to school in it.

The students go to different community agencies—law offices, elderly agencies, child care—on Thursday afternoons. You should have seen them the first day, dressed to the nines, with their resumes ready for their interviews. Not all the students go out. We had to think long and hard, but we decided if they were not doing well in their school work, they can't go out for community service. This serves as an incentive for them, they say to me, "Next semester I'm going out for community service; you just wait and see." And they have.

We have a course called "Community Action," where students are taught community organizing skills—change, power, leadership, vision. That's tied into the community service, and we have EBC members come in and talk to the students about how they got involved in community organizing.

I've combined my life with my activism. As Marion Wright Edelman says, "Service is the rent you pay to live on this earth." I really believe this. You're here to serve; we were all put here to serve each other, to help each other out.

Anger can be used in a positive way. Rosa Parks was angry. Anger made us get in those stores and stop them from selling rotten meat. Anger made us sign up people to vote. Anger got us to build affordable housing when the city said we couldn't. Anger made us go around closing crack houses. You can't just sit by. To not take the risk is to risk everything.

---

## Notes

[1] It is due to the perseverance of trade unions and the tenacity of ordinary ad hoc groups of workers that we enjoy important concessions from our employers: a five-day work week, instead of six or seven; an eight-hour work day, instead of ten or twelve; minimum wage protection; child labor restrictions.

[2] Mitzi Henderson, "My Son Is a Homosexual," *Parents*, November 1993, vol. 68, no. 11, p. 332.

[3] Barbara Presley Nobel, "Unhealthy Prospects for Women," *New York Times*, May 22, 1994, p. F23.

[4] Rosemary Wallner, *Girls and Young Women Leading the Way: Twenty True Stories About Leadership* (Minneapolis: Free Spirit Publisher, 1993), pp. 120–125.

[5] Women's Voices Poll: A Joint Project by the Ms. Foundation for Women and the Center for Policy Alternatives, Washington, D.C., 1992.

[6] From the National School Board Association, Alexandria, Va.

[7] Robert Pear, "Surgeon General Says Medicaid Enslaves Poor Pregnant Women," *New York Times*, February 26, 1994, p. 7.

[8] *Current Biography*, vol. 55, no. 3, March 1994, p. 8.

[9] Rianne Eisler, United Nations Commission on the Status of Women.

[10] Ben Lilliston, "Aid for Dependent Corporations," *Multinational Monitor*, January–February, 1994, pp. 11–12.

[11] Ronald K. Fitten, "Surprises in Welfare Study—Many Women Get off Aid within Two years—and Stay Off," *Seattle Times*, July 9, 1991, p. E1.

[12] National Committee on Pay Equity Fact Sheet "Key Facts About Unequal Pay," 1992. Washington, D.C.

[13] The wage gap is particularly severe for women over 30 years old, because at the younger ages *both* men and women are poorly paid.

[14] Nina Schuyler, "On the Line: Power for Poor Women," *The Progressive*, October 1992, p. 14.

[15] Anna Quindlen, "Inside the System," *New York Times*, February 26, 1994, p. 15.

# 5

# Ten Tales of Political Activism: Take on the System, and Win!

L ong before and since Harriet Tubman and hundreds of others set up the Underground Railroad, a network of activists that led at least 100,000 southern blacks from slavery, determined women have strategized, initiated, and directed momentous efforts for positive change. They've struggled, confronted, boycotted, picketed, and persisted against those who meant to deprive women, children, and families of fair treatment. They've taken on the government, the corporations, the media, and the churches to make room for equality and justice.

In this chapter, we'll tell ten stories of women who have chosen to work for change. Some are lifelong pursuits; others involve thousands of people, or are only as large as the community, neighborhood, or constituency at risk. All of them help comprise an instruction manual on how successful activism produces results. Not only do the issues differ across the ten avenues taken, so too do the approaches, tactics, and strategies selected/undertaken. In essence, activism comes in every size, shape, color and can fit each personal experience, style, and comfort level.

## 1.

### THINK GLOBALLY, ACT LOCALLY

## Is there Something in the Water? It's a Matter of Life and Death

Kendale Lakes, Florida is a community of 20,000 people that covers roughly two and a half square miles. Before its development as a residential community, the land was agricultural. In the late 1980s, three women tennis players, under the age of 45 and in good health, were all diagnosed with breast cancer. Upon investigation, the women discovered several others in this small community with the same diagnosis.[1]

The high incidence of cancer among women who were not otherwise high-risk made them believe the cause might be environmental. In fact, the prior agricultural use of the land included the spraying of pesticides and insecticides. Further, not long before, a sewage treatment plant in the community had been closed with no explanation.

The women reached out to their neighbors to gather more information and include others in the effort to determine the cause of such a high incidence of cancer. They formed the Kendale Lakes Women Against Cancer (KLWAC) with the initial goal of raising funds to study local breast cancer incidence. As a long-term goal, the group desired an increase in research on breast cancer at the federal level.

The Kendale Lakes women were discouraged by researchers from pursuing a link between an environmental agent and breast cancer. The scientists they approached weren't convinced of the presence of a cancer cluster in the community. That is, according to the experts proof of enough documented cases was needed to declare an epidemic. The women persisted.

Public meetings were organized. A total of 15 women came forward to volunteer information regarding their own breast cancer. Homeowners meetings drew attendances of over 100 local residents who wanted to get involved. Due to the momentum of citizen participation of the Kendale Lakes community cancer researchers were invited to a local meeting, as was the local media (television, radio, and newspapers), and asked to help initiate funding to research the problem. The severity of the problem was crystallizing. A large per capita level of breast cancer incidence led to community reaction and fear. Homeowners attended meetings to find out what was in the water. Real estate agents and prospective buyers became nervous about potential dangers and the impact on property values.

The growing publicity generated by the organizing of the Kendale Lakes Women convinced the University of Miami's Cancer Center that a study was essential. To gain funding for the study, the Kendale Lakes Women learned how to lobby state legislators for state budget monies. They also organized allied groups to join in the lobbying effort, including the Dade County chapter of the National Organization for Women, United Way, and a committee within the local police and fire departments. Eventually the group found a legislator willing to spearhead the effort at the capitol to get funding.[2]

Over the course of the years necessary to complete the studies, a couple of the most active Kendale Lakes women died of breast cancer. The KLWAC continued its campaign to win attention to the problem until its short-term goal was met: funding a study of the seemingly high incidence of breast cancer among young women residents. The process of community organization and agitation caused government and academic officials to respond to a critical need raised by the activists. The attention brought to this issue in southern Florida in turn adds urgency to the activism of those seeking more national scrutiny on the problem.

The Kendale Lakes women contributed to an important movement. A raised consciousness galvanized scores of women to join and take action. In 1992, pressure from hundreds of thousands of letters to and contacts with the United States Congress resulted in the doubling of the national budget for breast cancer research.

America is undergoing a breast cancer epidemic. Today, one of every eight women will develop breast cancer in her lifetime, compared to one in twenty in 1940. Every three minutes a woman is diagnosed with breast cancer—that's about five hundred new cases a day.

Take action! The National Breast Cancer Coalition, comprised of nearly two hundred activist groups from all over the United States, brings together women concerned about the issue to advocate more research dollars and greater public attention to the disease. Join the local grassroots organization to pressure the government to devote more money and time to breast cancer research, prevention, and quality care for women. Be hopeful. The treatment of breast cancer is changing rapidly, and more and more women are surviving breast cancer and living long and happy lives.

*"AFTER BREAST CANCER, I AM A WARRIOR, NOT A VICTIM . . I am saving my life in the service of what must be done . . . Sometimes we are blessed with being able to choose the time and the arena and the manner of our revolution, but more usually we must do battle wherever we are standing . . .*[3]

—AUDRE LORDE[4]

## 2.

## FROM THE STOCK EXCHANGE TO A JOB WITH MEANING

Beverley Cooper of Salt Lake City, Utah describes her new job as a professional activist:

It makes me high. I don't know how many hours I worked until I come home and sit on the couch and sigh. I get high from what I've done.

After I got my business degree, I worked as a commodities broker for ten years. It didn't fulfill me—my heart has been in working in something that changes the world. Since I was employed part-time, I decided to work as a legislative aide after the Utah state legislature passed an obnoxious anti-abortion bill.

Then the state senator I volunteered for ran for U.S. Congress, and asked me to work on her campaign. Because she was a wonderful pro-choice candidate, I worked closely with Utahns for Choice. After my candidate won her seat in Congress, I went to work in her district office and I became a volunteer with Utahns for Choice. I was recruited by that organization when they needed a new Executive Director.

Now as Executive Director of Utahns for Choice, I work to elect pro-choice officials in the state of Utah. I feel my business skills, such as not being shy about asking for money, are really valuable now. Our program is to use pro-choice Voter ID (voter identification) and education. Voter ID is the process of calling up voters and identifying the people who are already with us. We do a lot of speaking engagements, we do voter registration, we organize booths at fairs and public events and we meet with legislators. We want to make this issue not so tough to talk about in Utah.

Time, ideas, and money are the three ways people can help our organization. Almost always we can find a fit. Our board is made up mostly of women who haven't done anything political before. We found people who hadn't been tapped, haven't been involved in politics, or in an issue.

It seems women are much more willing to make the time to be involved as activists. I don't know if they *have* more time, but they are much more willing to *make* the time. Their organizational skills are incredible. No matter what background, whether it's managing a house or whatever, women have great organizational skills. When a woman decides this is something she really believes in she has the commitment and willingness to do what needs to be done. It's just amazing what we already know that we don't even know that we know and the skills we have that transfer into being successful activists or as part of an organization. I'm very excited about it.

When I was 18 or 19 years old I wanted to go out and change the world. Whether it's volunteer or paid staff, I am a walking advertisement for it all the time. I tell everyone you need to do it. If nothing else you're going to make contacts like you never have before and end up working in an environment you *like* to work in instead of an environment you *have* to work in.

Many women are unaware that activism can be a career, and a fulfilling, long-term one at that. Chapter 10 takes you to the next step in changing your life to include more meaningful work, for which you can get paid.

# 3.

## SINGLE ISSUES EXPERTS

Judith Vladeck is a seventy-year-old terror on skates to those perpetrating sexual discrimination in the workplace. An activist attorney for forty years, Vladeck has devoted much of her career to battling workplace discrimination and winning vindication, damages and pride for women done wrong. It is rumored that she still puts in eleven hour days, close to seven days a week. Vladeck represents those who want to fight injustices, including women who are professors denied tenure on the basis of gender; women denied promotions; women sexually harassed; women denied partnerships in firms on the basis of gender; and women dragged to the front of the line when it comes to company layoffs due to their lack of seniority. Vladeck's cases have taken on E. F. Hutton, the Union Carbide Corporation, Chase Manhattan Bank, and the City University of New York.

Not only is she unafraid of the giants, she is clearly compassionate toward her clients. "I think what distinguishes me has been that I really do care," explains Vladeck. "I've focused on this issue because women came to me for my assistance and the more I found out about workplace discrimination the angrier I got."[5] In fact, her successes are as much related to her ability to identify with her clients as they are with her incredible skills as a lawyer. Vladeck graduated from law school as one of 26 women in a class of 174. She went to work for the only law firm that would hire her.

"In the City University case, in which Vladeck painstakingly documented past faculty salaries, the judge ruled that the university had discriminated against women for 15 years."[6] In 1983, when the *New York Times* asked whether Ms. Vladeck thought the multimillion-dollar settlement was equitable, her response hit the nail on the head, "If we were to calculate the real back pay in this case, they'd have to take Brooklyn College and City College and auction them off to pay the damages."[7]

Vladeck advanced the training and self-image of women along the way. She has mentored young women lawyers (including her daughter), many of whom have come to her to practice this particular type of law. Judith Vladeck has taught her clients that they are worth big money. "I try to teach women that they should not be afraid of big numbers," she said. "The first time I settled something in the $1 million range, I was in a panic. I discovered then that it's a hell of a lot easier to get $100,000 in damages than to get five cents an hour [raises] for blue-collar workers."

Vladeck emphasizes the value of employment law. "The level of ignorance in our lives about our rights of employment is shocking. It is very significant because of the endemic discrimination we suffer due to our gender. Each case I take is serious and has far-reaching ramifications. Women need to know and use the laws that protect them." Ask if she'd ever represented an employer, and Ms. Vladeck is incredulous. "Are you kidding? Never."[8]

*The most absurd hazardous waste incinerator on the planet is up and running. It is four hundred yards from an elementary school, three hundred feet from nearby houses, and a stone's throw from the Ohio River which supplies drinking water to millions of people.*[9]

Terri Swearingen was born and raised in East Liverpool, Ohio, located west of Pittsburgh, Pennsylvania. An economically depressed area, the community became home to the largest hazardous waste incinerator in the world. Dangerously close to the homes and schools of East Liverpool's families as well as on the border of the mighty Ohio River, the plant burns 60,000 tons of toxic wastes annually.

Advocates for the plant cite the advantage of providing 150 jobs to a community suffering from high unemployment. They claim that the stuff spewed from the smokestack is mostly harmless and only a small amount of hazardous material is not destroyed.

Swearingen and other opponents of the plant don't believe that even so-called small amounts of known carcinogenic chemicals such as dioxin, mercury, and lead can be ignored. Further, research and investigation reveals that not only is the plant's discharge incredibly dangerous, but it is operated with blatant disregard of government regulations.

Swearingen continues to fight. She organizes protests and confronts local, state, and federal environmental authorities. She won the support of Al Gore who campaigned as a vice-presidential candidate against the plant and attracted the participation of such actors as Martin Sheen in public events. Swearingen is the leader of a movement that will not give up.

The plant suffers from many problems, including the potential cancer threat resulting from food chain contamination of one thousand to ten thousand times greater than simple inhalation of the emissions, an efficiency rate for mercury burning of 7%, which federal law requires to be 99.99%, and storage of the hazardous waste in open containers.[10]

What success can an activist have when one of the primary investors in this project also provided two last-minute, desperation loans to Bill Clinton's presidential campaign? She just keeps going. In November 1993, Swearingen organized East Liverpool residents to rally across from the Capitol Building in Washington, D.C. to again call for action from the so-called environmental president and vice president. In April 1994, the television news magazine *60 Minutes* did a lengthy piece on the issue and the woman leading the outcry against the plant. "This is my home. I was born here. *They* are the trespassers here," explained Swearingen.

Sometimes, our blood boils about a single occurrence or series of similar incidents. Many women activists like Terri Swearingen and Judith Vladeck have devoted years standing up against what they find to be just plain wrong. Their strategies and tactics, and ability to focus and persist, show us how we can undertake and succeed with a single-issue approach.

## 4.

### THE HEART OF THE COUNTRY ENJOYS ACTIVISTS WITH HEART

Rural America may be different than you think:

■ About 27% of the U.S. population, or approximately 62 million people, resides in rural areas.[11]

- Contrary to public opinion, less than 10% of the rural population lives on farms.[12]
- About 77% of our nation's counties are defined as nonmetropolitan.
- There are nearly 15,000 towns with populations of fewer than 2,500 people.[13]

Rural communities face staggering problems: continual net migration to the cities, unequal public services (such as roads and water), inadequate access to health care and doctors and the loss of family farms—a large source of economic livelihood. Often rural communities lack a powerful voice other than that of the agriculture industry, which does not address the full range of rural residents' needs. Due to the diffuse nature of rural populations, they are not adequately considered or given attention when national policies are formulated.

Some activists believe that the large businesses—agricultural, mining, and logging,—who make huge profits from rural areas, should put something back into those communities. These groups want to hold business and government accountable for their treatment of rural people and their towns. One organization with that priority is Save Our Cumberland Mountains (SOCM) located in the rural Tennessee Valley. One woman, Maureen O'Connell, has devoted over 20 years to help build the leadership skills of SOCM members in confronting government and corporate America. This is a story of success based on the courage and tenacity of ordinary people facing horrible odds.

For the 20 years that I've been an organizer, I've been bringing people together who have problems, issues, concerns, or something they want to accomplish. I work with local people on immediate, urgent issues giving them the tools and confidence to approach them. I help them think through the strategy and to take on the organizing tasks themselves as well as helping them get the training they need to be successful in their strategies.

Save Our Cumberland Mountains is a membership organization started in the rural communities of the Tennessee Appalachian Mountains, the Cumberlands. We work on local issues, such as strip mining, which are of desperate importance.

Strip-mining removes all the land above a seam of coal, including trees, soil, everything, to uncover the coal seam and make it accessible to the surface. In the process, the companies dig up the land, haul it out and throw the waste down into valleys. This causes enormous landslides, which tumble into creeks, fills them up with the overburden and eventually causes floods. In the early days of SOCM (pronounced Sock 'Em) there was absolutely no regulation of strip mining. This is not just an issue of it not being pretty—people's safety, homes, and communities, their wells, were threatened. The landslides completely covered county roads, with no care for the lives of people.

We won many victories for regulation around this issue. Fifty communities were fighting to enforce regulations of mining companies. They changed the law and carried out a lot of campaigns on enforcement. Winning involved lots of pressure and embarrassment tactics as well as getting good media coverage.

Through SOCM people in many other rural areas come to recognize there are similar problems in their communities. Members will form strategies to find the root of the problem. For example, what's needed at the state level? Who is the target, the person in power, who can do something to change the situation? Is there a state agency that needs to buck up enforcement? Are there people who just haven't been doing their job? Is there a new law needed?

This style of organizing has kept SOCM around for 22 years: We're a very high morale organization. It is an organization that is always freshly renewing itself; an organization to which great people join and belong, many of whom didn't have a clue they could ever get involved and win change. They're ordinary folks from rural communities and small towns. There's so much potential in so many people, and in all people, to assume leadership roles if they're given the chance.

That's our secret, we really put an emphasis on leadership development. It is our instinct that while people say they can't do something, we know they really can. Our organization doesn't do anything just to win on an issue. Our emphasis is on building a strong organization of people which means developing more and more leadership. We create places and ways for leaders and members to be involved and develop their skills. We lay out stepping stones to build up leadership. And then we increase the levels of responsibility that people take on. As important as winning on an issue is developing the capacity of people. People who never thought they would be leaders, who have come into the organization baking a cake, have become the president of the organization.

There are people in SOCM taking things on that you wouldn't think in your right mind you can affect. They take on powers whom you are told from birth that you cannot budge. It's just amazing, their courage. I learned from the people here that you need to handle the intensity of organizing, either you can burn yourself out or you can see this is going to take a long time. It's been this way since 1890 in the Cumberland Mountains; it's not going to change in a day. Local folks really taught me how to laugh in this work. No matter how bleak it seems, you can find something to laugh at.

Currently we're working on a host of issues: the dramatic increase in temporary work with no benefits and low pay, equalizing the public revenues that go into rural communities with those that go to urban areas, and trying to stop the southern part of Tennessee from becoming the toxic dump of the state, with landfills, incinerators, and dump sites. Also, we continue to address very local issues like getting water systems put in where the wells and creeks are too polluted.

Now, I couldn't get a normal job and feel that I could live with it: I love waking up in the morning and doing something I believe in and, I get paid for it! I am one of 11 children, and my father raised me with the sense that you don't let people push you around and you don't push other people around. Everybody's as good as everyone else. It's wonderful to have a job when you get to live that out.

# 5.

## USING THE POWER OF LIFELONG EXPERIENCE

*We who are older have enormous freedom to speak out, and equally great responsibility to take the risks that are needed to heal and humanize our sick society . . . we can try new things and take on entirely new roles—dangerous roles. Let me describe some of them: builders of new coalitions, watchdogs of public bodies—guardians of the public interest and the common good, advocates of consumer's rights and whistle blowers on fraud, corruption, and poor services, and monitors of corporate power and responsibility.*
—MAGGIE KUHN, FOUNDER, GRAY PANTHERS[14]

Maggie Kuhn started the Gray Panthers with five others, in 1971, when they were all forced to retire at age 65. This nationwide group was the first to highlight the need for citizen action on critical issues of importance to the elderly, such as substandard nursing home conditions, the inequity of mandatory retirement—"age-ism," regulation of the hearing aid industry, the complexity of Medicare forms, and saving Social Security cost-of-living adjustments (COLA).

We have a special opportunity when we work with senior citizens. They have valuable experience and insight to share:

Modjeska Simkins began as an activist in 1971, joining South Carolina's first NAACP branch to work on issues of justice for blacks. She ran for public office twice after the age of sixty-five.

Sam Peake, a retired electrician, participated with other elders in the Solutions to Issues of Concern to Knoxvillians (SICK) program to register voters in Tennessee. The group registered 30,000 new voters throughout the state, partly by taking on the powerholders and winning the right to register people in unemployment lines.

Equally important, elders are able to be active on difficult issues and exploitative conditions with no fear of job loss:

Lucille Thornburgh, semi-retired from a vigorous career in union organizing, explains: "We're more of an activist group than others around here—mainly because we have old union organizers like me. We're doing it in what to me is now the American way. We don't do it by writing letters, being nice little boys and girls. We've got to demonstrate, and embarrass somebody before we can get anything done."[15]

Senior activists have time that many younger people are unwilling or unable to give:

Eleanor Stopps put her retirement years to work saving the native sea bird population of Protection Island off Washington's Olympic Peninsula. Nearly three-quarters of the state's sea birds nest on this island, and Eleanor pressured every level of government to gain them a national wildlife refuge and bird sanctuary status. In her 70s, she persuaded county government to stop issuing building permits for the land on Protection Island, due to the lack of fresh water available. Then, with unrelenting persistence, she moved a bill through the United States Congress to create the refuge. Now she is working to educate recreational boaters in the area to the fact that the island is a wildlife refuge, and as such should remain undisturbed. Explains Stopps, "You have constant pressure to get anything done. You can't let anything sit on the back burner."[16]

Many retired people don't think of themselves that way:

"These government officials are not only breaking laws. They are perpetuating an act of fraud against the citizens of the U.S. who own the forests."[17] Gaby Moyer and a friend founded Friends of Dixie National Forest in Utah, working to keep the forests of many mountains and valleys protected. Their efforts involve limiting the size and number of timber sales, in which timber-cutting rights are sold with the right for the buyers to log. They are particularly focused on saving the giant Ponderosa pines and Douglas firs which are critical components of habitats for several species of local wildlife. And they have won several fights.[18]

Many organizations enjoy great diversity in the ages of their active members, because a coalition of *all* ages represents more accurately the true spectrum of any community. For example, the Gray Panther's membership has always included all ages.

Our society is one which, shamefully, tends to marginalize those euphemistically dubbed "senior citizens." The amazing amount of experience and wisdom built up into our elders is a resource that activists and their groups absolutely must better employ. Older persons know we can organize and change things; they've seen it happen. From the union organizers, to the women's rights advocates, to the consumer watchdog movement, to the civil rights protesters, seniors have lessons to share that can become the core of current activist motivation and power.

## 6.

### WORKING PEOPLE ARE NOTHING WITHOUT EACH OTHER

Discrimination, double standards, and outright sexism are nothing new to women. Yet, as women's percentage of the country's workforce grows from its current level of 46%, the need grows for women to have the skills to take on unfair working conditions and win greater respect and better treatment. Most women in this country work for low wages, in exploitative environments. Many, like those you'll meet here, are willing to risk their meager livelihood to fight for better pay and a safer workplace.

You may never think about where your soiled linens from hospitals and nursing homes, from public rest rooms, and restaurants go to be cleaned, but you might be surprised at how unsafe and difficult that place can be for the women who work there. The American Linen Company manufactures, sells, and cleans linens for a large number of commercial industries and services in about 100 plants world-wide. A family-owned company, one hundred years old, it has an annual income of about $250 million.

The company's employees, primarily women, work in conditions that anyone would call a disgrace. Some plants have been cited numerous times by the federal government for serious health and safety regulation violations.[19]

At the Bemidji, Minnesota plant, one woman was told she could never be promoted to being a driver because of her gender. Others have been forced to quit due to injuries on the job and have no recourse, other than their own pocketbooks. Still others have been hired part-time with no benefits, only to be scheduled with full-time hours.

Eleven women employees at this plant went on strike in the late 1980s, demanding a 5% pay increase (which averaged $5.00), and retention of the pension plan. American Linen countered that proposal with their own, offering to reduce employee break times with no pay increase for three years. The strike went on for nine months, at the end of which the company hired new workers who voted against keeping the union.

However, at another American Linen plant in Hibbing, Minnesota, the strike was much more successful. A group of seven women strikers, known as the "Hibbing 7," also went out on strike in the late 1980s. They held out for a year before the National Labor Relations Board ruled against the company for firing the striking workers. (Federal law prohibits companies from firing workers before hiring their replacements). While the company appealed the ruling, allies of the workers—in the community and in other unions—helped carry out a campaign to get city government, local school districts, and businesses to cancel contracts with American Linen. Four years after they first struck and began picketing, the Hibbing women were awarded a settlement of almost one-half million dollars to cover back pay and benefits. American Linen was found guilty of firing workers because their union voted to strike.

In the industrial plants of the southeastern United States, the situation is frequently even more exploitative, as Early Mae Wallace explains:

In 1975, I was 25 years old, chopping cotton for a living and a single parent with 4 children. I got tired of going to the cotton field to get paid $13 for a 10-hour day.

One night it rained, and I didn't go to the field because it was wet. I do believe I heard the voice of God say, "Go to Earle Industry and put an application in."

They called me to go to work the next day at the plastic factory, where they make garment bags from plastic. They put me on the floor as a service girl, to supply the sewers with thread, needles—whatever they needed, and to carry the finished work to the shipping department. All I wanted was to do my job and take care of my four babies. But the company treated people bad, just terrible.

In 1977, two people came in to talk with us about organizing a union— the International Ladies Garment Workers' Union (ILGWU). We got people to sign cards and we won election by one vote, but they fired me because I was one of the ring leaders.

The company stalled on negotiations, and in the meantime were hiring non-union people, trying to stack it with those who would be against the union. They told people not to talk to me if they wanted to keep their jobs!

Finally they got these non-union people to go for a decertification election, by promising them a raise. They voted out the union by three or four votes, and a minimum wage raise was all they got.

I continued to work with my head up. Things began to get real bad. People were harassed, violently. All this time I had two girls in college. I went into the bathroom and cried in the stall and asked God for strength because I had to work. I did that for four years.

One cold Saturday evening in 1991, two women from Amalgamated Clothing and Textile Workers' Union (ACTWU) came to my house and said, "We've been investigating this plant and did some research. Earle Industries made $18 million last year, $16 million the year before. Some other girls are going to come in and sign people up for the union." I needed the work, and I knew I was going to get fired again, but I wanted to help my people. The people signed those cards like crazy and the next Sunday night there were over a hundred people at the union meeting. We had never seen that many before.

The lead woman said, "You all want a union?" And everyone cried, "Yes!" She said, "Well, we can't get a union with this many people. I want you to go back to work tomorrow and get more people to sign." I had to get my cards signed after work, because I was constantly begin watched, but I got them all signed anyway. Then we filed for an election a few weeks away. We won the election, and everyone wore their red T-shirts saying "Union, yes!" The plant was like a sea of red, you could feel that union in your bones. You could feel the power all the way through the plant. I was sitting outside waiting for a ride home and I was singing, "I got victory over the enemy and the world can't do me no harm!" We went on and voted that union in, 172–101.

Well, we had a lot more struggles after that, but there has never been a battle won without a struggle. Nelson Mandela spent 27 years in a South African prison for standing up for what is right. So I say stand strong no matter how hard it gets. Because if you don't stand for something, you'll fall for anything.


Diamond Walnut supplies the country with half of its walnuts. Five hundred women, mostly Hispanic, have been on strike from the company for more than two years. All have been permanently replaced with other workers, which *is* legal for a company to do. But hardly any of the 500 have given up on regaining their jobs *with* better compensation. Having accepted pay cuts of up to 40% during the 1980s, workers wanted more than the ten-cent-per-hour wage increase offered in the early 1990s, when Diamond's profits reached over $170 million. Refused higher pay, the women voted to strike. Since then, they have convinced the General Mills Corporation to stop using the walnuts in its Betty Crocker brownies and Godiva Chocolatiers to stop using them in their products. Kellogg and Kraft are users of Diamond walnuts that are currently being targeted for support.[20]

Women like the Diamond Walnut strikers, Early Mae Wallace and the workers at Earle Industries, and the American Linen employees cannot just give up. If they don't stand up and demand fairer treatment at the job, all they have to look forward to are equally unfair conditions at the next. At some point, poorly treated women workers won't and don't take it anymore. Dignity and the need to heat their homes, eat, and be healthy are on the line.

# 7.

## CHALLENGED WOMEN TAKE ON CHALLENGES

*Groups and individuals make a difference . . . We women with disabilities have the same hopes and dreams and ambitions as our non-disabled sisters. We are neither weak or heroic. We are normal. And we are boat rockers.*[21]

Approximately 43 million Americans have some form of disability. That's one out of every 6 or 7 people. Yet people with disabilities are blatantly missing from the media, from leadership positions, and often from our daily lives. Some women activists have worked long and hard to include disabled persons in our institutions, and communities. Their goal is to replace attitudes of sympathy with those that accept the disabled for what they have to offer to all aspects of everyday life.

Typical of the treatment many disabled initially receive, Judith Heumann was turned down at her local school at age five on the grounds that her wheelchair was a potential fire hazard. She had polio. Her youth was riddled with segregation and discrimination. When she was 22 years old, Heumann was judged medically unqualified to be a public school teacher in New York City. She filed a lawsuit and became the first wheelchair-bound teacher in the school district. Her activism escalated when she became the deputy director of the Center for Independent Living in Berkeley, California five years later. Heumann organized many disability-rights demonstrations, won numerous awards for her work, and was the co-founder and vice president of the World Institute on Disability. Her outspokenness and activism paid off. Now, after being appointed in 1993 by President Bill Clinton, Judith Heumann is the assistant secretary for the office of special education and rehabilitative services in the U. S. Department of Education.[22]

Patti Mullins, an Indianapolis, Indiana lawyer, devotes the majority of her work to activism for the rights and needs of the disabled. Serving as the executive director of Access International, Inc., Mullins put extraordinary time into lobbying for the passage of the Americans with Disabilities Act (ADA). The ADA requires that businesses and public service facilities provide accessibility to disabled persons.[23]

Mullins believes that these measures will allow people to become more tolerant and accepting of those with disabilities when they see and interact with the handicapped in workplaces, schools, and communities. Access International was created to offer input to facilities on achieving accessibility for the disabled. It is comprised of and controlled by, people with disabilities and their families.

Why is Mullins involved in this issue? As a former nursing home staffer putting herself through college, Mullins witnessed the extreme abuse of elderly residents. Later, while pushing friends in wheelchairs through campus, she found how much of the area was entirely inaccessible to the disabled. Explains Mullins, "These are human rights we're dealing with. It's only because people kept violating them that it became necessary to legislate something to enforce those rights."[24]

Activism pays off. At a time when disabled students are prodding colleges for better accommodation, Cheryl Ann Fischer fought until she won a court decision admitting her to medical school. Clearly qualified academically, Fischer's blindness prevents her from becoming a surgeon, although she feels she can be successful in other areas of the profession, such as psychiatry or preventive medicine.

Adriana Duffy was a world champion gymnast until she slipped off a piece of equipment in 1989. Her legs permanently paralyzed, Adriana has hardly slowed down. At Stanford University, Duffy is an iconoclast of misperceptions of the disabled. "People have this conception that it's supposed to be the end of the world. You have to explain to them that most things in your life don't change at all."[25] Duffy has been a campus leader promoting rights for students with disabilities, including efforts to make the dormitories and campus facilities wheelchair accessible.

Even the federal government understands the importance of activism by parents of the disabled. The Department of Health and Human Services developed a program to teach disabled adults and their parents how to confront difficult government bureaucracies. The boat-rocking continues.[26]

## 8.

### DON'T MOURN, ORGANIZE!

*The main reason I joined was sexual harassment—there's a lot of it in high school.*

—MARINA GRINBERG, AGE 17

High school women are currently forming groups across the country to address women's issues. The National Organization for Women (NOW) has high school chapters in 12 states, all of which were organized recently. A California group, Females Unifying Teens to Undertake Responsible Education (FUTURE), surveyed 400 young women, and found these top five issues: stress, sexuality, sexual assault, suicide, and pregnancy. Groups focus on discussion and problem solving. Some women have turned to activism to wield change in their own high schools.[27]

Campus organizing is alive and well. While the freshness and excitement of the 1960s college activism seems long gone, we find young women and men activists are as committed and productive as ever.

The students of the current decade came of age during the Reagan-Bush era of conservative values. Yet, we find that women students are joining many progressive activist efforts: protecting a woman's rights to choose a safe and legal abortion, ending violence against women, halting discrimination against women in every aspect of life, and getting more of their brothers and sisters to vote. Students are also forging campus campaigns: against ROTC programs that promote militarism, against date and acquaintance rape, on a variety of environmental issues, and in favor of the national community service program created by the Clinton administration.

Student activities are prolific and varied: carrying out marches, lobbying, organizing discussion groups, training leaders for advocacy, developing leadership, and registering voters. Many point to the importance of the youth vote giving the Clinton-Gore ticket a 20% margin of support over the Bush-Quayle slate.

Halle Brenner grew up thinking she had to operate on her own as an activist, because the era of group activism—like that of the 60s—seemed to be over. Then she was contacted by the Long Island Alliance for Peaceful Alternatives.

It was the eighties and we felt like outcasts, because the Republicans had been in power nationally since we were nine, and there didn't seem to be an outcry in the schools for peace, justice, and activism on progressive issues. Then, a group of students along with their faculty adviser formed a political affairs club and contacted many other schools on Long Island about meeting to talk about issues.

We talked about what we had done privately and that we felt isolated as activists. Then we moved into action. With the help of the adult organization that had originally contacted us, we formed a group called the Long Island Coalition for Peace and Justice, in which over 100 colleges, high schools, and junior highs were represented. At first, we didn't really know what we were doing. And we all came with different issues. We realized right from the start that we needed to educate ourselves about the issues we were concerned with: do research, invite speakers in, and contact other organizations that worked on the same stuff. I realized that every generation can get involved in helping on issues and that I had been waiting for someone else to call me into action instead of calling myself into action.

The issues we concentrated on were hunger, homelessness, the environment, human rights, and peace. We organized lots of activities: working with local soup kitchens and shelters both as advocates and as volunteers; conducting educational campaign teach-ins at school so people could learn what homelessness was; fundraising; and working with children in the shelters. We also got to know the Central American community on Long Island. Previously, many of us didn't even know where El Salvador was. We worked with Central American organizations both for relief for refugees and to advance political views. We met our congresspeople to lobby to stop military aid to El Salvador. Every year we did a mass walk for peace, the Long Island Peace Walk for a Better World. It was inspirational and fun, a multigenerational event with everyone from children to senior citizens.

Our coalition spoke at assemblies at elementary schools because these issues need to be explored at an earlier age than they usually are. Students need to start getting active when their impressions are first forming. We found younger students had already become somewhat cynical, but they went through a significant transformation when they saw that young people like us were doing something and not just talking about it—that we were getting some results. They realized they had a voice too, and they started putting on plays and writing letters, and getting active around issues.

## 9.

## POLITICS THROUGH THE ARTS

*"We are the singing voice of the community, and it's a voice that must be heard."*

—BERNICE JOHNSON REAGON

It's hard to describe the fullness of sound, emotion, and sweetness of the a cappella voices of these six African-American artists. Sweet Honey in the Rock was organized by Bernice Johnson Reagon in 1973, and has for over 20 years melted the hearts, and soothed the souls of audiences around the world. As a musical group, Sweet Honey is unique. Through their 20 albums, Sweet Honey uses music to communicate their political activism and attract others. Their songs take on issues like apartheid, economic justice, AIDS, homelessness, political prisoners, and the global struggle for human rights.

"Spirituality, consciousness-raising, social responsibility, healing, and—most of all—love resonate at the heart of Sweet Honey's repertoire." And they call people to action. Many of their pieces are updated versions of old hymns or songs of their youth; others are innovative new compositions. The way the group operates is as important and political as their songs. Each singer covers unique singing ranges. As Audreen Buffalo describes, "Each serves as a master teacher in at least one repertoire or singing style and apprentices in an area covered by another member. . . . They are required to act organizationally and musically as both leaders and followers."[28]

Twenty-one singers have been members of the group since its inception including Reagon and Carol Maillard. Today's ensemble includes one woman who performs her singing in American sign language for the deaf.

Sweet Honey wants people to be galvanized in their lives, and help to provoke that action through their songs. The singers explain that it was the activism of other black women who moved them to take action, and they want to serve in the same role for others: "I think of my life as walking a path and being on a journey," Reagon says. "I'm going over tracks woven by Harriet Tubman, Sojourner Truth, W. E. B. Du Bois and Frederick Douglass. So yes, I live a full life, but I'm grateful."[29]

Signe Wilkinson has a great job. She is a *Philadelphia Daily News* political cartoonist; the first woman to win the Pulitzer prize for editorial cartooning. Combining her art with politics, Wilkinson is well known for her series of cartoons, *Abortion Cartoons on Demand.* ("No parental notification, waiting period, or counseling required for purchase.") Her work is provocative and challenges the latest trend to restrict abortion access in America. The cartoons make others aware that the newly proposed abortion restrictions—24-hour waiting periods, spousal notification, and threats to public funding for poor women's abortions—are, what Wilkinson calls, "thinly veiled harassment."[30]

This unique use of political cartoons both informs readers in a spirit that promotes activism, and addresses politics with a sense of humor. She understands that the fight around abortion is not yet won.

Wilhelmina Cole Holladay was frustrated with the dearth of information available about women artists. An art collector along with her husband, Holladay spent close to twenty years assembling the work of dozens of women artists. This became the core collection of the National Museum of Women in the Arts in Washington, D.C., founded in 1982.

"Everyone knows Michelangelo and Da Vinci, but even well-educated adults can't name more than five women artists," Holladay says. "They mention [Georgia] O'Keeffe and [Mary] Cassatt and then stop."[31]

The museum, which opened its doors in 1987, has the nation's third largest membership, one hundred thousand. It has provoked discussion about whether women's art should be segregated for viewing. It has given women a place to observe and study the expressions of their peers, predecessors, and previously unknown sisters.

The same year the National Museum of Women opened, Faith Ringgold initiated a group organizing and exhibiting art by women of color—Coast to Coast. Vistas Latinas (a coalition of Latina artists) and Godzilla (an artists group of Asian Americans) represent a growing number of art-related efforts on the part of many groups of women and feminists.

Some of these groups are refreshingly bold in their tactics. Women's Action Coalition (WAC), and Guerilla Girls, use out-front direct action maneuvers to make the point that women in the arts are not equitably represented. They conduct mass postcard campaigns to museums whose exhibits exclude women, and produce and distribute scintillating artistic posters, asserting messages such as the "Advantages of Being a Woman Artist." Many believe that groups like WAC, engaged in tactics in and out of the art world, have assisted the women's movement in regaining the momentum of the 1970s.

## 10.

### "ALL I KNOW ABOUT ORGANIZING, I LEARNED FROM MY MOTHER"
#### —Chesie Lee

At age 79, Frances Lee was asked to be president of her church women's group because they wanted to include more young women.

The people recognized the special organizing skills of Chesie Lee's mother.

Growing up on a chicken farm in a town of 250 people in southeastern Ohio, Chesie saw her mother start a 4H Club when she was nine years old. It was the 1950s and there was nothing for the youth of the community to do outside their homes, so Frances Lee went out and started something. Realizing there wasn't much for the women of the area to do, she started a community homemaker's club and later a garden club.

Looking back, Chesie knows how her mother avoided burn-out from being involved in too many things: Frances always brought in other women to do the work with her. Frances would initiate groups, and then agree to be president for one year. During that time she would identify and groom other women who could take over the leadership after that first year. Frances stayed active with the organizations she founded, but took on different aspects of the work, so that the new leaders could lead. She taught the new leaders that they should do the same; identify and groom future women leaders so that the group always enjoyed new blood and remained vital.

In many ways Frances was an adept organizer. She made certain that others always had a role in the proceedings and tasks to help carry out the work; she delegated wisely, nurturing true ownership of the group to others.

Frances had wanted to be a missionary, but grew up in a household where girls were not allowed to be highly educated. She married at age 17 and had six children, but she always worked as sort of a missionary in her own community. Frances was not afraid to stand up and take tough positions.

Chesie remembers when her mother attended a PTA meeting where the group was discussing which pastor in the community would give the invocation at the graduation ceremonies. Frances suggested that the students were quite capable of making that decision; some called her a "Communist" for that remark.

When Chesie was in high school, Frances served on a local development commission which was deliberating over a proposal to build a lake on Raccoon Creek. Frances' position was clear; she called the project "Tycoon Lake" because it was intended for rich weekend boat owners. It didn't even include a beach for the local folks to enjoy. Decades later, Chesie was visiting her childhood region and passed a sign indicating the way to "Tycoon Lake."

Perhaps most importantly, Frances Lee was both an organizer and a role model for other women. Bidwell, Ohio, had been a stop on the Underground Railroad during the Civil War. Subsequently many African-American families had settled in the area. When *Brown v. Board of Education* outlawed segregated schools, a local woman approached Frances to help organize resistance to integration of the local school. "It's the law of the land and that's how it has to be," responded Frances Lee.

Chesie Lee organized a statewide coalition in Wyoming that works on progressive issues and helps elect progressive activists to office. Pieces of her mother come out in her all the time, from her ability to develop the leadership of others, to her commitment to the power and potential of organized people. Every women has, or can find, another women role model who has helped pave the way for them to be an effective political activist.

Sometimes we overlook women—women as close as our mothers—who are the most meaningful role models.

## Notes

1 Virginia H. McCoy, et al. "Community Activism Relating to a Cluster of Breast Cancer," *Journal of Community Health*, February 1992, vol. 17, no. 1, pp. 27–36.
2 Ibid.
3 Audre Lorde, *The Cancer Journals* (San Francisco: Spinsters Press, 1980).
4 The National Breast Cancer Coalition 202 296-7477; Women's Community Cancer Project 617 354-9888.
5 Susan Antilla, "Profile: Workplace Discrimination? Don't Try it Around Her," *New York Times*, February 13, 1994, p. 7.
6 Ibid.
7 Ibid.
8 Ibid.
9 Information on this issue and activist was compiled by L. J. Davis and published as, "Where Are You Al?" in *Mother Jones*, vol. 18, no. 6, November 1993, pp. 44–49.
10 Ibid., p. 47.
11 Dennis U. Fisher, "Agriculture's Role in a New Rural Coalition," *Annals of the American Academy of Political Science*, September 1993, pp. 103–112.
12 Emery Castel, "Rural Diversity: An American Asset," *Annals of the American Academy of Political Science*, September 1993, pp. 12–21.
13 Priscilla Samuel Jones, "The Elderly in Rural America, *AGING*, 1993, no. 365, pp. 11–17.
14 Dieter Hessel, ed., *Maggie Kuhn on Aging: A Dialogue*. (Philadelphia: The Westminster Press, 1977), pp. 91, 92.
15 Ibid.
16 Mary Johnson, "Island Savior Eleanor Stopps Says, This is for the Birds," *New Choices for Retirement Living*, November 1992, p. 44.

[17] Mary Johnson. "Strike Tree and You're Out," *New Choices in Retirement Living*, July and August, 1992, p. 44.

[18] Ibid.

[19] Louise Mengelkoch. "The American Linen Story, A Special Report", *Z*, November 1993, pp. 36–44.

[20] Frances Rivers. "On the Walnut Bus," *The Progressive*, August 1993, p. 16.

[21] Sue S. Suter. "Women with Disabilities: How to Become a Boat Rocker in Life," *Vital Speeches of the Day*, December 1, 1993, p. 111.

[22] Debra Bladero, "Tireless Activist on Disability Rights, Nominee Has Battled Schools Before," *Education Week*, April 28, 1993, p. 19.

[23] There are tax incentives available for businesses that require structural alterations.

[24] Vicki Quade, "What Is the Value of a Human Life?" *Human Rights Quarterly*, Fall, 1993, pp. 12–16.

[25] Brian Cazeneuve, "Follow the Leader. A Day in the Life of Adriana Duffy: Full Speed Ahead." *International Gymnast*, November 1992, p. 48.

[26] Joe Shapiro, *No Pity: People with Disabilities Forging a New Civil Rights Movement*, (New York: Time Books, 1994).

[27] Melinda Henneberger, "Interest in Feminism Surges Among Teens," *Oregonian*, May 15, 1994, p. L11.

[28] Audreen Buffalo. "Sweet Honey: A Cappella Activists," *Ms.*, April 1993, pp. 25–29.

[29] Elsie B. Washington, "Bernice Johnson Reagon: Cultural Warrior," *Essence*, February 1994. p. 55.

[30] Mubarak S. Dahir, "Back to the Drawing Board on Abortion," *The Progressive*, May, 1993, p. 13.

[31] JoAnn Greco, "Women Artists Find Permanent Home in D.C.," *Variety*, March 24, 1994, p. E1.

# "This Is a Fight for Health Care with Dignity" Organizing to Win

*"I've had a taste of it and now I've got the bug. We had two strikes against us when we started and it was so invigorating to win."*

—JANET ROBIDEAU

In August 1989, Janet Robideau, a 38-year-old mother of one, went to work on the swing shift as a nurse's aide at the Hillside Manor Nursing Home in Missoula, Montana. Of the 102 total patients at Hillside Manor, 39 were under her care for several hours. As a relatively new employee at the home, Robideau had to make some quick and risky decisions. If Mrs. A needed assistance to get to the toilet, then cleaning up the vomit covering Mrs. B would have to wait. Other patients had not yet been initially checked. Robideau asked the director of nursing for help, but was told, "Help will be here in a couple of hours. In the meantime, you have to do, what you have to."

**106**

Staffing was consistently inadequate at Hillside Manor. The shortage contributed to predictable episodes of substandard care. One woman attempted to get to the bathroom herself, fell and broke her hip. Patients received cold dinners because there weren't enough staff to feed them. Baths were irregular, despite the routine many patients were accustomed to, of daily or weekly bathing. Dentures were left in a glass of water with a cleansing tablet each night, rather than brushed. Perhaps, most depressing of all, the staff shortage meant that patients were unable to accomplish their daily ambulation to keep their muscles working. As a result, Robideau and her co-workers saw many residents deteriorate shortly after moving into the home.

Robideau felt cheated. Her certified nurse's training assured her that patients would receive good care if there were adequate personnel with enough time to provide that care.

Our nurse's aide training told us to spend time with patients to do things like fix their hair, write letters for them, read to them, visit with them, but we just never had the time. It was very sad. We couldn't meet their most basic needs, let alone the little extras that make nursing home living bearable.

It was apparent that the staff could only do part of what was necessary to make life bearable for the residents. Staff were poorly paid and overworked. Aides were in charge of as many as 15 patients during their waking hours at a starting wage of only $3.90 an hour. As a result, Hillside Manor suffered from frequent staff turnover. How could Robideau proceed? How could she go on working in an environment that was supposed to be attentive, yet which provided poor care?

## ORGANIZING FOR POWER AND CHANGE

Fortunately, Robideau had great instincts. Understanding the impossible circumstances in which she found herself, she asked for help. Robideau gathered a number of co-workers for meetings in her home at the beginning of October 1989. The gatherings became a weekly support group, where staff began sharing stories of overwork, poor pay, and negligent treatment of nursing home residents. More information about the working conditions at Hillside Manor emerged. The nurse's aides enjoyed little respect from the other caregivers. Only some registered nurses would help aides alleviate the workload, most would not. The management hired college students, desperate for work, whose schedules did not fit with the shift timing at the home. One of the home's cooks reported that she had been reprimanded for allowing a patient to choose a certain dessert.

The support group became a complaint group. Fifty-five aides were employed at Hillside Manor; they wanted to direct their complaints about the lack of sufficient staff to someone who would do something about it. They approached the authorities, from their immediate supervisor to the charge nurse, to the director of nursing, to the Hillside administrators. The response was the same at each level; assurances that their complaints were heard and understood, but as managers of the home, "their hands were tied."

## Creating a Group Strategy

Often, groups of disgruntled neighbors or co-workers ask the boss to rectify particularly substandard conditions. Either they are turned down or assured of some action, they turn around and go back to work or, if they are financially able, they move or quit. Robideau's group persevered. They understood that conditions at Hillside Manor were an outrage. They felt certain that no one in the community would sit by quietly if they knew what kind of care the patients were receiving. Most important, they were motivated to gather strength to take on the power of the nursing home.

Power comes in two varieties: organized money or organized people. In this case, the corporation that owned this home and six others across the state, had the power of vast sums of money. The workers, the patients, and their families, lacked the power of money; they needed to exercise the power of well-organized numbers of people.

Understanding that large numbers of people must be recruited and organized effectively, Robideau's group created an organizing strategy. The organizing strategy is a plan, like a road map, showing how to get from here (where you are now) to your goal; it is a series of steps implemented in an ongoing process.

### Step One: List the goals that you want to achieve

You would never embark on a road trip without knowing something about where you're headed or approximately how many miles must be traveled. Similarly, you want to attain specific goals through your organizing efforts. The overall goal of Robideau's group was to achieve quality care for nursing home residents. The means to that end was an adequate number of nursing home staff. The group determined they could only win increased staffing levels by gaining public awareness of the problem through significant public outreach and education.

### Step Two: Research. Gather information about the situation in order to bring a substantial case to the public

*a. Find out the true financial picture:*

- Hillside Manor is owned by the SAGE Corporation. The SAGE homes in Missoula are two of the six nursing homes owned by the company in Montana in 1991. The six homes cleared a profit of $2.2 million for SAGE.
- SAGE owns facilities in Florida, California, and Oregon. Together the SAGE nursing homes netted a profit of over $9 million in 1991.
- SAGE owns no nursing homes in its home state of Minnesota.
- The nursing home business is only one component of the corporation's assets. SAGE also owns shopping malls, hair salons, and condominiums.

*b. How the company earns its profit:* Two kinds of patients comprise the Sage Nursing Home's clientele: Medicare and private pay patients. Medicare patients pay $1,200 to $1,500 a month. This money is state and federal funded for the elderly who qualify with a certain low level of income. To qualify as a Medicare pay patient, one must "spend down" assets to a level of compliance. Private pay patients use their own money to pay up to $3,000 a month. Nursing homes are a calculated business. Once someone's life savings are drained through high payments to the home, Medicaid and Medicare payments begin. The home never loses its patient fees. SAGE Corporation understands that the nursing home business is a recession-free industry.

In fact, there is a growing shortage of nursing home beds available across the country. Nursing home owners can profit by charging and accepting only the more affluent. This trend will continue since the number of people 85 years and above is the fastest growing segment of the elderly population. By the year 2000, their numbers are projected to rise by 40%. Some analysts contend that more than half of those over age 85 require long term care.[1]

In addition, SAGE operates pharmacies and profits by charging patients separately for pharmaceuticals. Although the drugs are available outside the nursing home for less, patients can't shop around for the best price. For example, simple milk of magnesia could be purchased from the local drug store for $2.98 (360cc); SAGE sold it for $8.10 (60cc).

  *c. Trickle down effect?* In the meantime, the payroll for the SAGE Corporation was not eating up its profits: the nursing staff of the homes were paid $7.10 per hour (licensed practical nurses) and $9.00 per hour (registered nurses). In 1989, the year Robideau started at Hillside Manor, nurses aides were paid the minimum wage of $3.90.

  *d. The Nursing Home Reform Amendments of the Omnibus Budget Reconciliation Act (OBRA), passed by Congress in 1990, sets specific and measurable standards that must be met by every nursing home across the nation to assure that quality of care and quality of life be provided for each nursing home resident.* There is a broad range of standards detailed in OBRA, including residents' rights—daily choices, privacy, social and recreational activities—as well as minimum standards for the staff. These amendments provide a tool for local watchdog organizations like the Montana Coalition for Nursing Home Reform to use to address the circumstances at individual homes. It is the job of the Coalition, and groups like it, to help enforce these standards. In fact, groups like the Coalition must train the members, staffs, and relatives of nursing home patients, to rate nursing homes and demand from the home owners and managers at least the kind of treatment outlined in the federal law.

  *e. Collect more reports from the front lines:*

*When an X-ray was taken on that day—23 days after the teeth were reported missing—they were found lodged in the man's esophagus.*
                    —FROM A STATE REPORT ON THE OPERATIONS OF A BILLINGS,
                    MONTANA NURSING HOME MANAGED BY
                    THE SAGE CORPORATION.

  *f. Contact the National Coalition for Nursing Home Reform:* Founded in 1975 by eleven citizens groups, the National Coalition coordinates the work of over 200 state and local member organizations concerned with the care of nursing home residents. The group provides important research information to activists and helps people initiate organizing drives to address nursing home issues. Local groups can utilize the resources of the National Coalition by joining it. Robideau's group felt the profit margin enjoyed by the SAGE Corporation was indeed comfortable enough to allow for an increase in the staff to help improve the quality of care for the patients of Hillside Manor.

### Step Three: Conduct outreach to gather other allies, individuals, and organizations to join your organizing effort

"The nursing home industry is formidable. One person can get out on a street corner and complain," explains Robideau, "but they're not going to get anything done. It requires a huge number of people to really get through to the big guys."

Initially the support group included about eight employees at Hillside Manor. From their research they realized they would need more people to go up against a major corporation and accomplish change.

First, they went to their union, the Hotel Employees and Restaurant Employees (HERE), Local 470. The union agreed to be part of any effort regarding nursing home working conditions, such as pay, benefits, worker's rights, and fair treatment. The union helped organize meetings of the workers from the other two nursing homes in Missoula. Many workers were skeptical of their ability to win any change because they had seen previous efforts fail. But Robideau's group kept going. They spoke with co-workers on breaks and on social occasions. They documented conditions in the other SAGE nursing home facilities which always led to the same conclusion. There were never enough workers employed to do an adequate, much less a quality, job for residents.

The group reached out to the families of the patients who had a large self-interest in quality care at the home. Flyers were printed, advertising public meetings on the issue. The flyers were distributed creatively; for example, put on car windshields in the nursing home parking lots. The public meetings were well attended—at least 150 people at each. Those who attended had their first opportunity to voice their complaints publicly about the quality of care at the three Missoula nursing homes owned by SAGE. The local media gave good coverage to the group and the issue of nursing home reform.

### Step Four: Create a formal group—a network, a committee, an organization, or the equivalent—so that others can, and will, join to be part of the strategy

Robideau's support group grew with both individuals and other organized groups anxious to join the effort. Together they formed the Montana Coalition for Nursing Home Reform in 1989. She recalls the importance of gaining additional participation, "When we started out we had two strikes against us. It was so critical to utilize the resources of other individuals and groups. The Coalition was more credible with

12 or 13 organizations. Without that we could have faded because at first people thought we had no chance of having an impact on the huge nursing home industry."

---

◆

### Ongoing research:

Relatives and families of the residents provided specific information about the care of patients in the homes. Some of the patients in residence supplied documentation.

*"My husband was in a home for two years. He was not always shaved, his hands and nails often were very dirty, and he was not washed before meals. He didn't get enough attention with toilet, often was very wet and had soiled clothing. Quality care is every resident's right, but not possible when there is not enough help."*
—*Wife of resident*

---

The mission statement of the Montana Coalition for Nursing Home Reform states that it will promote permanent, institutional change that will improve the quality of care and life for residents in nursing homes. The group's aim is to assure the implementation of nursing home residents' rights:

- The right to choose when to get up and retire
- The right to choose when and with whom to eat
- The right to be free from physical and mental abuse and the abuse of neglect
- The right to be free from chemical or physical restraints, except for safety's sake
- The right of access to all personal records

### Step Five: As an organization, determine the targets that have the power to make change

*a. The SAGE Corporation:* First, the Coalition tried to work with the corporation. They presented documentation of the lack of quality care at the Missoula nursing homes and the need for more workers. They discussed the problem of high turnover of staff in the homes due to the heavy work load and the low pay. SAGE Corporation managers claimed that they did not have the money to hire more workers or pay higher wages. They said the corporation was involved in the nursing home industry "out of the goodness of their hearts" because it was such a necessary community service, not because it was profitable.

*"Despite our best intentions, there will always be broken bones in nursing homes."*

—SAGE CORPORATION
NURSING HOME ADMINISTRATOR

### b. Government:

1. Elected officials: The Coalition sought out its local legislators to begin to work on state laws requiring certain minimum standards of care in nursing homes. The coalition contacted Congressman Pat Williams, who was concerned about the issue, and spoke out publicly for nursing home reform.
2. Government agencies: In Montana, the government agencies who regulate nursing homes are the Department of Health and Environmental Sciences (DHES), and the Department of Social and Rehabilitative Services (SRS). DHES certifies nursing homes and enforces state standards: SRS administers the state matching funds for Medicare and Medicaid patients.

### Ongoing research:

1. Montana gives tax breaks to out-of-state corporations, including the SAGE Corporation, that come in, set up business, and provide jobs to Montanans.
2. The SAGE Corporation provides no benefits for its workers. The nursing home caregivers are essentially health care providers with no health insurance.

*c. The media:* It was clear that when people learned the horror stories of patients at the nursing homes, they were galvanized to support the changes sought. The coalition approached and worked the media to provide coverage which assisted them in winning goals. *The Missoulian* newspaper assigned a reporter to the issue, although the paper tended to print generalities. The *Montana Independent*, a weekly, endorsed the Coalition's campaign and provided regular, in-depth, investigative coverage. The local public television station, MCAT, held call-in shows on which patients, workers, and families told their stories.

### Step Six: With the power of large numbers, undertake a series of tactics directed at your targets. Demand the specific changes sought

The organizing strategy is a plan comprised of a series of tactics allowing the coalition to confront targets with specific demands. Strategies are not hit and miss; rather they are part of a plan which builds toward achieving improvements in people's lives. The Montana Coalition for Nursing Home Reform used a variety of tactics.

**1.** Patients and their families were encouraged to file complaints about nursing home care with the Department of Environmental and Health Sciences.

**2.** Nursing home administrators were asked to improve staffing levels to these specific levels:

—One aide per 8 patients on the day shift
—One aide per 12 patients on the evening shift
—One aide per 15 patients on the night shift

At first, the administration tried to ignore the coalition, assuming that the group would disappear. As the coalition gained momentum, the administration tried to silence the group by disputing the claims of inadequate staff. In predictable form, the administrators tried to blame the problem on the workers. This didn't work because the Coalition was too large and had research and documentation to back up its claims. The workers, families of patients, and community supporters were already united.

**3.** When the administrators refused to consider higher staffing and wage levels, nursing homes were picketed to gain public attention. Workers at the unionized SAGE nursing home received a 10–25 cent per hour annual raise; workers at the non-unionized SAGE homes received a 10 cent per hour annual increase. Janet explains, "When the minimum wage was raised to $4.25 in the early 90s, I earned $4.35. At that time my daughter's wages at a fast food restaurant were $4.55 so she was making 20 cents an hour more flipping burgers than I was caring for human life."

**4.** The Coalition conducted literature drops throughout town, to inform the public about the issue.

**5.** The group approached the student senate at the local university to ask them to encourage students to refrain from working in nursing homes. The case was successfully made by explaining that it was easy for the management to exploit the student workers, who were somewhat desperate for jobs. Since students were willing to work at lower wages and did not intend a long-term commitment to the profession, they did not have a stake in the jobs and accepted the oppressive working conditions.

**6.** Congressman Pat Williams and local legislators helped the coalition get recognized in the Montana state legislature, where the group worked to pass laws requiring higher staffing levels in the state's nursing homes.

**7.** In 1990, the Coalition focused its activities on insuring enforcement of the 1990 Nursing Home Reform Amendments of the Federal Omnibus Budget Reconciliation Act (OBRA). They printed literature detailing OBRA standards set out for all nursing homes, and encouraged those who knew of substandard conditions to join the Montana Coalition campaign.

**8.** The Coalition members wanted to have a direct impact on the quality of care for nursing home residents. They delivered flowers to homes on Mother's Day, arranged visits to the homes by the union and members of the Coalition, and worked with resident's groups to help enforce the national reform law.

**9.** The Montana Coalition conducted tours of many of the 100 nursing homes across the state. They devised a grading system by which the homes were either "recommended" by the Coalition or "not recommended" by the Coalition.

**10.** The Coalition brought its activists to the state capitol to testify on behalf of increased staffing for nursing homes. In fact, one official complained to Robideau that she always brought different people. Robideau knew that he realized the group was large and therefore a force to be reckoned with.

**11.** The Montana Coalition worked to convince the Department of Health and Environmental Sciences that they should conduct bona fide surprise inspections of nursing homes. Previously, if DHES showed up at one local home, others in the area would be quickly notified by the first and have time to prepare for the inspection. Preparation included the purchase of new linens, curtains, and cereal bowls, and the short-lived substitution of better meals, but never of additional staff.

### Ongoing outreach

In 1992 the Montana Coalition for Nursing Home Reform began to conduct statewide outreach, encouraging people to file complaints about nursing home conditions in other parts of the state. Allies included: Unions, such as the Carpenters, Local 28, (Hotel Employees and Restaurant Employees International (H.E.R.E.), and those affiliated with the Montana AFL-CIO; citizens groups, such as Montana People's Action, the Coalition for Montanans Concerned with Disabilities, Montana's Senior Citizen's Organizations, and the state's ombudsman office.)

Through its intensive public outreach and education, the Montana Coalition was successfully getting out the word about the mistreatment of patients at nursing homes. The momentum of their organizing caused ripples in many people's daily lives. For example, pastors delivered church pulpit speeches, in which they advocated for people to join the organizing drive and the work of the Coalition.

## PRINCIPLES OF DIRECT ACTION ORGANIZING[2]

The goal of direct-action organizing is to gather and channel the power of people to win victory on an issue. It is a method which involves people directly confronting the issue and the respective powerholders, instead of allowing one person to advocate for them. Robideau was the volunteer chair and president of the Montana Coalition for Nursing Home Reform from 1990 until 1994. Beginning in her own living room and building up to an organization of three hundred people and many allied organizations, Robideau organized with other like-minded Montanans to win concrete change for nursing home residents and workers across the state. Most important, Robideau and others built an ongoing organization that directly confronted powerholders. By this process, the Coalition fulfilled the three principles of direct action organizing:

### 1. The coalition and its members won concrete victories

From increasing exposure of the issue by the public, to gaining specific improvements, the organization thrived. Specific victories included:

■ *Increased staffing levels at nursing homes.* Nursing home owners responded to the loud noise of the Coalition's tactics and instituted higher staffing levels.

As Robideau describes, "The Missoula nursing homes stated that wages were raised because they understood how hard workers toiled—they valued their workers and wanted to prove it. We at MCNHR knew that this was done because of our campaign and that we had won by pressuring the opposition into doing what was needed. It didn't matter that we didn't get the credit, we knew in our hearts that it was because of us."

■ *Better working conditions for nursing home caregivers.* The workers are now paid over $5.00 an hour and receive health care benefits. Further, because the union homes first won contracts that stipulated higher wages, wage increases, and health care benefits, other nursing homes in Missoula and across the state, did the same.

■ *More effective government inspections of nursing home facilities.* The Coalition won a change in DHES practices. They now inspect only one local nursing home per visit, and then return for subsequent visits on a different shift, and at a later date, to inspect others. Sometimes, inspectors will arrive unexpectedly at midnight. In addition, the workers won truly private interviews with inspectors. Previously, staff were questioned before nursing home supervisors, and were reluctant to be truthful.

### 2. People gained a sense of their own power

Alone, the nursing home residents, their families, and workers could not have made a significant difference in the quality of nursing home care. Instead, those citizens with a common self-interest in quality nursing home care banded together, made specific demands of powerholders, and in many cases, won. They experienced their own strength, which motivated them to keep going.

### 3. The coalition altered the relations of power in society

The victories benefited those who previously enjoyed little or no power in relation to the SAGE Corporation. Now the coalition and the public have more power vis-a-vis the SAGE Corporation, the media, and government officials and agencies that were pulled into this effort. The lesson learned is that the power of organized people works,

achieves results, and builds organization for the next issue people want
to confront.

## Leadership Development

Direct action organizing is based on the belief that leaders are not
born, they are made. Rather than assuming that anyone who has a title
or who speaks charismatically is de facto a leader, direct action community organizing defines a leader as, "a person with a following, who
learns the skills necessary to help win concrete victories on specific
issues."

Equally important as organizational victories, the drive to improve
nursing home care in Montana developed the leadership skills of many
individuals. Robideau had never headed an organization, but had
served on the periphery of some issues. She had never formulated ideas
to be carried out by the group. Her leadership in the Coalition involved
her in almost every aspect of the organizing drive. She conducted ongoing outreach, served as chair and lead spokeswoman, raised money,
and developed the skills of other citizen leaders.

In these roles, Robideau was part of a leadership team. Others involved in the organizing brought a variety of skills to the group: how to
determine strategy, who potential funders were for the organization,
and how to work with the media.

The development of leadership skills requires training. The Montana
Coalition attended organizing training sessions conducted by the Northern Plains Resource Council in Wyoming; others were held at the local
university in Missoula or the citizen group Montana People's Action.
Coalition board members and individual activists were sent to the
classes.

Robideau and her board valued and assisted in the development of
the leadership skills of the Coalition membership. They believed the
most important goal was to have the members feel "ownership" over
the organizing. "I have to have a stake in the organization in order to
care about sticking with the issue," Robideau explains, "People were
involved with the Coalition for a number of reasons. Once they felt
they were part of the solution, they took ownership." Members felt the
Coalition was *their* organization, one in which they could win victories,
as well as develop skills.

The power to win change in our neighborhoods, workplaces, and
across the country lies in our ability and effort to bring like-minded
people together, to create the pressure which will bring about change.

As citizens who believe in democracy, we have the right to as much power as the governmental, corporate, and media sectors. There is no great mystery to the organizing work that must be done to take that power and win improvements on the causes we care about. We just need to do it.

## ◼◼◼ WOMEN WHO DARE ▭▭▭

### Janet Robideau

After several years of hard work and good results, I've moved on to work in other citizen organizations and other human rights issues. As a member of the Northern Cheyenne Tribe from eastern Montana, I'm getting involved in organizing around Native American rights. I'm also active with local groups countering bigotry and the religious right. Now I find that I'm a leader in the groups I'm involved with instead of a novice, because of my experience with the Coalition.

It is so critical to build leadership and learn how to share that leadership role. For the first two years of the Coalition, I jealously guarded my position as head of the organization, and I didn't want to share the limelight. I think I believed that no one could do it as well as I. And because I am an aggressive style organizer, people were willing to sit back and let me do almost everything. Eventually it taxed me heavily, and I realized as the organization grew that I couldn't be everywhere at once; that in fact I had to share leadership with others. Then I began to reach out into the membership and develop other leaders. Now the leadership is there in the Coalition to carry on without me.

My advice to others is to keep at it, reach out to others; your power is in your numbers. The nursing home industry was tough to take on. Other people and groups discouraged us and told us that we'd never get anywhere, that we didn't know what we were doing. But we kept going. And we won.

## Notes

1. Kenneth N. Gilpin, "Vital Signs Improve for the Nursing Home Industry," *New York Times*, February 27, 1994, p. F5.
2. We gratefully acknowledge the insight and values of the father of direct action organizing, Saul Alinsky. Please see Chapter 8 for books by and about this important, legendary figure in U.S. history.

# Sharpen Your Activist Skills

W hat do dynamic leaders have? Are they born with the ability to walk into a room, greet multitudes by name, stride confidently to the podium, make stirring speeches, analyze problems, and propose innovative solutions? Seasoned activists know almost instinctively how to develop strategy; veteran fundraisers deliver the big bucks with aplomb, effective organizers open a spigot and produce a crowd.

Accomplished leaders, organizers, fundraisers, and activists are not born that way: Over time each has developed a repertoire of skills that she employs to accomplish her goals. Few leaders or activists are good at everything, yet they all have gained one or more of the key skills described in this chapter.

You, too, can enhance your volunteer or paid career and win victories on issues by developing new skills. The ability to raise money, speak out in public, organize an effective meeting or campaign, lobby public officials, research the implications of public proposals, work with the media, put together an effective meeting or convention, and develop or analyze strategy can be learned on the job, by working inside an organization or campaign, or at widely available training sessions.

## Activist skill inventory

| Skill | My Current Ability | My Interest in Learning More | (Total) |
|---|---|---|---|
| | (Rate 0–10) | | (Add: Ability and Interest) |
| Organizing | | | |
| Public Speaking | | | |
| Fundraising | | | |
| Citizen Lobbying | | | |
| Research and Policy Analysis | | | |
| Media and Press Relations | | | |
| Meeting Facilitation | | | |
| Event Planning and Management | | | |
| Computers and Information Systems | | | |
| Networking | | | |

## Skill Inventory

One place to begin honing your skills is by completing the inventory above. Review the skills listed in the first column, and rate your current abilities in each area, as well as your interest in learning more, using 1 as the lowest in ability or interest. If you're not sure what a term means, just place a question mark in that column. As you read the rest of this chapter, learn those new terms, and come back and adjust the ratings as necessary. Select your top two or three priorities, those that received the highest combined scores to develop.

## ORGANIZING

If you get a thrill out of seeing a roomful of people crowded into a meeting because *you* convinced each one to be there, or if all your list making for the meeting has paid off by having every detail anticipated, perhaps you'd like to be an organizer.

Organizing is an ancient profession with a very low public profile. Organizers bring people together, those with the same problems, concerns, or self interest, to create strategy that will find solutions and gain power in numbers. The result is direct democracy in action.

As Janet Robideau and the Montana Coalition for Nursing Home Reform demonstrated so effectively by challenging nursing home abuses, organizers build groups, help members of the group choose and carry out their own objectives, and provide training to volunteers in a process known as leadership development.

Organizing drives can hold government, private institutions, or businesses accountable for their actions. Use lobbying strategies to enact changes in the law, or heighten public awareness of issues through media visibility.

Some people become organizers when critical events intervene in their lives.

Janice Dickerson jumped into action when her home town of Revilletown, Louisiana, a community founded by ex-slaves after the Civil War, was poisoned by chloride emissions from a Georgia Gulf plastics plant. The Gulf Coast Tenants Leadership Development Project alerted environmental groups to the fact that three out of every five African Americans and Hispanic Americans live in communities with uncontrolled toxic waste sites. The project won a settlement from the company, and now it leads in multi-racial environmental organizing.

Organizers approach problems systematically, analyze power, and seek strategies to exert pressure. The best organizers encourage and develop leadership and create greater effectiveness and power for the group. They break down overall goals into smaller steps, make lists, and work intensively with group members.

Organizers are paid, professional staff, who often maintain a low profile because the most important aspect of their job is to encourage others to take leadership. Leaders are those who have a following, they are more visible in the group, and gain training and support from the paid staff.

Rosalinda Lugo was an activist leader of United Neighbors Organization (UNO) in Los Angeles for 11 years. Through UNO and its affiliated national organizing network, the Industrial Areas Foundation (IAF), Rosalinda received training and support for her leadership roles.

IAF gave me something I never received in the schools I attended. It gave me an opportunity to become a public person, and the skills I needed to become an activist. UNO provided a vehicle by which I could change things in LA, and the state.

I learned that there are two kinds of power: organized money and organized people. We don't have money. But we can have organized people. I found that leaders are not born, they are made. Community organizations can take a person like myself, with no political training, and give them skills and teach them to do political analysis, strategic analysis, how to connect with others in the community, how to discover the self-interest of people in order to motivate them. I started out as someone who was afraid to speak in public, and I learned how to be a leader.

In 1935, Millie Jeffrey got her first job as a union organizer with the Amalgamated Clothing Workers of America, at a salary of $25 a week. Dedicated to a lifetime of organizing, she marched with Rev. Martin Luther King, Jr. in Alabama, helped organize the National Women's Political Caucus, was an early member of the National Organization for Women, served on the Board of the National Abortion and Reproductive Rights Action League, and presided over the board of the Michigan Women's Foundation. Many times encouraged to run for political office, she preferred to remain an organizer.

Jeffrey is now 82, and her name is not yet a household word. Still, she is considered the godmother and mentor of many women in American politics, including Representative Pat Schroeder, and former Vice Presidential candidate Geraldine Ferraro. Jeffrey told the *Detroit Free Press*, "I enjoy working with people for collective action. I've always said, the first thing is, to recognize power. And then you have to use power—collectively. And use it for the good."[1]

Jeffrey has spent her life behind the scenes, organizing, canvassing, leafleting, and making telephone calls—"to make democracy work," she explains.[2] Organizers may work with particular neighborhoods or communities, build union membership, run political campaigns, or focus on single issues or constituencies.

Maureen O'Connell of Save Our Cumberland Mountains explains the role of an organizer this way:

Organizers like me do not do the work ourselves. Rather we help form an organization of people who work to meet the goals that they themselves have set. If organizers do well, there will be more and more members with more and more skills to address problems. Eventually the experienced leaders learn most of the skills of a talented organizer—how to analyze power, create strategy, recruit members, organize meetings, and work with the media. Organizers are careful to help new people determine what can they do right now, and what they can learn to do next. We watch to see when they will be ready to chair the meetings, or chair the chapter, and think about how to convince them that they can do it, too.

### Young organizers

- Twelve year old Kory Johnson of Phoenix, Arizona read *50 Simple Things Kids Can Do to Save the Earth.* When she heard that a local incinerator was scheduled to burn hazardous waste, she organized a campaign which generated thousands of protest letters, helped organize a rally and candlelight vigil, and garnered so much support that the governor finally called the project off. She is profiled in *Kid Heroes of the Environment.*[3]

- Kristen Belanger, a 12 year old from Woodbury, Conn., decided to do something about hunger and homelessness. She raised over $700 for a local soup kitchen, organized an Easter egg hunt for homeless children, and appeared on radio to promote a winter clothing drive which gathered 1355 pounds of clothing for the homeless. For her efforts, she was honored with a J.C. Penney Humanitarian Award, and was recognized by the Giraffe Project as one who "sticks their neck out."[4]

- The Giraffe Project has a *Standing Tall Teaching Guide,* an education curriculum for students in kindergarten through high school, which encourages students to become involved in their communities.

## Organizing Tips

- Organizers help people with similar concerns gather to win victories.

- Organizers never do for others what they can do themselves. Instead, they educate and encourage members to take leadership.

### In order to win victories, choose issues that are:

- Immediate—something that relates to people's daily lives—the issue that will get heads nodding when discussed. While everyone at a meeting may be genuinely concerned about war or famine in a far-off land, car theft in their own neighborhood is of equal immediate concern.

■ Specific—not vague or generalized. If the issue is car theft, ask why are police patrols infrequent, missing streetlights not replaced, or are there vacant houses that attract crime?

■ Realizable—of the three specific concerns above, solving the vacant house problem is more complex and long-term; replacing bulbs in broken streetlights, on the other hand, seems quickly attainable. More frequent police patrols are probably winnable in the near future.

## How to Get Training as an Organizer

**Community Organizers** build local power through campaigns which hold elected officials, government agencies, and large corporations accountable to the public. They push for streetlights and stop signs, make sure that banks issue mortgage loans in those neighborhoods where people deposit their savings, and convince public entities to invest in small business districts.

Join, or get more active, in a neighborhood or community organization for skills training, look for groups listed under community organizations in your telephone directory, or attend a session at one of these training schools for organizers:

*Association of Community Organizations for Reform Now (ACORN)*
739 8th St. SE, Washington, DC 20003; 201/547-2500. ACORN works in low income communities, and has created homestead programs in several cities to turn vacant houses over to neighborhood residents.

*Center for Third World Organizing*
3861 Martin Luther King Jr. Way, Oakland, CA 94609; 415/654-9601. CTWO provides training and support for organizers of color, and works to build organizations which promote the interests of minority communities.

*Highlander Research and Education Center*
1959 Highlander Way, New Market, TN 37820; 615/933-3443. Highlander is a research and popular education institution, established in 1932 to help Southern communities deal with the structural causes of economic, environmental, and social problems in a democratic, practi-

cal and effective manner. Rosa Parks attended a training at Highlander not long before she sat down and initiated the Montgomery bus boycott.

*The Industrial Areas Foundation*
36 New Hyde Park Road, Franklin Square, NY 11010; 516/354-1076. The IAF works with church-based groups to tackle community problems, including jobs, education reform, abandoned housing, and crime.

*The Midwest Academy*
225 West Ohio St., Suite 250, Chicago, IL 60610; 312/645-6010. The Academy is the training center for Citizen Action (a national network of grassroots groups), which is dedicated to enabling low and moderate income people to win concrete benefits and develop a sense of their own power and after the relations of power in order to build a more just and humane society.

*National Training and Information Center*
810 N. Milwaukee Avenue, Chicago, IL 60622; 312/243-3094. NTIC is a resource center which offers training, consulting, technical assistance and research to those working on neighborhood revitalization. Issues such as housing, toxics, community reinvestment, crime, and drugs are stressed.

**Issue/constituency organizers** build power for their particular group or cause. Lesbian and gay rights' organizations, women's rights (including reproductive rights groups), groups organized around race and ethnicity issues (for African Americans, Native Americans, Hispanics, Asian Americans, Arab Americans, and Jews), all have networks that provide training opportunities for those who are involved and seek higher levels of commitment.

There are many organizations that work on the local and national level. Contact local chapters of national groups to find out what type of training may be available, or seek more information from:

*National Abortion and Reproductive Rights Action League (NARAL).* Write or call for a list of the 40 affiliated state and local organizations, which provide training and opportunities for involvement for state and local activists. 1156 15th St. NW, Suite 700, Washington, DC 20005; 202/973-3000.

*Public Interest Research Groups (PIRG's)* are campus-based organizations active on 175 campuses in 25 U.S. states and in Canada. PIRG students use research to expose auto repair rip-offs, dangerous children's toys, the lack of planning for emergency evacuation near nuclear power plants, as well as many other environmental issues. PIRGs teach students how to plan a rally, run a campaign, do research and attract media attention. Contact their national office at U.S. PIRG, 215 Pennsylvania Avenue SE, Washington, DC 20003; 202/546-9707.

*The National Association for the Advancement of Colored People (NAACP)* has over 1800 local chapters working to achieve equal rights through the democratic process, and eliminate racial prejudice in housing, employment, voting, and schools. The NAACP holds seminars, conducts voter education and registration drives, and sponsors an annual convention each summer. 4805 Mt. Hope Drive, Baltimore, MD 21215; 410/358-8900.

*The National Council of La Raza* is an umbrella organization of 147 member groups which work for civil rights, and economic opportunities for Hispanic-Americans. 810 1st St. NE, Suite 300, Washington, DC 20002; 202/289-1380.

*The National Gay and Lesbian Task Force (NGLTF)* sponsors an annual training conference, *Creating Change*, with an institute for people of color, and day-long workshops on gay and lesbian activist issues. 2320 17th St. NW, Washington, DC 20009; 202/332-6483.

*The National Urban League*, with over 100 chapters in cities across the country, works to eliminate racial discrimination and institutional racism, and provides direct services to minorities. They have a summer internship program and a Seniors in Community Service program. Some affiliates offer Parent Council Training Programs to help parents effectively confront local school policies and practices. 500 E. 62nd St., New York, NY 10021; 212/310-9000.

This is just a sampling of the hundreds of groups that organize on issues or for constituencies. For a more complete listing, see *Good Works*, edited by Jessica Cowan, or *The Activist's Almanac* by David Walls.

***Union organizers*** build power by bringing new members into the union and fighting for workers rights. Many organizers start out as rank and file workers, whose activism leads them to take jobs with the union. Here's how Nita Brueggeman got involved with the Amalgamated Clothing and Textile Workers:

I was working full-time at a garment factory—it was my second or third industrial job. Because of a negative experience in a union in California, I was essentially anti-union. I was convinced they would take my dues dollars and not do a damn thing for me. So I was a really hard case when I went to work at that factory. I didn't know anything about the Clothing and Textile workers. For two years I was a pain in the neck to the union; I gave them a really bad time.

I was a very high producing worker—the plant paid a minimum wage of $1.20 an hour with an incentive for production, and I was among the top three operators. We made very expensive down-filled ski garments, and I would sew the tunnels through the different parts to keep the down from falling towards the bottom.

Then arbitrarily one day, the employer switched my machine and my job. They moved me to putting in zippers, on a completely different piece of equipment—a double-needle machine that didn't work half the time—which meant that I could not make any money.

I just couldn't get through to the company, they wouldn't listen. Then the president of the local union, an older woman, came up to me and said, "I don't think they're treating you right, do you want some help?"

At that point, I said, "I've gotta have some help, I cannot afford to stay here for a $1.20 an hour." My husband was unemployed and going to school at the time, I had two kids, one of them a young baby, and I was really supporting the family.

So she helped me, and it took a couple of months. After that, in all good conscience, I just couldn't walk away. I said, "You had no reason to help me, I have been your absolute nemesis for two years—I was the kind of union member you hate. The kind of member who said, we don't need a union, I'm doing just fine. And you know, she handled it perfectly, she never asked me for anything. She only said, "I'm just glad we were able to help, that's what we're here for.

Right then, I got hooked. And that's how I got involved with the union.

If you are a union member and want to become more active or even get a job as a part- or full-time union organizer, talk to your union representative, or find out if there is a women's caucus or women's committee in the union. One in eight women is a public employee.

*The Coalition of Labor Union Women (CLUW),* was formed to help increase the participation of women in union leadership and politics. 1126 16th Street NW, Washington, DC 20036; 202/466-4610. Nine to Five, the union of women office workers, was founded in 1973 and affiliated with the Service Employees International Union two years later. 614 Superior Ave NW, Cleveland, OH 44113; 216/566-9308.

Unions whose membership is predominantly female include:

*The Service Employees International Union (SEIU),* has one million members and 300 locals in the US and Canada. They hold regional training conferences focusing on women's organizing, civil and human rights. 1313 L St. NW, Washington, DC 20005; 202/898-3200.

*The American Federation of State, County and Municipal Employees (AFSCME)* has 3000 locals, 1.3 million members, and a special women's rights department. 1625 L St. NW, Washington, DC 20036; 202/429-1000.

*The Communication Workers of America (CWA)* offers a steward school and an organizing school for its members, of which 52% are women. 501 3rd St. NW, Washington, DC 20001; 202/434-1100.

*The AFL-CIO Organizing Institute* recruits and trains new union organizers in a multi-stage program. Anyone can submit an application and be interviewed. Once accepted, you attend a three day intensive training course on basic union organizing. After training you may be offered an internship, and be placed with an actual campaign for several weeks. Upon successful completion of the internship, you may continue training as an apprentice organizer for up to three months. At the completion of the training program, you will get help finding a job as a full-time organizer with an AFL-CIO union. Women, minorities, bilingual individuals, and union members are strongly encouraged to apply. 1444 Eye Street NW, Washington, DC 20005; 800/848-3021.

**Campaign organizers** build volunteer organizations for electoral victories. As more and more women step forward to seek public office, they will need an ever-larger cadre of skilled organizers to run their campaigns. If you enjoy campaigning but don't see yourself as a candidate, get involved as a volunteer or seek training as a campaign staffer or manager. (See Chapters 11 and 12 for more on running and winning campaigns.) Both the Democratic and Republican parties hold campaign schools locally and nationally, and specialized campaign training for women is available from:

*The National Women's Political Caucus (NWPC)* conducts sessions for candidates and campaign workers in cities across the country through its local affiliates, including special trainings to meet the needs of young women and women of color. Contact your local branch of the Caucus, or the Director of Training, 1275 K Street, Suite 750, Washington, DC 20009; 800/729-6972.

*The Women's Campaign Fund,* the oldest women's political action committee in the country, recruits, trains, and provides funds for women candidates. 120 Maryland Avenue NE, Washington, DC 20002; 202/544-4484.

*The YWCA Institute for Public Leadership* trains women for political leadership roles, including running for office, managing a campaign, or lobbying on issues. YWCA of the USA, 726 Broadway, New York, NY 10003; 212/614-2779.

Or, organize your own training by asking a successful campaign organizer from your area to spend time with you or your group.

## To Find Out More about Organizing

Read the classic texts of community organizing, by Saul Alinsky, the master of strategy—*Reveille for Radicals*[5] and *Rules for Radicals*.[6] For an instructive biography of Alinsky, read *Let Them Call Me a Rebel: Saul Alinsky—His Life and Legacy* by Sanford D. Horwitt.[7]

Before you start to organize, pick up a copy of *Organizing for Social Change: A Manual for Activists in the 1990's*, by Kim Bobo, Jackie Kendall, and Steve Max.[8]

Read *The Activist's Almanac: The Concerned Citizen's Guide to the Leading Advocacy Organizations in America* by David Walls, for historical background and descriptions of current project of national networks of community organizations.[9]

Read Harry Boyte's *The Backyard Revolution*, for more examples of grassroots organizing.[10]

## PUBLIC SPEAKING

If your secret dream is to stand up before a crowd and utter the words that stir hearts and minds to action, perhaps you should consider speaking in public. From talking at a crowded PTA meeting to testifying before a state legislature, few things can be as effective, or as intimidating, as public speaking. Public speaking is a learned skill, and those who want to be leaders of organizations or movements, or seek elective or appointed political office, should develop and practice their public speaking skills.

Helen Caldicott, an Australian pediatrician, helped start the movement to end atmospheric testing of nuclear weapons in the Pacific Ocean. Caldicott founded Physicians for Social Responsibility and Women's Action for New Directions while practicing medicine in the United States; her speeches galvanized thousands to take action against nuclear proliferation.

Caldicott says that she engages her audiences, "by breaking through the psychic numbing, hitting them on the head with a two-by-four, so to speak, dropping nuclear weapons on them (verbally) by describing that their eyes will melt and their babies get vaporized."[11] She explains how she got started as an activist, and a speaker:

I first read about nuclear war when I was fifteen, sitting on a beach in Melbourne. That image of waiting for the fallout to come down from the northern hemisphere, and the end of our good earth, has never left me.

As a young mother, I was scared that my children would be killed. And then in medicine I learned about radiation and mutation, and saw deformed babies. I treated children with cystic fibrosis, a disease that's increased in incidence because of nuclear power, and I've comforted children dying of leukemia, with their bellies swollen and their hair falling out.

I stood up to deliver my first public speech at the YWCA in Adelaide, to a group of older women who were knitting and eating lunch out of brown paper bags. I think my passion mitigated against being scared. There's always one face that stands out in an audience, and as I talk to that one face, that one soul that rivets me, everybody else is drawn in with the energy. It's really energy that I speak with, not just words. And people resonate with the energy and the passion as much as with what I actually say.

The other thing I do is to watch the sleepiest person in the audience, and I wake them up. I might do something outrageous, or simply change the subject. You can use long pauses, raise your voice or drop it down very low.

## Tips on Public Speaking

■ Observe others who are effective speakers, and note what makes them so powerful—do they use their voices well? do they look their audience in the eye? present precise information and concrete facts?

■ Develop your speaking style by offering to talk one-to-one with volunteers or voters during a campaign. Move on to speaking before small groups—invite some friends to your home to practice your speech before you speak in public.

■ Organize your thoughts; present them with a beginning, a middle, and an end. Think of the three key points you want to convey.

■ Try to use a written outline rather than reading a prepared speech—you'll have more visual contact with the audience. Practice in front of a mirror at home to get comfortable with your outline. Can you speak without notes?

■ Vary your body language, voice, and cadence to create dramatic interest in your speech.

■ Take yourself seriously, and others will too—in your style of speech and the way you dress. Avoid trivializing yourself or your opinions—eliminate words such as "really," or "just," as well as unnecessary questions such as "Isn't it?" from your speech.

Public speaking really does get easier with practice. If, during this process, you discover that creating the speech is more thrilling than delivering it, you may want to focus on speech writing as a related skill.

## For Speaker's Training

Join Toastmasters, a national organization which helps people build self confidence, develop their speaking skills, and learn how to run meetings. After completing ten step-by-step lessons, you will have an opportunity to practice and get feedback in a supportive environment. Toastmasters has 7,600 clubs in 50 countries. Some locales have separate chapters or make special efforts to include women. Contact: Toastmasters International, PO Box 9052, Mission Viejo, CA 92690; 714/ 858-8255.

Look for organizations and political campaigns with public education efforts (sometimes called Speakers Bureaus) which train volunteers to give talks to small groups at house meetings, coffees, or neighborhood meetings. The training program usually provides a basic outline of the talk, along with helpful hints and practice sessions for new speakers.

Sign up for speech or communications classes at your local community college. Be video-taped, review your performance, and make notes for improvement. This can provide the single most effective feedback you will receive as a public speaker.

## To Find Out More

*Rise Up: A New Guide to Public Speaking*, by Sandie Barnard, includes interviews with effective modern speakers, and special tips on speech preparation and delivery for women speakers.[12]

*How to Present Like a Pro: Getting People to See Things Your Way*, by Lani Arredondo.[13]

## FUNDRAISING

Are you gutsy and persuasive? Tenacious and able to follow through? Can you talk to anyone about anything? You could be highly successful as a fundraiser. Even the most crucial issues cannot be addressed without the money needed to get them before the public eye. Because so many people find fundraising intimidating, those willing to bring in the cash to finance a cause or campaign are highly prized in every organization.

There are as many ways to raise money as there are to give it: through the mail, at fundraising events, over the phone, through memberships or pledges, raffles, bake sales, by selling ads for a newsletter or program. One-on-one solicitation of large donations, or major gifts, present some of the greatest challenges, and rewards, to novice fundraisers.

## Tips for Effective Fundraising

- Do your homework—know your cause, what the money will be used for, and something about the donor.
- When you're ready to ask, *ask* for a specific amount, then *wait* for a response.
- Often donors like to fund specific programs, or pieces of equipment, rather than seed money or operations. Peruse your organizational budget and raise money for as many specific projects as possible.
- See Chapter 13 of this book for more tips on fundraising.

## How to Get Training in Fundraising

Join and participate in a committee sponsoring a fundraising event for a cause. Offer to assist the chairperson or coordinator, so you can get an overview of the process.

Direct mail fundraising—the solicitation of gifts through letters to donors, is a highly specialized field. Volunteer to help someone who writes direct mail appeals, and manage the lists in your organization in order to gain a better understanding of the tasks involved.

For one-on-one fundraising, set yourself a modest goal and try to achieve it. Ask staff or leaders or your group for help in figuring out how to ask for money. Many churches have effective fundraising programs, and can be a source of free training. Or, join a major gifts committee, which usually offers training as part of the fundraising program.

## To Find Out More

*Fundraising for Social Change,* by Kim Klein, provides plans and tips for small events, intermediate level fundraisers, and annual events.[14]

*The Grass Roots Fundraising Book: How to Raise Money in Your Community,* by Joan Flanagan, has step-by-step instruction for beginning, intermediate, and advanced level events and other activities.[15]

*Getting Major Gifts*, is an excellent resource for major gifts for fund-raising.[16]

The Fund Raising School, part of the Indiana University Center on Philanthropy, is the only university-based national program in fundraising education. The program travels to 21 cities across the United States, offering seven separate courses ranging from basic principles and techniques of fundraising, to proposal writing and major gift programs. Contact: The Fund Raising School, Indiana University Center on Philanthropy, 550 West North Street, Suite 301, Indianapolis, IN 46202-3162; 800/962-6692.

The Grantsmanship Center conducts workshops in obtaining grants, proposal writing, and fundraising in cities across the US. PO Box 17220, Los Angeles, CA 90017; 213/482-9860.

## CITIZEN LOBBYING

Can you see yourself walking the halls of the state capitol or city hall, using just the right arguments to convince an elected official to vote your way, despite heavy opposition? Or, organizing droves of constituents from every legislative district in the state to visit the Capitol to speak out on a crucial issue? Lobbying involves presenting persuasive arguments to, as well as putting political pressure on, decision-makers in local, state, or federal government.

Most of us have an image of paid professional lobbyists—people with large expense accounts who take elected officials to upscale lunches to promote the interests of big business and other powerful interests. Citizen or public interest lobbyists create another type of lobbying; they invite hundreds of constituents to the Capitol on lobby days, and unceasingly provide information otherwise missing from public debates. They also inform grassroots activists about how to affect the legislative process.

Many elected officials started their careers as volunteer lobbyists. Congresswoman Maxine Waters of California was a Head Start parent who visited the state capitol in Sacramento to advocate for increased funding for the Head Start program. Former Governor Barbara Roberts of Oregon was a bookkeeper for a construction company who lobbied tirelessly for her autistic child's right to a public education.

Most citizens are surprised to learn how a few people can dramatically make a change in the process. Multnomah County Chair Beverly

Stein points out, "I had put $100,000 in my budget for family support and retaining kids in school, and the Hispanic community has done a really good job of turning people out to testify in support of that item. They have people testifying in Spanish who have to be translated, and that's powerful. The Asian Community brought little kids who've just come to the country to testify in support of an Asian Acculturation Center, and that makes a difference. If ten people come and testify on each of these issues, they can really turn things around. It doesn't take a lot."

Even elected officials who agree with your position rely on citizen lobbyists to increase pressure on fellow decision-makers because they recognize it as a powerful way to effect change. President Franklin D. Roosevelt once told a delegation that came seeking reform, "Okay, you've convinced me. Now go on out and bring pressure on me!"

## Tips for Citizen Lobbyists

Convincing legislators to pass a bill or fund a program requires a combination of facts, political pressure, and an understanding of:

■ *Process* The legislative process can seem complex and confusing to first-timers. Find someone inside the system—a supportive elected official, a volunteer or paid lobbyist—to keep you informed of what's going on and, more important, what has to happen next.

■ *Politics* Understand the politics of the issue; who has power and a vested interest in the outcome? Remember, there are likely to be many stakeholders. What is the political climate on this issue? Who is the opposition, and what strategies are they likely to pursue? Who are your allies on this issue?

■ *Personality* Legislators and policy makers have a set of life experiences that may or may not make them responsive to your appeal. Those with a disabled sibling may be more responsive to a parent talking about the problems of children with disabilities. Find out all you can about the attitudes, concerns, and contacts of legislators you are lobbying. Who is the elected official responsive to in their district? Make sure that is the person who comes to lobby them.

■ *People* Motivate and mobilize regular citizens in support of the issues. Meet individually with legislators, phone them, send letters, testify at and attend public hearings in great numbers to bring attention to your issues. Be specific about why you support the legislation, and ask directly for their support.

■ *Perseverance*  Keep the pressure on from many different angles. Testify, bring constituents in, send letters, organize telephone campaigns. Since you don't know which combination of actions will work, you must work them all.

## Learning to Lobby

Lobbying is a skill usually learned on the job; look for a mentor—a paid or citizen lobbyist who knows her way around the state house or city hall. Offer to be her assistant, and find ways to make yourself useful. Help put together fact sheets and prepare other written materials to be used in lobbying.

Look for organizations that sponsor or oppose legislation you care about. Attend a "Lobby Day" or workshop, and learn how constituent pressure can be the most persuasive argument. Many states have women's coalition lobbyists who work on a range of issues of interest to women—does yours?

## To Find Out More

Two low-cost publications are available from the League of Women Voters. *Tell It to Washington* is a pamphlet with tips on how to lobby effectively in person, by phone, and by letter, lists Washington, DC phone numbers of Members of Congress, the Supreme Court, and the Cabinet. *Anatomy of a Hearing* will help you present your case effectively in a public hearing. Call 202/429-1965 or write; LWV 1730 M. St. NW, Suite 1000, Washington, DC 20036.

*The Non-Profit Lobbying Guide: Advocating Your Cause and Getting Results*, by Bob Smucker.[17]

*How to Lobby Congress: A Guide for the Citizen Lobbyist*, by Donald E. del Kieffer.[18]

*Testifying with Impact*, by Arch Lustberg of the United States Chamber of Commerce.[19]

## RESEARCH AND POLICY ANALYSIS

Does finding all the facts about an issue intrigue you, and make you want to seek more? Would you like to dig through the library, or interview an expert to find essential information that will shed new light on a local problem?

*Tactical research* is used for organizing purposes. A great deal of information is readily available to the public—we need only ask. In fact, comparing information from various public sources is one easy way to document existing problems. For example, a local government applying for federal funds to clean up a river, may document in great detail the pollutants in the river. In the report to potential new companies moving into town, the information will be presented in a very different way.

*Policy research and analysis* studies the status and needs of various groups in society, looks at how governmental programs and social practices affect those groups, and develops new policies to solve problems. For example:

■ What percentage of women will be in the workforce in the next ten years? How does that affect the need for affordable child care?

■ One in four women will be elderly by the year 2030. 8 out of 10 persons aged 65 or older, and living alone, are women. What are social and economic implications of these facts?

■ Breast cancer has reached epidemic proportions in the United States—it is the most common form of cancer among women. Over 950,000 American women have died of breast cancer since 1960— twice the number of Americans who died in World Wars I and II, the Korean, Vietnam, and Persian Gulf wars combined. A historic funding bias against breast cancer and other women's health concerns is now being reversed due to an analysis of public policies on breast cancer, and an increase in the number of women in Congress. Higher allocations of federal funds, increased public education efforts, grassroots activism, and political leadership all contribute to new public policy on the issue of breast cancer.

Policy involves having a goal or vision—know where you want to go— then find the best strategy to get there. Start with a vision of where you want to be, work backwards to goals you want to achieve, and then develop strategies to achieve those goals.

## Research Tips

■ Reporters know how to find information and obtain access to sources. If appropriate, try to enlist someone from the media in your research effort. If there's a story in it for them, they might help do your work.

■ Research can be an effective component of a lobbying effort. Legislators may consider a certain approach to a problem. If you can show that approach has either succeeded or failed in other states, you are contributing valuable information to the development of policy.

## How to Learn about Public Policy

Map out a personal learning campaign to find out about public policy:

As you read the newspaper or watch the news, identify one or two issue areas about which you are deeply concerned.

Talk to people, read books,and attend conferences relating to those topics. Become a local expert on the issue; become familiar with current policy alternatives.

Subscribe to publications such as *Governing* magazine, Times Publishing Co., 2300 N St. NW, Washington, DC 20037; 202/887-6261 to find out how other jurisdictions (towns, cities, or states) are solving similar problems.

Synthesize information from many sources to come up with new innovative ways to solve problems.

## To Find Out More

*Tactical Investigations for People's Struggles*, by Barry Greever.[20]

*The Center for Women Policy Studies* was founded in 1972 to educate the public and policy makers on women's equity issues. The Center sponsors policy seminars, and publishes research and position papers. 2000 P St. NW, Suite 508, Washington, DC 20036; 202/872-1770.

*The League of Women Voters* has published a series of public policy books which review issues such as plastic and nuclear waste, drinking water quality, US farm policy, health care, child care, and offer concrete suggestions for change. Call 202/429-1965 or write; LWV 1730 M St. NW, Suite 1000, Washington, DC 20036.

*The Center for Responsive Politics* conducts research and educational programs on campaign finance, voter registration, ethics in government, and congressional reform. 1320 19th St. NW, 7th Floor, Washington, DC 20036; 202/857-0044.

*The Center for Responsive Governance* conducts research and sponsors trainings in citizen participation in government and voluntary organizations. Holds an annual conference on management for citizen organizations. 1000 16th St. NW, Suite 500, Washington, DC 20036; 202/857-0044.

## MEDIA AND PRESS RELATIONS

Do you lie awake at night, wondering why your side of the issue doesn't get more attention from the press? Do you yell back at the television when you feel your position has been misrepresented or ignored? Developing a press strategy and building press relations can be highly rewarding roles, especially for organizations and campaigns short on money for paid advertising. Media and press relations are areas where almost every organization can use additional help.

Press people are typically highly overworked professionals with too little time to adequately research and report most stories. (Press traditionally refers to print mediums only—newspapers, magazines, etc.—while media refers to print as well as broadcast media.) They appreciate well-organized information and groups who understand the attributes of a legitimate news story. They want fact sheets, updates, and documented research so that they can write intelligently about an issue.

The *editorial page* is where editors and columnists express opinions and take stands on issues. Set a meeting with the editorial board to seek their endorsement during a campaign or broad public debate. The *news section* in charged with reporting both sides of every issue. Don't spend your time trying to convince a reporter that you are right, but be sure to present your case as effectively as you can. Even if you disagree with the press coverage, you don't want to make enemies of them.

Aspects of a media or press plan that you will want to learn about include *background briefings* to educate the press, and help shape the language they use to characterize the issues. For example, encouraging the press to use the phrase "pro-choice" rather than "pro-abortion" defines the issue in the minds of many voters. *Press conferences* cover announcements of news stories that include organizational and issue developments, and responses to ongoing events in the news. *Press releases* are written statements distributed to the press at news conferences or otherwise, and must be written in a standard format.

## How to Get Experience in Working with the Press

As a way of getting acquainted, ask organizations you are involved with if you can attend future press conferences. Volunteer to help set up chairs, or sign in media representatives.

Spot local organizations which get good media coverage and volunteer to be on their media team, or assist the media relations person to gain basic skills.

Political campaigns depend heavily on "free" or "earned media" (as opposed to paid advertising) to help carry their message to the voters. Volunteer during a campaign as a press aide, or assistant to the press team.

Organize an internship with a local political writer.

Offer to serve as a volunteer intern to the press person of your political party.

Visit your community radio or cable television station, and get involved with news reporting.

Monitor press coverage and clip news stories. Get a copy of *Doing Your Own Newspaper Survey* to determine how hometown and regional newspapers cover news of and by women. Contact the National Network of Women's Funds, 1821 University Ave., Suite 409N, St. Paul, MN 55104; 612/641-0742.

## To Find Out More

Read *Prime Time Activism: Media Strategies for Grassroots Organizing*, by Charlotte Ryan, for analysis of what's newsworthy, with solid tips on how to create a media strategy.[21]

Get the *Talk Show Directory*, by Accuracy in Media, if you want to know how to approach radio shows with ideas; from AIM, 12675 K St. NW, #1150, Washington, DC 20005; 202/371-6710

The League of Women Voters has an excellent *Guide to Getting Good Media Coverage*, available from LWV, 1730 M Street NW, Washington, DC 20036; 202/249-1965.

## MEETING FACILITATION

Are you tired of disorganized meetings where nothing ever seems to get accomplished? Have you watched people drop out of the action because of "death from meetings?"

The reason to hold a meeting is to plan action and make decisions. Inaction breeds discontent. Meetings can make or break an organization. Pam Gallina of southern Nevada recalls the time she tried to become active in an association of businesswomen, "At the meetings, the same three or four women were always talking and making decisions. Everyone else was intimidated by the parliamentary rules. We weren't encouraged to participate, and I quickly dropped out."

Meeting skills are helpful for those who seek leadership in organizations, or career positions in management of non-profit groups. *Parliamentary procedure*, a formal set of rules which governs the meetings of legislative bodies, political parties, and other groups, is worth learning if you aspire to be an elected official, party officer, or lobbyist, or participate in any organization which uses that set of rules to govern its meetings. Yet, parliamentary procedure can often be an "insiders game" which benefits the good old boys (or gals) who know it best.

Meetings can be made highly efficient, and very effective, by using alternative sets of meeting rules. The rules can be simple, and stated at the beginning of the meeting. Examples are, "Only one person may speak at a time. The chair will recognize each speaker. All members of the organization are allowed to vote, and a simple majority will carry an issue. Non-members are invited to observe and participate, but may not vote."

Meeting *facilitators* are trained to get input from all participants, and use modified forms of consensus decision-making, or simple majority. It is quite common for professional facilitators to be hired to run large or complex meetings. Experienced facilitators know that open-ended discussion can lead to a lack of focus and direction. They use their skills to get input from participants which leads to decisions.

Everyone can develop expertise in facilitating meetings, and these basic skills are useful in an unending number of situations. Helping groups accomplish their work in effective ways can build confidence and contacts for you, the facilitator, as well.

## Tips for Effective Meetings

- Be sure that the meeting has a written agenda, with realistic time limits for each item. Stick to the time limits, or engage in a brief discussion about extending them.
- The chair or facilitator should clearly explain the rules for participation.
- Try to encourage participation from everyone during the meeting. Be sure to call on those who have not yet spoken—be aware that .

women may need support and encouragement to speak in meetings that are dominated by men.

■ Summarize key points, decisions, or actions periodically. Be sure to resolve each matter before another is taken up.

---

### Steps to preparing for a great meeting

The Board of Directors or Chair of the Meeting will:

1. Pre-plan with key leaders around important or controversial issues or decisions.
2. Choose a purpose for the meeting. Set clear goals.
3. Ask people to attend the meeting. Remind those who plan to attend.
4. Plan the agenda and distribute beforehand, if possible.
5. Select a fair chair.
6. Choose helpful rules.
7. Select a person to make a written record of the meeting, and mail it to committee members.[22]

---

## How to Get Experience in Running Meetings

Observe effective meetings, the use of written agendas, and techniques used to gain input from participants. Tell staff or leaders of your organization that you would like to try running a simple meeting, and ask for their help in putting together an agenda.

Assist in a large meeting, or retreat, by taking minutes or recording notes on an easel pad.

If you are interested in parliamentary procedure, attend meetings of your political party, or other groups that use these rules.

## To Find Out More

*Democracy in Small Groups: Participation, Decision-Making and Communication,* by John Gaits.[23]

*Leadership for Change: Toward a Feminist Model,* by Bruce Kokopeli and George Lakey, is a pamphlet that demystifies leadership functions, and has a handy checklist.[24]

*Robert's Rules of Order,* by Henry M. Robert, or look for alternative books or charts on how to use *Robert's Rules* during a meeting.[25]

*Simplified Parliamentary Procedure,* an 11-page pamphlet available from the League of Women Voters. 1730 M Street NW, Suite 1000, Washington, DC 20036; 202/249-1965.

*The American Society for Training and Development* offers networking and professional development, along with classes and workshops on organizational and training skills. Some of the 150 local chapters offer mentorship programs. 1640 King St., PO Box 1443, Alexandria, VA 22313; 703/683-8100.

## EVENT PLANNING AND MANAGEMENT

Do you enjoy organizing parties? Planning and managing small or large events is a specialty skill with multiple uses in the political world. Meetings, conferences, fundraising events, lobby days at the state capitol or city hall, training sessions, and press conferences, all need detailed planning and superb execution to build the credibility of the organization and to get the job done. Most organizations have an annual calendar that includes one or more large annual events. The ability to produce events is a marketable skill; free-lance event producers organize conferences and meetings for numerous clients. Many professionals in the field of event management started out as volunteers.

### Tips on Organizing Events

■ Start early and recruit plenty of people. Divide the group into subcommittees—facility, program, turnout, food—and recruit a chairperson for each subcommittee. Make clear agreements and set realistic goals.

■ Create a "backwards timeline" starting from the day of the event, listing everything that will need to be done by that day, and the intermediate steps needed to make it happen. For example, "food delivered 2 p.m." also requires "food ordered" (two weeks before), "menu planned and decided" (three weeks before), and "food committee meeting" (four weeks before event). Do the same thing for organizing the program and the logistics of the site. Then go back and write someone's name beside each task on the list.

## How to Get Experience in Event Planning and Management

Join the committee for a large annual event, such as a fundraising auction, and offer to chair a subcommittee.

Create and organize a small event of your own design. Make a written plan and ask an experienced event organizer to review that plan with you.

Host a house party for an organization you care about.

## To Find Out More

See information on events in Joan Flanagan's *Grassroots Fundraising*.

Read *Creating Special Events: The Ultimate Guide to Producing Successful Events*, by Linda Surbeck.[26]

Check out *A Comprehensive Guide to Successful Conferences and Meetings: Detailed Instructions and Step-by-Step Checklists*, by Leonard Nadler and Zeace Nadler.[27]

## COMPUTERS AND INFORMATION SYSTEMS

Keeping track of members, contributors, and community contacts is a crucial aspect of every campaign or organization's work. For those who like to be on the inside of an organization, and not assume a public role, computer and information projects can help you gain familiarity with computer systems that may be useful in other areas of your life.

For those with computer expertise, helping groups choose and purchase hardware and software, designing programs, and training staff and members to use computer technology, can be an invaluable contribution to any cause. Design a database system, or help a statewide group set up an on-line network for improved communication. A computer data base can be highly effective in running an electoral campaign or fundraising drive. Be sure to match appropriate levels of need with the system and do not encourage groups to over-invest in a system that is too complex.

## Gaining Experience with Computers and Information Systems

If you are new to computers and are seeking to develop computer literacy, volunteer to input data or perform other basic computer tasks. If you want to develop familiarity with a particular computer program or system, call and find out which organizations use that system.

If you have a computer and a modem, you can go on-line and get access to tutorial help in many computer subjects. The two best known on-line services are CompuServe (800/848-8199) and American Online (800/827-6364). Many grassroots activists are discovering the benefits of on-line networks for communication.

If you are familiar with computers and information systems, and want to offer your help to a nonprofit organization, be prepared to make a major time commitment. If you talk a group into getting a new or upgraded computer system, or a new software program, you will want to be available to help them learn how to use it effectively and to trouble-shoot problems.

## Activism On-Line

The Ms. Foundation's Coalition Connections suggests these networks for activists:

*ChoiceNet,* a weekly reproductive rights electronic newsletter, is shared over the host system Internet. Call 415/546-7211.

*HandsNet* is an on-line system used primarily by nonprofits in community development, legal services, food, and shelter provision. Call 408/257-4500.

*Public Forum\*NonProfit Connection,* is part of the GENIE host system and links nonprofit organizations. 800/638-9636.

*The Well (Whole Earth 'Lectronic Link)* is used by nonprofit groups working on a variety of issues. 415/332-6106.

*The Women's Information Resource and Exchange (WIRE),* is the only on-line network dedicated to women's issues. Keep up to date on women's politics and travel, get news and information on women's health. 800/210-9999.

## For More Information

*Electronic Networking for Nonprofit Groups: A Guide to Getting Started,* by Tom Sherman, Washington, DC: Apple Computer Community Affairs and the Benton Foundation, 1994.

*How to Connect,* by Chris Shipley, Emeryville, CA: Ziff-Davis Press, 1994.

## NETWORKING

The old boy's network doesn't have a listing in the phone book, an office, or official club meetings. The network exists in men's clubs, in board rooms, and on the golf course. Men have used business, social, and political contacts for years for a variety of purposes. Networks are based on the simple principle that through sharing information, each person in the network gains more power.

Since networks function to introduce younger members and help them get started, women are at a disadvantage when not included. As women strive for new positions, they find it can be a bit lonely to be one of the first women senators (the United States Senate installed a women's restroom in 1993 after the number of women tripled from two to six), or the lone female on a board or commission.

Women's networks are organized to help women gain power, contacts, and support in many situations. They help women promote each other's businesses, gain visibility, share information, and technical assistance. Specialized networks connect women in business, the professions, sports and athletics, politics, and labor.

Networks of women public officials are highly successful in increasing the effectiveness of women officeholders.[28] Such networks include: the Black Women Mayors' Caucus, the Congressional Caucus for Women's Issues, Women Executives in State Government, California Elected Women, and Women in Municipal Government. These groups help women elected to public office, and who may be isolated in their own region, track information about strategies that do and do not work.

Other networks for women interested in politics include the National Women's Political Caucus, and the Washington (DC) Women's Network, which help women get political appointments and jobs. In 1993, Republican women set up the Republican Network to Elect Women (RENEW), expressly to serve as "an old boy's network for Republican women."[29]

## Tips for Networking

■ Start with the network you already have—that includes everyone on your phone list who you call regularly to get ideas or to help solve problems. Send them copies of interesting articles you read, suggest that they get together with others who you have met who share common interests. Exchange names with interesting people you meet at conferences and events.

■ Expand your contacts, either by joining a women's network or creating your own. Look for networks that represent who you are, or what you do. The Third Wave is a multicultural network of young women feminists across the country. African-American Women in Defense of Ourselves seeks to heighten the visibility of black feminists. Find out about the Coalition of Labor Union Women, or the American Association of University Women.

■ Join legislative alert networks, make phone calls, or write letters at crucial times, on issues of concern.

■■■■■■■■■■■■■■ **WOMEN WHO DARE** ▭▭▭▭▭▭▭▭▭

### Rosalinda Lugo

Since last November, I have been a staff person for a project called HOPING Youth, a program funded by city, state, and county monies to reduce gang violence. Before that, I had been a leader with UNO, (United Neighbors Organization) for about 11 years, as a volunteer. During that time I taught in the Los Angeles Unified School District, working with a mix of African American, Mexican and Central American students. I decided to make this job switch because of something that happened in my classroom.

A child who had been at my school for eight years came to my classroom for 6th grade and he was unable to read or write in English or in Spanish. Through my involvement with UNO, I had been working to reform the school system. And I thought, why am I wasting my time as a volunteer trying to make the public schools more responsive to kids' lives when this boy could not read or write? This was not an isolated case—there were hundreds and hundreds of children this was happening to.

I decided to make this career change to prove—as I believe firmly—that the only way to change schools is if the parents are involved. Not just parents, but *organized* parents. The communities where parents are well-organized, and where they approach the schools in an organized fashion, have good schools. Where parents are not connected or organized, the schools are not good.

My job with HOPING youth is to try to change the power structure so that parents have more power. As the Associate Director for School Parent Organizing, I supervise the teams of organizers who go out to work with youth and parents. I train them in how to run better meetings, how to identify leadership, how to do a power analysis and strategic analysis. We've hired 65 people already, a very diverse group of Hispanic, White, African-American, women and men, from their early 20s to their early 60s. I got involved with UNO through my church, when the pastor invited me to attend a couple of meetings. At one meeting we broke into committees because UNO was preparing for a forum with the candidates for governor. I sat in the committee talking about Tom Bradley, because he was the only candidate I had heard of. A few days later, a fellow called to ask me to meet with Tom Bradley's campaign manager, to invite Bradley to the candidate's forum.

When I got there, I thought there would be a lot of people, but it was just the other fellow and I. I told him I would go in, but that I wasn't willing to speak about anything. He said he'd do all the talking. We met with Bradley's campaign manager, and this was a moment that really changed me. We invited Bradley to the candidate's forum and explained that this was an important event, because the people from East LA should have a say in who was the next governor of California.

"Wait a minute, why should Mr. Bradley go to an event in East LA You people don't vote and you can't give money. So why should he go?" When he said that, something happened in me and I felt this anger. I thought about my parish—Lourdes—my community . . . and I spoke up and I said, "Why should he come? He should come because we're important and we're taxpayers." I got angry.

I got more involved and was still feeling that anger, the kind that drives you. In October we had the forum and none of the candidates showed up. I spoke about Tom Bradley, and people who knew me could not believe I'd spoken up. I did it because he made me so angry.

All this time, I knew that I was poor, that was a given. But it was always in the back of my mind that if you get a good education you can move out of East LA, then things would get better. What that man said made me realize that in the eyes of powerful people, people like me and my family, and the people in my church who were very important to me, didn't count. That meeting changed my life.

I became chair of the education committee. These events made me into a political person. Working with UNO gave me something I never received in school. It gave me an opportunity to become a public person, the skills I needed to be an activist, and the vehicle by which I could change things in LA and in the state. I learned the difference between public and private.

Private is where you want to be liked. And public is where you want to be respected.

---

## Notes

[1] Sheryl James, "Thoroughly Modest Millie," *Detroit Free Press Magazine*, January 23, 1994, p. 8.

[2] Ibid.

[3] EarthWorks Group, *Kid Heroes of the Environment*, (Berkeley, Calif.: EarthWorks Press, 1991).

[4] Frances Chamberlain, "A Young Volunteer with a Gift for Giving," *New York Times*, October 17, 1993, p. 1CN.

[5] Saul Alinsky, *Reveille for Radicals* (New York: Vintage Books, 1969).

[6] Saul Alinsky, *Rules for Radicals* (New York: Random House, 1972).

[7] Sanford D. Horwitt, *Let Them Call Me Rebel: Saul Alinsky, His Life and Legacy* (New York: Knopf, 1989).

[8] Kim Bobo, Jackie Kendall, and Steve Max, *Organizing for Social Change: A Manual for Activists in the 1990's* (Arlington, Va: Seven Locks Press, 1990).

[9] David Walls, *The Activist's Almanac: The Concerned Citizen's Guide to the Leading Advocacy Organizations in America* (New York: Simon and Schuster, 1993).

[10] Harry C. Boyte, *The Backyard Revolution* (Philadelphia: Temple University Press, 1980).

[11] Julie Hutchinson, "Crusading Doctor Offers Prescription for Saving Earth," *Toronto Star*, May 22, 1992, p. C16.

[12] Sandie Barnard, *Rise Up: A New Guide to Public Speaking* (Englewood Cliffs, N.J.: Prentice-Hall, 1993).

[13] Lani Arrendondo, *How to Present Like a Pro: Getting People to See Things Your Way* (New York: McGraw Hill, 1991).

[14] Kim Klein, *Fundraising for Social Change*, 2nd ed. (Inverness, Calif: Chardon Press, 1988).

[15] Joan Flanagan, *The Grass Roots Fundraising Book: How to Raise Money in Your Community* (Chicago: Contemporary Books, 1992).

[16] Grassroots Fundraising Journal, *Getting Major Gifts* (Berkeley, Calif., 1990).

[17] Bob Smucker, *The Non-Profit Lobbying Guide: Advocating Your Cause and Getting Results* (San Francisco: Jossey-Bass, 1991).

[18] Donald E. del Kieffer, *Hot to Lobby Congress: A Guide for the Citizen Lobbyist* (New York: Dodd, Mead and Co., 1981).

[19] Arch Lustberg, *Testifying with Impact* (Washington, D.C.: United States Chamber of Commerce, 1983).

[20] Barry Greever, "Tactical Investigations for People's Struggles," reprinted in *Organizing for Social Change, A Manual for Activists of the 1990's* by Kim Bobo, Jackie Kendall, and Steve Max (Arlington, Va.: Seven Locks Press, 1990).

[21] Charlotte Ryan, *Prime Time Activism: Media Strategies for Grassroots Organizing* (Boston: South End Press, 1991).

22 Adapted from Joan Flanagan's "Steps to Preparing for a Great Meeting," in *The Successful Volunteer Organization: Getting Started and Getting Results in Nonprofit, Charitable, Grassroots and Community Groups* (Chicago: Contemporary Books, 1981).

23 John Gastil, *Democracy in Small Groups: Participation, Decision-Making and Communication* (Philadelphia: New Society, 1993).

24 Bruce Kokopeli and George Lakey, *Leadership for Change: Toward a Feminist Model* (Philadelphia: New Society, 1984).

25 Henry M. Robert, *Robert's Rules of Order*, revised ed. by Darwin Patnode (Nashville: T. Nelson, 1989).

26 Linda Surbeck, *Creating Special Events: The Ultimate Guide to Producing Successful Events* (Louisville, Ky.: Master Publications, 1991).

27 Leonard Nadler and Zeace Nadler, *A Comprehensive Guide to Successful Conferences and Meetings: Detailed Instructions and Step-by-Step Checklists* (San Francisco: Jossey-Bass, 1988).

28 Katherine E. Kleeman, "Women Officials' National Policy Network," *The Center for American Women in Politics Newsletter*, October 1993, vol. 9, no. 2.

29 Gail Russell Chaddock, "More Women Run for US Offices While Campaign Money Rises," *Christian Science Monitor*, May 6, 1994, p. 1.

# CHAPTER

# 8

# Changing the World in One Hour per Week

*I'm busier now than I ever was before I got active—these days I'm working and going to school. I don't know what triggered my activism. The feminist had been there, but the activist had not. I hated politics, let me tell you. But now I'm really into it.*

*In a way, I have less time to get involved now than ever before. But I feel very passionate about women's rights and women's role in society, about the inequities in our legal system, and in society at large. This is something that's very important to me, and that's where my energy comes from.*

—PAM GALLINA
PRESIDENT OF SOUTHERN NEVADA NOW

Something is calling you to take action—it may be a local issue that needs attention, a wrong that needs to be righted, or simply the feeling that you want to get involved in your community, or do something more meaningful with your life. Another voice reminds you that you don't have much time to get involved in politics. You're busy, and you have so many other priorities.

Even with a limited amount of time, you can have a significant impact on issues and events around you. You *can* change the world by

**151**

taking a stand, inspiring others to join a cause, and working systematically toward a goal, *even* with just an hour each week. If you can't
jump into politics head first, you can still throw a few pebbles into the
pond and create some ripples.

## SERVICE VERSUS SOCIAL CHANGE

Before you decide how to focus your time, consider the distinction
between service work and working for social change. The compassionate often feel the call to do *service work*—meeting the direct needs of
those in our society who have the greatest need, such as delivering
meals to elderly shut-ins, caring for foster children, or collecting clothing and shoes for the homeless.

Service work often becomes a catalyst for political advocacy and
social change. After cleaning up one too many oil spills from beaches,
the activist wonders if regulations on oil tankers are strong enough, or
if they are properly enforced. Someone who serves meals to the homeless week after week, comes to the conclusion that there simply are
not enough jobs or housing for the working poor. Volunteer tutors realize that hungry children will never be able to learn. While service work
has its own very rich rewards, those involved may end up feeling that
they are continually placing band-aids on the wounds of society, without really treating our major social ills. Service workers who move into
advocacy provide compelling testimony about the need for reform, as
well as the front-line experience to help shape social policy.

Throughout this chapter, we present ideas for how you can help
those most in need through service, as well as ways to shake up the
system via social change so that those desperate needs will eventually
be met. The choice is yours.

## MAXIMIZING THE IMPACT OF LIMITED TIME

You can achieve significant results from as little as one hour per week
of volunteer or activist work. The keys to maximizing your impact with
limited time are *planning, focus,* and *follow-through.*

Each minute you invest in *planning* your activities makes the rest
of your time much more productive. Make a plan and separate the
tasks into small pieces that you can accomplish on a weekly basis;
don't try to start a new endeavor each week.

Look for one specific problem to solve, one person to help, one organization to get involved with. The more you *focus* your efforts, the better chance you have of achieving results. With limited time available, take on a project of limited scope.

With the proper *follow-through*, you can weave your one or two hours each week into a consistent pattern that will yield greater long-term results. Use a written plan to identify a weekly course of action. Keep your plan in a file folder with notes and contact names readily available, so that you can use the time you do have most efficiently. Steal a minute or two each day to return phone messages, drop a note to a crucial contact, or clip newspaper articles on a topic of interest.

## What You Can Do with One Hour Per Week

One person can change the world by changing other people. One hour a week can be enough to start a chain reaction—you could get one new person involved, who, in turn, may get another, who goes on to recruit another.

### Organize a visibility campaign

Let's say you want to heighten public awareness about a dangerous intersection near the public school. You believe a stop light is needed to prevent further traffic accidents, and protect the safety of children. Spend your very first hour organizing a small *planning session* with others who share the same concern—make phone calls and invite several neighbors to your house. The next week, use the group's time to brainstorm five to ten activities which will heighten awareness of the problem. Divide the tasks among the group; sign up for some task yourself, or volunteer to check in on everyone else's progress. Some activities that take an hour or less are:

- Call or write the police department to document accidents at the intersection.
- Find out who in city hall has the power to authorize a new stop light; it may be the traffic or transportation department.
- Write a letter to city hall requesting a traffic light study.
- Recruit a neighbor to attend a local PTA meeting and pass around a petition requesting the new stop light.
- Call a radio talk show and ask for support.
- Write a letter to the editor of the local newspaper.

- Invite neighborhood youth to make warning signs; post them at the intersection.
- Alert the media about the petition and the children's signs.
- During an election year, encourage others to attend public forums and ask candidates to take a stand on the issue.

Each one of these activities may take no more than one hour. Yet, the combined effect of each one, over the course of several weeks, could result in a highly effective public education campaign. By organizing several neighbors who share your concern, you will dramatically multiply the impact of your efforts.

### Research and lobby on an issue

Don't just talk back to the television, or mutter a response to the radio news. If an issue is coming up for a vote in the state legislature, city council, or United States Congress, take action to influence the votes of your elected officials.

During your *research* phase, read newspaper or magazine articles, call local and national organizations for fact sheets, subscribe to a newsletter, and ask to join an activist alert network so you can quickly learn who the key decision makers are, and what actions need to be taken to affect their votes.

Contact your elected officials—they do read and count their mail. Often an undecided legislator will let the mail count be the final factor in making a decision.

*The mood and tenor of the daily mail from home is a recurring topic of conversation in the rear of the House and Senate Chambers or around the coffee cups in the dining room of the Capitol.*

—JAMES WRIGHT,[1]
FORMER SPEAKER OF THE HOUSE

Some ways that you can *lobby* include:

- Make phone calls to the city hall, state capitol, or Congress. Any member of the Congress can be reached at: 202/224-3121. (On-line subscribers to Compuserve can send e-mail messages: GO-CONGRESSGRAM, Prodigy subscribers: JUMP LETTERS TO CONGRESS). If you don't know the phone number, call your public library or local chapter of the League of Women Voters. If a crucial vote is about to take place, get five others to make calls, and have each ask five more people.

■ Write a letter to the editor of your local newspaper. Focus on one or two points, and express your feelings on the issue. You don't have to be an expert to have an opinion.

■ Send a telegram to the White House. Messages to the president are tallied regularly as a measure of public opinion on issues of the day. A Public Opinion Message of up to 20 words can be sent to the president, vice president, or any member of Congress for $9.95 by calling Western Union at 1-800/325-6000.

■ If that's too expensive, send a postcard or letter to:

President of the United States
1600 Pennsylvania Avenue
Washington, DC 20500

The president receives 40,000–50,000 letters a week, which are tallied by staffers and used as a barometer of public sentiment on the issues. Routine correspondence receives form-letter responses, unusual questions or issues receive original responses drafted by the staff. All letters to the White House get a response.

■ Call the White House! The White House receives about 1,000 phone calls each day, and a special phone comment line records pro and con responses on topical issues. Public comments are tallied daily, and a report is given to the president. The White House switchboard (answered 24 hours a day) can be reached at 202/456-1414. The comment line (answered 9 A.M. to 5 P.M. Eastern Standard Time) is 202/456-1111.

■ Call or write a letter to your congressional representatives, stating your position on the issue. Keep the letter brief; ask one specific question, so they will have to respond to you personally.

Representative _____
U.S. Capitol
Washington, DC 20515

Senator _____
U.S. Capitol
Washington, DC 20510

Capitol telephone: 202/224-3121

Call your representative or senator's office, ask for their FAX number, and send them a FAX.

■ Distribute copies of legislative alerts to neighbors, friends, church members, or day-care parents.

■ Have lunch with three friends and ask them to write letters; bring paper or postcards for them to use.

■ Testify at a legislative hearing. (Take one or two hours to prepare your testimony and another hour or two to present it.) When a bill was proposed in the Illinois state legislature to increase wages for personal attendants for elderly and handicapped persons, in order to help reduce high rates of turnover, many rehabilitation organizations testified in favor of the legislation. But it was consumer Terry Gutterman who made the issue clear to the committee by explaining, "Imagine giving the keys to your house to 14 different people in a single year." The bill passed.[2]

■ Don't overlook your most powerful contact. Request a personal meeting with your member of Congress the next time she or he is back home in the district. Be prepared to state your opinion succinctly, and ask for support.

---

◈

### The League of Women Voters' do's and dont's for letter writing

**DO** write legibly, be brief, and to the point. Identify yourself by district if possible, and state any personal, family, or business interest you have in the issue. State your opinion or concern, and give the reasons or personal experience that led you to that position.

**DO** identify a bill by title or number if you can. Specify your problem or concern about a government department. Ask a specific question to which you would like to receive a specific answer.

**DO** write if you approve of something, not just to complain or oppose.

**DON'T** be righteous or apologetic. Your elected officials will assume that you're a taxpayer. And they are happy to hear from you.

**DON'T** Be vague, rude, or threatening; those tactics won't help your cause.[3]

---

### Just make phone calls

One of the most crucial tools of organizing is the reminder call. If it is difficult for you to spend time away from home, offer to make reminder calls once a week on behalf of your favorite organization. You can contact hosts or attendees to confirm the details of a meeting or event. It is possible to make fifty reminder calls in one hour; those calls can assure the success of a meeting or fundraising event.

### Raise money for your favorite cause

Set a goal of raising $100 during one hour a week for several weeks. Here's how you can do it:

Ask twenty friends for $5 each, ten friends for $10 or solicit five $20 contributions. (More likely, you will raise some combination of donations, such as one $20 donor, four $10 givers and eight $5 donors.) State your case, and convince others why they should support the cause. Deliver the money to the group and ask how else you can help.

If $100 is not enough, set your sights on a bigger number. If your own resources and contacts cannot generate major contributions, use your time to research potential donors, and help leverage large donations to the cause.

### How to raise $10,000

Here's a plan to raise $10,000 in about ten hours: This process assumes there are people in the community who are capable of making such a large donation, and that at least one of them will be sympathetic to your cause. This situation is more likely than you may think!

**Week 1**—Meet with staff of the organization you're seeking money for and review your plan. Bring along the list of sponsors of a large charity event in town. The program of the event should list all their names.

**Week 2**—Go to the library and research newspapers to determine the background, political and civic interests, board positions, and memberships of the charity event sponsors. Use the information you've gathered to narrow the list to the eight names most likely to support your cause.

**Week 3**—Meet with staff to review your research on prospective donors and narrow the list of eight names down to the four most likely prospects.

**Week 4**—Conduct additional research on the four prospects—find out their key issues, and try to determine who will be most sympathetic to your group's program.

**Week 5**—Write a memo to the staff of the organization summarizing your research on the top four; propose a particular project or aspect of the organization that each potential donor would be most likely to support with a gift of $5–10,000.

**Week 6**—Encourage the staff to set up a meeting with the prospective donor. if appropriate, go along yourself.

**Week 7**—Drive over to pick up the check; deposit $10,000 donation in bank.

---

Don't overlook any possible avenue of support. "If your time is limited, focus on leveraging donations," advises Susan Kaufman of Portland, Oregon. She and two friends from Art AIDS raised over $160,000 to provide housing assistance for people with AIDS, by getting the organization listed as a voluntary check-off on the Oregon state income tax return.[4] They spent less than 20 hours writing the application and appearing before the Oregon Charitable Check-Off Commission and netted a return of $9000 per hour. "It's great because the state sends out the mailing, and collects the money. We just deposit the checks," says Kaufman.

### Incorporate new ideas into your current work

Ask how your current paid or volunteer involvements can be utilized for greater effect. Kathy Thurber was vice president of the Minneapolis Parks and Recreation Board when she decided to find out what percentage of girls actually used city playgrounds. In 1990, she found that less than 20% of playground users were girls. The Girls Initiative, a plan to promote girls' participation in recreation programs, links sports and self-esteem. Today 45% of those using city recreation facilities are girls. In 1991, 30 girls played volleyball; one year later there were 300.

### Vote and convince others to vote

No matter what else you do, maintain your registration and exercise your right to vote. Elections occur more often than every November; every state has a primary as well, and special elections may be called at any time. Before every election, make a list of two-to-three key issues of importance to you. Use your "activist" hour each week to:

■ *Register others to vote.* The League of Women Voters estimates that almost a third of all Americans change residences every two years. Some states automatically register voters when they change the address on their driver's license (this program is known as "Motor-Voter"). Elsewhere, people must re-register. Find out if your state accepts mail-in registrations, or if you must be deputized to register voters.

■ *Call the candidates,* or their campaign offices, to determine where they stand on your issues.

■ *Attend political debates or candidate forums,* and ask a question if your concerns have not been addressed. Call the local chapter of the League of Women Voters to find out where and when debates will take place.

■ *Influence the votes of others* by writing a letter to the editor; wearing campaign buttons; placing a sign in your yard or on your door; or endorsing a candidate at meetings of other clubs, groups, or gatherings of friends you attend.

■ *Set a personal goal of convincing ten voters* to support your candidate, and remind them all to go to the polls on election day.

The Louisville Coalition of 100 Black Women holds a Power and Influence Breakfast each year. About a month before election day, the Coalition invites candidates to speak to its members and answer questions. One of 60 local chapters of the National Coalition of 100 Black Women, the group has a goal of getting more minority women interested, and involved, in politics. "We do have political strength," said Dr. Betty Bibbins, chapter president, "We just have to use it."[5]

You may find that your own successes and the encouragement of others will stimulate your interest in doing more. Take another look at your current commitments, reframe some of your priorities, and free more time for activist work. After spending some time on the front lines with members of society who are most under attack, you can turn your first-hand observations into stronger arguments for greater funding and more support.

## WHAT YOU CAN DO WITH THREE HOURS PER WEEK

With three hours per week, you can undertake a more complex issue. Take on a bigger goal, and organize more people!

### Set Up Individual Meetings to Further Your Activist or Political Career

Identify and meet with opinion leaders. A leader is someone with a base or following, *not* just a person with a title. Make a list of opinion leaders in your area—the kind of folks that other people respect, and listen to. Set up a series of one-on-one meetings, for 30 minutes each.

Ask their opinions, and find out why they are involved in the community. Tell them about yourself, and discuss issues of mutual concern.

## Organize an Annual Event

Large annual events take months of careful planning and preparation. Choose an event and dedicate yourself to making it better. The Race for the Cure is sponsored annually to raise funds and awareness for breast cancer research. To help organize the race in your area, call the Susan B. Komen Foundation at 800/I'M AWARE (800/462-9273).

Take Our Daughters to Work Day, April 28, has exploded on the scene as a national day to show girls some of their career options. Spend three hours a week building momentum for next April. For information and ideas, call the Ms. Foundation for Women at 212/353-8580.

## Organize or Join an Issue Campaign

Use your initial three-to-six hours to do research on your area of concern. Search periodical and newspaper indexes at the public library to find news stories about the issue. Call reporters to find out if they will share information. Contact people who have worked on the issue in another town or state. Write a fact sheet, make copies, and use it to get people to take action.

## Volunteer for a Political Campaign

Walk into campaign headquarters and offer to help answer phones, stuff envelopes or paint signs. Go door to door with the candidate to get the inside scoop on the issues, or join the committee for a gala fundraising event. Find out what ongoing projects need attention, and make a weekly commitment to the campaign. No previous experience is necessary.

## Serve on a Board or Commission

Expand your leadership skills, network, and serve the community by joining the board of directors of a nonprofit organization or a publicly appointed commission. Read the newspaper, or ask your local library to find out the names of boards, commissions, and task forces in your area, and start to track their progress.

Two states, Iowa and Montana, now require gender balance on all publicly appointed boards and commission, further opening up many possibilities for women. Many states are increasingly searching for women with expertise in many areas to serve.

It can be challenging to be the first woman appointed to a previously all-male board, as Nita Brueggeman explains:

When I was appointed to the Board of Tri-Met (a regional mass transit authority), I was the only woman, and more than that, I was a woman who was not from business, and a woman who was not wealthy.

They had absolutely nothing to say to me for about six months, and I survived by being tenacious. I took on a committee that I think the chair wanted to pass off to a woman—the Committee on Accessible Transportation (CAT), at a very opportune time, although I didn't know it then.

The ADA (Americans with Disabilities Act) was a-coming, and I helped CAT organize so that it stopped being a committee that would decide between three bad choices of accessible transportation and became a committee that says, "Here's what we want and need."

After a while I was representing a pretty vocal constituency, with the force of federal law behind it, and eight or nine percent of a $155 million a year budget, and people did take notice. And start to listen. And now I am truly the expert on the board on accessible transportation issues. It was good timing, and I was fortunate to get that committee. I don't think that was the chair's intent, I think they imagined they would sideline me there.

The other thing I've worked really hard on is, getting women on the board—there are now three. These are four-year appointments, and while sometimes people fight to stay on these boards, I'm looking towards who they can select to replace me. I think we need new blood and new ideas.

Brueggeman beautifully demonstrates how she developed a single area of expertise to establish her credibility and expand her power on the board.

---◆---

### How to Get Appointed to a Board or Commission

- Find out who arranges for appointments at the local and state level, and what openings are, or are likely to become, available.
- If you are interested in a specific board, first find out exactly what qualifications are required, and how often the board meets—weekly, monthly, quarterly? Ask for a job description for the position and a complete financial update.

- Observe a meeting of the commission. Do members of the group represent particular constituencies? (i.e. women, small business owners, immigrants, the taxpaying public) Talk to current and past board members and staff about their experiences. Review written reports or financial statements.

- Prepare your resume, highlighting relevant experience. Submit an application or search for someone to nominate you.

- Do some research to determine if the commission has been set up to "rubber-stamp" a pre-arranged political outcome, for example, a citizen review board which has been set up to give the public hospital a clean bill of health. Do you want to be a part of such a situation?

Read *Don't Miss That Appointment!* a National Women's Political Caucus Guide for those interested in being appointed to a federal board or commission.

---

## Join and Get Active in Your Local Political Party

In some places, party meetings and caucuses are where the action is electorally. In other regions, party organizations play a more limited role. What's the case in your area? If you haven't already done so, attend several meetings of your party's central committee, and obtain a copy of the platform. If you are so motivated, get active in party politics. One way to get started is to become a precinct worker or captain.

## Give Yourself a Political Education

*Create your own six-week program.* Orient yourself on a political map—your home is included in several legislative districts, because you are represented by elected officials at the local, county, state, and federal level. Find out your district number, and who represents you at each level. Do your representatives vote the way you would? If neither of the major parties seems to represent your interests, explore the alternative political parties, such as the Green Party (environmental) the Women's Party (feminist) and the New Party (multi-issue progressive).

*Research the district where you reside.* Look for census data to determine the demographics of who lives there; get information from the Board of Elections on voting patterns and history, and see how you match up with typical voters where you live.

*Visit your city or county council, and your state legislature.* Find out when public hearings will be held on issues and attend the hearings—sometimes hearings are held around the state, making them more accessible to those who live far from the capitol. Make notes on your opinion, sign up, and testify at the hearing.

*Visit and join the League of Women Voters.* The League is non-partisan; it does not support or oppose candidates of either party for any level of government. The League studies and take stands on public policy issues such as health care, reproductive choice, child care, clean air, and water. They have excellent materials about the process of government. Ask for information on how a bill becomes a law, or find out what current issues are being studied in your area. You can do research, lobby on an issue, meet community leaders, and network with other activist women through the League. If you have difficulty locating one of the 1,300 local, state, or regional chapters of the League, call the national headquarters at 202/429-1965.

*Read* Civics for Democracy: A Journey for Teachers and Students by Katherine Isaac.[6] This is an excellent guidebook to participatory politics, and a textbook that all high schools should be using.

## Take a Stand

Actor Charmaine Blakely was sexually attacked during a meeting with Hollywood talent agent Wallace Kaye. Although the Screen Actor's Guild (which licenses and franchises talent agents) told Blakely that the agent's file was confidential, she decided to brave possible reprisals in the entertainment industry and contacted the police. She worked with the police to conduct a sting operation. Two years later the talent agent was convicted and sent to jail after 50 additional women came forward to report similar attacks. "This experience has taught me how much good can be accomplished if you choose action over fear. Sexual harassment and sexual assault don't have to be 'business as usual' in the entertainment industry."[7]

## Follow Your Kids

Join your children in getting involved with activist groups. Arlene Victor of Bloomfield Township, Michigan, went to a meeting on nuclear disarmament with her daughter because, "She shouldn't have to fight for her future alone." Victor subsequently went on to become the national President of Women's Action for New Directions, which has 10,000 members nationwide. The group works to convince Congress to cut the military budget and redirect funds to social and environmental programs.[8]

## Service Work

Directly affect the quality or direction of another person's life by taking a role in mentoring that individual. A growing movement matches volunteer mentors with young people at risk, who may not have an adult role model or be getting the one-on-one attention they need to succeed. Sandy Lawrence, a vice president of an investment banking firm, describes why she chose to mentor Teri, a high school student in Cleveland, Ohio:

> I've done a lot of volunteer work and work with nonprofits, like sitting on boards, but wasn't getting the right satisfaction out of it. I wanted to try a one-on-one situation. With all the other efforts we make with youth and education, it all comes back to one-on-one. I think mentoring is so important.[9]

Whenever you go out to volunteer, take a young person with you!

The Women's Prison Association is a group of volunteers that works with women inmates in New York State, providing individual counseling, a half-way house for previously incarcerated homeless women, and prison nursery volunteers, who provide a sense of community spirit and caring.

Suzette Brooks, a corporate lawyer with a conscience, had a hard time finding ways to volunteer in New York City. At age 29 she started New York Cares, an organization that matches busy young professionals with volunteer tasks they can carry out in limited amounts of time, and on short notice.

Use lessons from your own difficult experiences to help others. Gerri Peper of Colorado first got cancer at age 16. She fought it off, but 20 years later, found she had malignant breast cancer. She got involved in several support groups, including *Can Surmount*, a program of the American Cancer Society, where she offers peer support as a one-on-one counselor to new cancer patients.[10]

Ten years ago, Mary Alice Norton started inviting hungry neighbors over for meals remembering how her mother often set two extra places at the dinner table in case a neighbor dropped by. As more friends went in and out of the hospital, and became unable to prepare food themselves, Norton sought a way to take care of them. "I don't know how it happened, but people just started to call and say that they needed a meal, or that they knew someone who needed a meal." Norton said. "It has just been word of mouth from the beginning."[11] At age 87 she still runs a Meals on Wheels program which provides about 200 lunches and dinners each month to homebound senior citizens in the semi-rural hills of Southern California's Topanga Canyon. People like Norton have served over 100 million home delivered meals in cities and towns all over the U.S. since 1972.[12] To find the Meals on Wheels program nearest you, call the National Association of Meal Programs at 202/547-6157.

If you feel hesitant about getting involved in a formal program, why not just "adopt" an older person in your neighborhood who may need extra help with grocery shopping, garden chores, even putting out trash cans on a weekly basis?

Become a literacy tutor or volunteer one morning or afternoon a week at a public school in your area. Or, volunteer for a shift at a crisis line—you will receive training in how to deal with the calls that come in.

### Get Paid to Volunteer

Large employers, as well as many smaller businesses, increasingly recognize the value of having their employees involved in community projects. Over 600 U.S. corporations have community service programs for their employees, with several (such as IBM, Xerox and Wells Fargo Bank) offering "social service sabbaticals" for those who want to take a job leave to perform community service. Find out if your employer has a similar program, or convince them to match volunteer time, granting you up to 10 hours a month as a paid volunteer.

## WHAT YOU CAN DO WITH SIX TO EIGHT HOURS PER WEEK

### Volunteer One Day a Week at the Organization of Your Choice

With such a significant time commitment, you should be able to get an interesting ongoing assignment. Coordinate a major fundraising event, chair a legislative committee, or take charge of an annual membership drive.

Keep a special program running smoothly, as Freddie Nixon does. Freddie, a United Methodist volunteer, works every Wednesday at the Women's Project in Little Rock, Arkansas. She coordinates the Ministries to Incarcerated Women and Their Children Program, which brings children to prison on visiting days to maintain relationships with their mothers. Freddie runs all aspects of the program, from arranging with prison officials, to contacting the children's caregivers, and scheduling the volunteers who provide transportation. She also oversees an annual retreat for the volunteers, the children, their caregivers, and mothers who have been released. Freddie makes an enormous difference in many people's lives, all in just one day each week.

## Join a Speaker's Bureau to Get the Word Out

Conduct public presentations for school classes, neighborhood, civic, and community groups to build public support for your favorite issues. Get trained by an organized speaker's bureau, or research and organize your own presentation. Volunteer to be a guest on radio talk shows, or sign up to testify at public hearings. For example, you can call your local office of Planned Parenthood, or contact the ACLU to make presentations about the Bill of Rights.

## Take Leadership

Go ahead, accept that nomination to be president of the neighborhood association, chair of an annual fundraising banquet, or speaker for an activist group. If you've found yourself standing on the sidelines and second guessing other people's leadership, perhaps it's your turn to try.

## Become a Media Intern

Offer to be an intern two mornings a week at your newspaper. Sign up for free training at a community cable access station and become the host of a weekly cable television talk show. Volunteer at a listener-sponsored community radio station, and help produce a show on a regular basis.

## Sign Up for a Class, Workshop, or Training

Go back to school and find out what's being offered on the subjects of politics, community organizing, organizational development, leadership, assertiveness training, or women's studies. Check the options at your local community college or university—many have special centers of continuing education for women. They help women of all ages and at all stages of life continue their education, and make career changes through workshops, seminars, and internships.

## Meet Your Role Model

That's what Terry Vinco did. While taking a business seminar at Northwood University in southeastern Michigan, she wrote a paper about the real "Norma Rae," a textile worker named Crystal Lee Sutton who challenged the power of JP Stevens, and helped organize the local textile workers union in the 1970s. After writing the paper, Vinco was inspired to locate her role model. Many phone calls later, Sutton invited Vinco to visit her in North Carolina. Vinco spent a weekend with Sutton, and learned first-hand the story of her life, hearing all the details the movie never told.[13]

# HOW TO CREATE YOUR OWN TWO-TO-THREE WEEK INTERNSHIP

If you like to dive into new situations, focus intently on issues, or want to explore the idea of working full time in politics, consider taking two-to-three weeks from your work or personal schedule to become a full time, unpaid staffer for an issue, organization, or campaign you care deeply about. By making such a strong commitment, you should be able to garner an assignment that will be both interesting and educational. Here are some ideas for creating your internship:

## Offer to Join the Staff of Your Favorite Nonprofit Organization

Think about the calendar of major upcoming events, and help with the annual banquet or lobby day. Work on turnout for the event; call through the membership list, and get as many people as possible to attend the event. Help with publicity by drafting a circulating press release, or arranging transportation for the event.

## Intern for Your State Representative or Other Local Elected Official

Send a written survey to constituents on a hot issue; tally the results.

Research a topic, and draft a speech for the official to give on the subject.

Read and sort mail from the district; draft responses to letters.

## Join a Political Campaign

Early help makes women candidates visible, and allows you to stand out among a smaller campaign staff. If you join the campaign early on, you won't get lost in the shuffle.

If you find you enjoy campaigning, remember that the last few weeks before an election are critical. Huge areas of responsibility are available to those willing to carry them out. Volunteer on an ongoing basis to establish your credibility, and let the campaign know that you will make yourself available full-time for the last two weeks. Offer to help "Get Out The Vote."

## Pack Your Bags and Go!

Many national organizations based in Washington, D.C., as well as local groups based in any state, offer internships with a small stipend. Join the staff of 9 to 5, the National Association of Working Women, the National Wildlife Federation, or the National Committee for Responsive Philanthropy. Find out about available internships by subscribing to *Community Jobs, the National Employment Newspaper for the Non Profit Sector*, 50 Beacon Street, Boston, MA 02108; 212/ 475–1001.

━━━━━━━━━ **WOMEN WHO DARE** ▭▭▭▭▭▭

## Evangeline Brown

I was born in Norwood, Louisiana, on February 23, 1909. My parents brought me to Dermott, Arkansas when I was about seven years old, and I've been here ever since. I grew up here and finished high school with an average of 98.75. I got my first grade teaching license, but I didn't feel I was anything till I went to college in Pine Bluff. I taught school for about 44 years altogether.

And since that time, oh, I've participated in so many things. I have about 33 plaques on my wall. Mostly from community service and education, things like that. I was the only African American elected president of the Arkansas Education Classroom Teachers. The National Education Association sent me across six states, teaching workshops on human relations when integration first came. At the Seven Star Missionary Baptist Church, I'm chair of the department of education and of the program committee, and I am supervisor of the children's division.

Politically, I work with the Democratic Party, and have helped organize workshops for voter education since about 1972. I was a member of the board of the Voter Education Project down in Atlanta before I retired. I ran for Mayor at one time, and I lost by 108 votes.

The incumbent was white, and he wasn't doing a proficient job, but nobody else would run. The African American man we tried to get to run would not do it. And I said, "I will not be in this world and let people think I don't know any better." So I just ran, and to tell you the truth, we all know I won. But they have a way of fixing things down here. A lot of people voted for me, and the next morning, everyone said, 'How you doing, Mayor?' And I had to remind them, I'm not the Mayor."

I am Vice President of Arkansas Legal Services. I represent the clients, the poor people, on their board. There are about eleven lawyers on the Board, and four of us represent the indigent from 24 counties. I'm not intimidated by the lawyers—when they get going with that jargon, I say, "Now wait a minute, you've got to break that down for me." I've been over there so long, they just turn to me and say, "Ms. Brown, is that down enough?"

I'm chair of the Education Committee for the local chapter of the NAACP, and I am chairman of the Legislative Committee for the PTA. And what else?

I started raising foster kids in the 60s. When I was teaching 7th–12th grade, I would have kids who needed help, and they would follow me home. Then a woman died and left five kids with their grandfather. The human services counselor asked me if I would take them, and I did. Then I started taking in more and more kids; all together I reared about 34 foster kids. Most of them are doing very nicely. They come back and visit and call this home, I have good relationships with them.

The biggest challenge in my life is to get these Delta people to understand that they should look up and live. I just hate to see people oppressed, and I hate to see people who don't have enough self esteem to come out from under. I'm just here trying to help those who need help. And lately, the days begin to look a little brighter.

## Notes

[1] League of Women Voters, *Impact on Congress: A Grassroots Lobbying Handbook for Local League Activists* (Washington, D.C.: League of Women Voters, 1987), p. 5.

[2] Sue S. Suter, "Women with Disabilities: How to Become a Boat Rocker in Life," *Vital Speeches of the Day*, December 1, 1993, p. 111.

[3] League of Women Voters Education Fund, *Voicing Your Choice* (Washington, D.C.: League of Women Voters, 1994), pp. 14–15.

[4] This program allows several nonprofit organizations to be listed on the bottom of the state income tax return each year; taxpayers can make a voluntary contribution of $1, $5, or $10 to any or all of the groups listed. If your state collects income taxes but doesn't have a voluntary checkoff system for non-profit organizations, you may want to pursue legislation to create such a system.

[5] Kim Wessel, "Power Breakfast Dishes Up Politics, Cholesterol," *Louisville Courier-Journal*, October 8, 1993, p. 4B.

[6] Katherine Isaac, *Civics for Democracy: A Journey for Teachers and Students* (Washington, D.C.: Essential Books, 1992).

[7] Charmaine Blakeley, "Rewriting the Script," *Ms.*, March–April 1994, p. 31.

[8] Kwan Mun, "Activist Wants to Wave Wand, Make War Disappear," *Plain Dealer*, March 18, 1994, p. 14B.

[9] Marc Freedman, *The Kindness of Strangers: Adult Mentors, Urban Youth, and the New Voluntarism* (San Francisco: Jossey-Bass, 1993), p. 39.

[10] Jeanne Malmgren, "Dancing with the Dolphins," *St. Petersburg Times*, May 7, 1989, p. 1F.

[11] Kurt Pitzer, "Still Hungry to Help Others," *Los Angeles Times*, August 13, 1993, p. 1.

[12] Alan Balsam, Joseph Carlin, and Beatrice Rogers, "Weekend Home Delivered Meals in Elderly Nutrition Programs," *Journal of the American Dietetic Association*, September 1992, p. 1125.

[13] Michael Funke, "Looking for 'Norma Rae,' " *Solidarity*, March 1994, p. 16.

# 9

# Finding or Creating
# Your Niche

The history of the United States is the history of women taking
action.

In the 1700s, grassroots efforts by American women included charities and social aid societies. The first women's charity in the United
States was the Free African Society, organized in 1778 by freed slaves
in Philadelphia. Members deposited 25 cents per week into an insurance pool that was used to help get through emergencies. The Society
for the Relief of Poor Widows and Children, founded in 1797 by Isa-
bella Graham in New York City, recruited over two hundred members
in its first year. The membership fee of $3 was used both to train 98
widows with sewing skills so they could be self-supporting, and enroll
200 small children in school.[1]

By the 1830s many women turned their efforts to organizing for the
abolition of slavery. Underground networks linked freed and escaped
slaves, with Harriet Tubman leading dangerous missions to freedom.
White women did support work in abolition societies, and more than
one thousand were organized by 1837. The abolition movement was a
grassroots effort, based in churches, and funded through thousands of
small contributions.[2]

As activists for abolition, women learned they could be effective in making change. There was no male opposition to their organizing in parlors, but women who spoke out in public were harshly rebuked. The first American woman to attempt a public speaking career was Maria Steward, a freeborn black woman, who spoke in Boston in favor of abolition.[3] The Grimke sisters used the podium to present eyewitness accounts of the horrors of slavery. All were criticized by male leaders for speaking in public. In 1840, Elizabeth Cady Stanton and Lucretia Mott traveled to London as delegates to the World Anti-Slavery Convention. They had to sit behind a curtain in a gallery where they could listen to men debate, but were not allowed to participate.

Women activists chafed at their unequal status among abolitionists and in society, and the suffragette movement was born. It took 70 years of organizing, 47 state campaigns and constitutional conventions, 19 successive Congresses, and tireless petition gathering, marching, and lobbying to gain the vote for women in 1920. After winning its campaign for suffrage, The National American Women's Suffrage Association changed its name to the League of Women Voters and dedicated itself to educating women to be effective participants in the electoral process.

Dorothea Dix organized a one-woman national crusade in the 1840s to reform the way society treated the mentally ill. She traveled alone throughout the Northeast and the South, inspecting prisons and poorhouses, and lobbying state legislatures for reform. Her work led to the first publicly funded institutions to care for the mentally ill.[4]

The Young Women's Christian Association was founded in Boston in 1868 to provide shelter and "moral guidance" to country girls who came seeking jobs in the big cities. Chapters of the "Y" were quickly formed in cities all across the country.[5]

In the 1870s, a huge grassroots women's movement grew around the issue of temperance. The most prominent organization, the Women's Christian Temperance Union, organized "parlor meetings," a precursor of the house meeting strategy still employed today, to raise awareness and funds for the cause. In 1889, the Chicago chapter of the WCTU raised enough money to support two day nurseries, two Sunday schools, an industrial school, a shelter for four thousand homeless or destitute women, a free medical dispensary that treated more than 1,600 patients, a boarding house that over the years provided shelter for more than 50,000 men, and a low-cost restaurant.[6]

The National Women's Trade Union League, founded in 1903, was an unusual cross-class alliance in which middle class women helped support women of the working class, especially those in the garment industry, in their efforts to become unionized.[7]

Women were active in consumer rights, as well. In 1911, women in New York formed the Housewives League, agreeing to shop only at stores that charged the lowest prices. In 1912, they successfully boycotted butter, and fought for the labeling of packaged goods for weight or volume of contents. At its height, the League had 800,000 active members nationwide.[8]

Take it from the thousands of women who have dedicated themselves to activist lives before you—there's no shortage of important work to be done. All you have to do is decide to get involved. Follow a two hundred year tradition of American women and step off the sidelines and onto the playing field of politics. But how and where do you start?

The best place to start is by volunteering some of your time. Citizen action groups, public interest organizations, and political campaigns depend on volunteers to perform essential tasks, make contacts, and get the word out to the general public. Although you can start with very simple tasks, volunteers also assume high levels of responsibility in many organizations. Since aligning yourself with a particular group puts your own credibility on the line, you will want to find a group that you feel comfortable with, and that offers you interesting and rewarding work. In return, you should be well-treated and respected, and have your time used efficiently.

How do you find the group that's right for you?

## 1. Determine Your Priority Issues

Ask yourself which issues you'd like to work on. Do one or two issues or campaigns come instantly to mind? Write those down, and try to expand the list to include three to four possibilities. If the issues on your list seem immense and impossible—*save the environment* or *end homelessness*—try to break them down into more do-able parts—*clean up a neighborhood stream* or *convince a local corporation to hire ten homeless people.* If you want to learn about different styles of organizing, consider joining a multi-issue organization or a coalition. Maybe you want to get more active in a group that already represents you—your political party, union, or neighborhood association.

Next, determine what you want to do or learn (public speaking) or get from the group *(I'm new in town and want to meet others who share my values).* You may have many goals in this area.

## 2. Find Out Which Organizations or Campaigns Address Your Issues

For each issue on your initial list, write the names of one or more organizations or campaigns that address the issue. Get a name and phone number of someone to call in order to get involved. If you don't know the names of the organizations, use these sources for information:

- Approach one activist or organizer and ask for names of contacts.
- Visit or call the reference librarian at the public library for help.
- Clip stories from your local newspaper related to the issue; note the names of individuals or groups who make statements to the press.
- Look under Community Service or Community Organizations, or check the consumer guide section of your white or yellow pages.
- Call the Women's Lobby in your state, a hotline, the United Way, or another central clearinghouse for volunteers.
- Attend public hearings, meetings, or rallies on the issue and look for opportunities to sign up as a volunteer. Don't just give your name, get someone's name and phone number, and contact them the day after the rally or hearing.

Once you have a list of contact names and telephone numbers, call and make an appointment with each group. (You may want to space these appointments over several weeks.) Ask to speak with the volunteer coordinator, and say that you are thinking about getting involved, want more information, and ask how you can help.

## 3. Interview Each Organization by Talking to a Staff Member or Volunteer

Try to set up a brief personal meeting with a representative of the group or organization. Unless the group is dealing with a major crisis, someone should be willing to schedule 20 minutes to talk with you. During that initial visit to an organization or campaign, you may want to achieve several goals:

- Get basic information about the issue or candidate, including written materials that you can take home to read.
- Join the organization, or make a donation to the candidate, if you feel willing and motivated to do so.

- Ask about how you can become actively involved by volunteering some of your time. What jobs are available to volunteers? How much of a time commitment is required for each task? Is training available as part of the project?

Effective organizations interview volunteers as seriously as they would interview part-time staff. The volunteer interview may be formal or informal, brief or extended, but there should be some process to match the interests, skills, and needs of volunteers with the organization.

Groups mobilizing huge numbers of volunteers for a one-time task—like a group which recruits hundreds of people to clean up public parks or beaches on a single day—may not be willing to spend a half hour talking with each one. Campaigns facing election deadlines may ask you to just "come on down and help out." All volunteer groups may operate less formally than organizations with staff, and may only tell you where and when to show up to get started. If you feel comfortable donating a couple of hours for a one-time task, you will get a good feel for the organization and some answers to your questions by talking to others involved, or coordinating activities.

### Sample question for your volunteer interview

1. What are the main goals of your organization? What strategies do you use to accomplish those goals? What victories have you achieved?

2. How many staff does the organization have? How many volunteers? Who is on the board of directors? How did board members get those positions?

3. What jobs do new volunteers perform in the organization? Experienced or veteran volunteers? What skills are you looking for in volunteers?

4. How much time commitment is requested of volunteers? How are they scheduled?

5. Do you offer training or leadership development opportunities for volunteers?

6. Who else can I speak with who has volunteered here for a year or longer? Has she risen through the ranks of the organization?

## 4. Volunteer at One or More Organizations

Every organization has a style of operating—some are formal, with many titles and specific roles. Others are very informal, where everyone just pitches in to get tasks done. No matter how compelling the issue, you will feel happiest in an organization with a style that feels comfortable. By volunteering once or twice for several different groups, you can find one which has both the style and issues that you want to continue working with.

Just as with a paid staff position in private business, each volunteer job requires a certain level of knowledge or training to complete. Most organizations have entry level tasks that are routinely assigned to first-time volunteers. These are usually non-threatening tasks which are easy to learn quickly, and are often completed in a group setting, so you can meet others involved in the organization. Typical volunteer tasks in this category are:

- volunteering at an event (staffing a booth or table, helping to set up or take money, selling tickets)
- helping with a large mailing
- answering phones or making phone calls
- working in the office, making copies or filing
- clipping newspapers
- data entry on computers

You may be asked your preference, or told that one project is "all we have to do right now." For your first or second time volunteering, you should be willing to perform any of these entry level tasks.

## HOW DO I KNOW WHICH ORGANIZATION IS RIGHT FOR ME?

As you volunteer for various groups, you will also be informally evaluating each one. No matter how good the cause, you want to have a good experience, learn new things, and make contacts.

The best match for you will be to find a well organized group or campaign that is working on a compelling issue, has room for a new activist, and offers the training or contacts you seek.

Here are some things that you can, and should, expect from a well-organized group:

- New volunteers are welcomed, introduced to others, and given brief training on their job for the day. As a first-time volunteer, you are made to feel part of the group.
- A range of volunteer roles and positions are available within the group, with some type of training or support, to learn how to perform those roles. You may have to ask a leader or staff person for information about this.
- Someone from the organization makes the effort to find out who you are, what you have to offer, and what kind of skills you may want to develop by working with the group.
- Current leaders of the organization have moved up through the ranks, creating opportunities for others to do the same.

After visiting several organizations, one will feel right for you. It may be a combination of the group you think is most effective on the issues, which has a good system for working with volunteers, and will offer training, opportunities, or the type of personal contacts that you want to make. No group may seem perfect, because no group is perfect. Find the one that is the best match for you, and strive to make it better.

## What Kind of Groups Should I Stay Away From?

No matter how important the issue, an ineffective organization will not offer you positive experiences, and may be frustrating to work with. Here are some warning signs to watch out for:

- *Coordinators are chronically disorganized.* You show up on time, but they're never ready to put you to work. You're asked to sit around and wait, while others organize themselves and prepare your work. This situation quickly leads to feelings of resentment and burn-out among volunteers.

- *The organization is constantly in crisis.* Learn to differentiate between an externally created political crisis—*The governor just announced a new plan to eliminate a crucial program, and we're going all out to convince her to change her mind*—and an internally created crisis—*We printed the tickets too late, and now we have to personally deliver them to each of our members, rather than send them in the mail as planned.* Anyone can make a mistake once in a while, but you don't want to be associated with a group that bumbles from one crisis to another.

■ *You are immediately invited to join the board of directors, head a major task force, or committee.* Effective groups should have leadership development plans which help people rise through the ranks with training and support. If many leaders at the top have quit because of burn-out, you may not want to inherit their place.

There are, however, legitimate reasons for recruiting for major leadership positions outside the organization. If you represent a constituency the group wants to reach, or offer special skills that are not available within the group, such an invitation may be appropriate.

■ *A small group of people run the show, and everyone else just does the work.* Have the top leadership of the group always been there? Do they complain that no one else wants to get involved, yet do not provide real opportunities or demonstrate a willingness to share power? Is the organizational culture one in which information is not shared?

## Make a Commitment to One Group.

Meet with a staffperson or leader, and tell her you want to join and get actively involved in the organization. This meeting should be a slightly longer version of the volunteer interview. Be clear about how much time you have available, *"I'd like to come in one morning a week, either Monday or Wednesday, and I can also make phone calls from home on Thursday nights."*

Be specific about what you'd like to get out of the experience. If organizers and leaders know what your needs are, they will try to meet them. Say things like, *"I'd like to develop my public speaking skills. Are there ways you can help me do that?"* Or, *"I'm interested in policy development, but don't know much about it, does the policy committee need help?"*

Come away from the meeting with a specific plan and agreements. First time volunteers should have an attitude of willingness to do whatever is necessary, and invest some time in the mundane tasks before moving onto more complex ones. Sometimes, stuffing envelopes *is* the most important work of the day, and everyone doing the task is overqualified for the job.

## How Can I Move Up in the Organization?

Don't be impatient if you are not rising through the ranks as quickly as you'd like. Staff and leaders of most groups have seen volunteers arrive with great enthusiasm, make huge commitments, and then disappear. Staff may be hesitant to invest training and time in a new member who has not proven her willingness to stay around.

Most organizations operate with an informal pyramid of volunteer tasks. Volunteers are given entry level tasks as a way of testing their commitment before they are invited to move up the pyramid. Positions of greater responsibility are usually offered to those who:

- show up on time, make calls or contacts as promised, and consistently meet, or exceed expectations
- take responsibility for coordinating others
- are willing to assume more difficult tasks, such as fundraising or lobbying
- have a base of support—a group of people they can "turn out" for activities

Sometimes new members join an organization because they care about the issue but feel the group is using the wrong strategy to reach its goals. It is unusual to walk in as a first-time volunteer and be able to affect organizational strategy. If you think that what the group is doing wrong, ask questions about why the strategy was chosen, and find out who in the group makes strategy decisions. Ask to meet with them, or write a letter or memo stating your ideas in a constructive way. State your qualifications or perspective for giving feedback, such as "I'm a public employee, the kind of person you're trying to attract to your campaign, yet what you're doing does not seem effective to me." Offer your suggestions for change.

## How Can I Create My Own Niche in an Organization?

What if you come in regularly, perform your assigned tasks, but can't seem to get out of your cubbyhole in the organization? If all the interesting volunteer jobs are filled, how can you create a new one?

The key is to be observant for unmet needs in the organization, and offer to fill them.

Here is one hypothetical example of how a volunteer can create her job; this experience could easily take place in hundreds of organizations around the country.

Jennifer answers the phones at a nonprofit organization each Wednesday afternoon. After several weeks, she notices that no one on the staff wants to take calls from students doing research papers on the issue. She asks some staff members about it, who all agree on the importance of giving information to those students, yet feel overloaded by other responsibilities and unwilling to take on this time-consuming task.

Jennifer offers to take the calls herself, and to put together a packet of materials to help answer the students questions. She feels that students are important future voters who need to be reached, wants to develop her own ability to speak about the issue, feels that talking to students one at a time will give her good practice, and wants to help the staff. The staff enthusiastically agrees, and one organizer sits in with Jennifer for her first one or two interviews with students.

After meeting with several students, Jennifer agrees to go and speak to some classes as well. Another volunteer is recruited to answer the phones at the office on Wednesday afternoons, and Jennifer becomes the Student Coordinator. Along with the staff, Jennifer sets goals for getting more students involved in the issue. She develops key contacts at each campus, and within a year has organized 3 campus chapters, registered 582 new voters, signed up over 75 new members, and recruited many enthusiastic volunteers for the cause.

Again, the right niche for you is one that matches your personal development goals with the needs of the organization. If you are interested in media relations, you may want to offer to put together materials and organize a special press briefing with the group's executive director. If you are interested in computers, you can offer to research database systems for the organization to consider as they strive to accommodate a growing membership.

## Time Management Tips—How Not to Let a New Organization Take Over Your Life

Working with a new organization can be exciting and fun. As your level of commitment increases, you may find yourself devoting more and more time to the activities of the group. You'll find you prefer doing activist work to watching television, walking the dog, or going to the supermarket. But at some point, everyone has a time limit. Here are some ways to manage your volunteer time commitments:

- Ask clearly how much time will be needed when you are offered a project. Commit to that amount of time, but be clear that you cannot do more. Prepare a back-up plan if the project demands more time than you have.

- If your task becomes overwhelming, request that other volunteers be assigned to work with you, or split off a meaningful piece of the work and re-negotiate to only do that piece.
- If you get multiple requests from the same organization, ask them to prioritize the task they'd rather have you do (or choose one yourself, and decline the others).
- Don't be afraid to say no—restate what your time commitment is, and your willingness to do work within that time frame.

*It is always easy for those in pursuit of ends which they consider of over-whelming importance to become themselves thin and impoverished in spirit and temper, to gradually develop a dark mistaken eagerness alternating with fatigue, which supersedes the "great and gracious ways" so much more congruous with worthy aims.*

—JANE ADDAMS
TWENTY YEARS AT HULL–HOUSE

Was Addams the first woman activist to describe burn-out?

## BLENDING YOUR PROFESSIONAL AND ACTIVIST LIVES

Another way to create your niche, is to use your professional skills for the public good. Ask your employer to release you for a certain number of hours each week for community service. Or use your professional skills to help others:

The Women's Development Corporation, a nonprofit Rhode Island group, began in 1979 when women architects decided to use their talents to help low-income mothers get housing. Founders Alma Felix Green and Susan Aitcheson chose Providence, a mid-size city for a low-income development project. WDC designs, finances, builds, and manages housing for low-income mothers and their children. By 1992, WDC had $13 million in real estate, including 200 new or renovated units, and was in the process of building 100 more.

Connie Spuruill, a homemaker with five children, started Central Ohio Forest Products, a subcontracting and supplier business, in 1980. She was one of the first women in the Ohio construction industry and, after finding it difficult to obtain a bank loan, organized the Association of Business and Professional Women in Construction. Within six months, the Association had attracted 12 members; it now counts hundreds of members throughout the Midwest. Spuruill explains, "What we do is educate women construction business owners on how to communicate with their legislators. The legislators are not being made aware of discriminatory practices—they have no idea unless we tell them."

Since many cities and states have set public policies to contract with more women and minority owned businesses, Spuruill points out, "It's common knowledge that some of the subcontractors have been set up as front companies. It's a company that a man owns, and he puts his wife's or secretary's name on the papers. We are going to have the definition changed of what is a legitimate female owned enterprise."

Spuruill combines what's good for her business with what's good for the community. "I spend many volunteer hours educating legislators and community organizations about how beneficial self-employment training can be for those on welfare or struggling on below-poverty incomes. As a former welfare mother, I became self-sufficient through starting my own business."[9]

Some other examples to consider:

- Phone professionals are well-suited for phone banks, and are usually very effective at raising money.
- Realtors can help find free or low-cost office space for campaigns and activist groups.
- Librarians are particularly effective in researching issues.
- Computer specialists have highly prized skills in setting up systems.
- Teachers are terrific trainers and may have the time to take on summer internships.
- Attorneys have polished public speaking and debating skills.
- Women in the building trades can repair safe houses (a term used in domestic violence work) and shelters, and construct signs for political campaigns.

Take another look at your own skills and workday; think about creative ways to apply them to make the world a better place.

■■■■■■■■■■■ **WOMEN WHO DARE** 🔲━━━━━━━━🔲

### Carrie Barnett

Surprisingly enough, I didn't define myself as an activist until other people gave me that label. I opened Chicago's only gay and lesbian bookstore because

I thought the business could be successful. I'm very rooted in marketing and in fulfilling market needs, and I perceived this as an opportunity for a successful business venture. It also gave me the opportunity to spend my professional life serving a community that I care very much about. But I never perceived it as activism, I felt that I was doing it for myself.

My business partner and I are concerned with creating an open place where everybody can come and explore their ideas. And maybe if they're lucky, while they're browsing through the shelves they will come across some new ideas that they might want to learn about.

You don't always have to agree with a person in order to understand, accept and support their right to have an opinion. I really have learned that from seeing all kinds of people come into my bookstore. Like straight men and women whose gay brother is coming home to die, and they want to know how to take care of him. I remember one man who came in, and was so nervous about being in the bookstore, who asked me "My brother says something about the concept of 'family' in the gay community and it seems very important to him—but I don't understand, what exactly is that?" What an amazing opportunity!

We get a lot of people in our bookstore who are "coming out," as well as relatives of people who are coming out, who stand out front and walk back and forth because they are afraid to come inside. We've created a very safe, comfortable space so people will not feel uncomfortable walking in with their head up.

I'm an open lesbian who is willing to put my name and my story out in the local media, so I can reach gays and lesbians who might not have the access to the gay papers. Unfortunately, that gave a chance to two people who are filled with hate to threaten my life on two different occasions. When the City Council was considering the hate crimes ordinance in this city. I was asked to describe those death threats. And I spoke in front of a committee, along with a dozen victims of hate crimes who came and told their stories. I told my story by letting them hear the vitriol and the anger of what I heard when I picked up the phone and someone screamed at me, "I'm going to come in there and kill you!" That's how I started my speech, and it got everyone's attention.

I also volunteer at Horizons, which is the gay and lesbian community service agency, as a youth center advisor. I feel very strongly about giving back to adolescents what people gave to keep me alive. I was a fairly disturbed teenager, and there were people who gave me a vision of the end of the tunnel that I want to pass on.

I think my parents gave me a sense of community and community spirit. Being raised as a Jew in a very Protestant and Catholic community, where in 1966 we couldn't join the swimming pool, teaches you who your community is. And I learned about justice, to fight for justice.

## Notes

[1] Henry A. Rosso and Associates, *Achieving Excellence in Fundraising: A Comprehensive Guide to Principles, Strategies and Methods* (San Francisco: Jossey-Bass, 1991), pp. 255–256.

[2] S. M. Evans, *Born for Liberty: A History of Women in America* (New York: Free Press, 1989), pp. 237–130.

[3] Wendy Kaminer, *Women Volunteering: The Pleasure, Pain and Politics of Unpaid Work from 1830 to the Present* (Garden City, N.Y.: Anchor Press, 1984), p. 33.

[4] Ibid., p. 26.

[5] Ibid., p. 37.

[6] Rosso, p. 256.

[7] Kaminer, p. 38. Kaminer notes that many middle-class women in the organization became politicized by providing service and charity work.

[8] Katherine Isaac, *Civics for Democracy: A Journey for Teachers and Students* (Washington, D.C.: Essential Books, 1992), p. 118.

[9] Georgia Mattison and Sandra Storey, *Women in Citizen Advocacy: Stories of 28 Shapers of Public Policy* (Jefferson, N.C.: McFarland and Co., 1992), pp. 111–273.

# CHAPTER
# 10

# From Volunteer
# to New Career

*Kelly Crawford, a 22-year-old college student, signed on as a volunteer for candidate Bill Clinton at the Democratic National Convention. She criss-crossed the country several times during the campaign. One year later, she was a member of the White House staff.*

*E. P. Jones was a bookkeeper with a story to tell. It took her two years to write the tale of what it was like to grow up in the foster care system of New York from the age of six. Three years after her book,* Where is Home? *was published, she is a national consultant and trainer to foster care and child welfare agencies.*[1]

*Shelley Reecher was attacked by four men while running in the park. She got and trained a dog for personal protection, and now operates Project Safe Run, which lends trained dogs for women to run or walk with.*

All of these women started out by volunteering time and energy to causes they passionately believed in. Now they all get paid to do the work they love.

Perhaps you too are at a point in your life where you want to serve your community, or change the world. Are your volunteer hours so captivating that you'd like to do that work full time? Are you ready to spend your work days really making a difference? Is it time to quit clock-punching and throw yourself into a cause you really believe in?

Caring about your work, enjoying it, or even loving it can be deeply rewarding—an experience that is all too rare in American workplaces. Through your work, you can a make a statement about yourself, and how you want the world to be. Because nonprofit and community organizations don't have high profiles, many people are unaware of the job opportunities available in this sector.

## WHY YOU SHOULD CONSIDER A CAREER IN SOCIAL CHANGE

### *It's interesting, challenging work, with opportunities to learn and grow*

For those with a strong social commitment, there's nothing better than putting your creativity to work making your community, country, or even the world a better place.

"Take your conscience to work," Ralph Nader urges. "There are positions that encourage people to be primary human beings, whose essence includes the right, if not the duty, to take your conscience to work every day."[2]

It's rare to find a staffperson of a social change organization who is bored with his or her job. You'll find yourself learning more about the issues, and how power works in our society, than you ever could in graduate school. Because many organizations are small, each staffer may be called upon to perform a variety of tasks. During a typical week, you may meet with prospective members, write newsletter articles, work on graphic design for a brochure, and brief the press on the issues.

The non-traditional nature of the organization usually allows for more fluid work conditions and liberal employment policies—you may be able to negotiate your own weekly schedule, bring your baby to the office, or arrange for a month off each year. Those without formal education can look forward to lots of on-the-job training, greater opportunities for advancement, and fewer barriers than in the business world.

Best of all, you can put every ounce of your imagination to good use, creating new ways to affect public policy and to fill seriously unmet needs in our society.

### There are plenty of jobs out there for those who are committed to the cause

Nearly one million nonprofit organizations exist in the United States, employing 8.7 million people and relying on the volunteer work of 5.8 million more.[3] While about half those jobs relate to health care delivery, that leaves more unique jobs that you may ever have dreamed of. We'll show you how to find out about these jobs later in this chapter.

### Job satisfaction is high when you can act on your beliefs

"I know for a fact that there would be more dead children in the Denver area if it weren't for our work. You don't get that kind of job satisfaction anywhere else," said Adrienne Anderson, a Rocky Mountain Regional Organizer for the National Toxics Campaign. When a door-to-door canvassing survey uncovered massive health problems and babies dying of rare birth defects, brain tumors, and leukemia, Anderson's organization started doing research. They discovered that Martin–Marietta corporation had been dumping deadly rocket fuel propellant into the Denver water supply since 1957. While city, state, and federal authorities knew about the toxic poisoning, none acted on the information until the National Toxics Campaign got involved. The organization teaches communities how to protect themselves against toxic hazards. "The basic things we learned in kindergarten are still things we're mobilizing around today," says Anderson. "It's not right to throw trash in your neighbor's yard. It's not right for Martin–Marietta to poison a neighboring water supply." And while those principles are basic, the job is immense. "It's a tremendous amount of work to mobilize people all across the country to reform America in ways it needs to be reformed. But it's happening. I want to be a part of that."[4]

## So What's the Catch?

### Salaries may be lower than in the private sector

The many organizations spearheaded by Ralph Nader have one thing in common—they're some of the most underpaid offices in Washington, D.C. Yet, even at $18,000 a year for entry level positions, scores of applicants chase every job. On the other hand, many organizations realize that to attract and retain a professional staff, they will have to pay wages somewhat competitive with the public, if not the private, sector. Experienced fundraising coordinators can earn $30–$40,000 per year; organizing jobs average $25,000 per year. National organizations tend to pay on a higher scale than local groups.

### Saving the world is hard work

Be sure to explore the less glamorous aspects of your potential new career; the hours can be long, and the pay lower than in the corporate sector. As a volunteer, you can go home whether the work is done or not. In a staff role, you could easily be the one who has to stay until midnight. Burnout is not uncommon among professional organizers. So take one more careful look at the rewards of volunteer activism, as well as the difficulties of a staff role, before you set your sights on making this transition.

## HOW PUBLIC INTEREST ORGANIZATIONS WORK

Non-profit groups range from the huge Sierra Club, with a national budget of $40 million and 250 staffpersons, to local all-volunteer groups with a shoe box treasury. Almost a thousand groups across the country have the budget and resources to hire one or more paid staff members. Each organization develops a structure designed to carry out its own work. Typically, some of the key roles in the organization are:

*Volunteers, Members, and Leaders* are those who give time and money to the cause, and are the building blocks of every organization. When the number of volunteers and paid members gets large enough, the organization may decide to hire a staff. In some groups, the *Volunteer Coordinator* keeps contact with volunteers and members, informing them of activities necessary to carry out the work of the organization. An effective volunteer coordinator is part cheerleader and part teacher, and understands that an activist's commitment may exceed the time available to volunteer. The Volunteer Coordinator's job is to make the best match between the time and skills of each activist and the work that needs to be done.

*Organizers* are trained professionals who work to implement the political strategy created by the members and leaders of the group. In some groups, the organizers are also responsible for fundraising; in others, a separate *Fundraising Staff* raises the money for the organization through a combination of memberships, direct mail solicitation, grant proposals, and events.

The *Executive Director or Coordinator* is responsible for the day-to-day running of the organization, often developing strategy and tactics to carry out the goals set by the Board of Directors. The Executive Director may serve as a primary spokesperson for the group. The *Board of Directors and Board President* are usually unpaid, volunteer positions of leadership. This group, elected by the membership, sets goals and direction for the organization, usually in an annual plan. The Executive Director and staff carry out the plans and decisions made by the Board. The Board is fiscally responsible for the organization.

Typical entry-level jobs in nonprofit organizations include volunteer coordinator, organizer trainee, entry-level fundraising (including door-to-door canvassing for membership and donations), and administrative assistant positions.

Those with management experience who have been active as volunteers on an issue may get hired as a director or coordinator of a nonprofit group.

Lawyers who wonder about justice beyond divorce cases should look into the Southern Poverty Law Center (which specializes in cases against the Ku Klux Klan), the Disabilities Rights Center, the National Senior Citizens Law Center, the Tobacco Products Liability Project, or the Environmental Law Institute.

Sometimes a member of the board of directors will resign a leadership position in order to take a staff job with the group. The transition from leadership to staff can be difficult, but it may be worthwhile to have someone with a strong organizational background take the position. Occasionally, a part-time project arises and a board member may be willing to take it on, as was the case with Sarah Gorin in Wyoming:

*I was one of the people that put the Equality State Coalition together in 1992. I'm chair of the board, and we had a project that we wanted to get done—it's a book on legislative accountability. Our other staffperson works thirty hours a week and this was kind of my baby, and I wanted to work on it.*

*I thought it wouldn't be right to be working part-time and still be on the board, even though I only work ten hours a week. I raised it twice, and even offered to resign, but everybody said, just forget it. Nobody had any concerns.*

## MAKING THE TRANSITION FROM VOLUNTEER TO STAFF

Many political organizers and staff start out as volunteer activists and work their way into full-time, paid, professional jobs. This transition can take time; a long-term plan may be necessary to carry it out. Here's a look at what kinds of jobs already exist, and some ways to create your own dream position.

## How to Get a Job in a Nonprofit Organization

**1.** If you know what group you want to work for, start by inquiring if any new positions will be opening, or other staff changes are anticipated. Let the staff know that you are interested in a paid job. Ask for a truthful analysis of your chances to get hired, and be prepared for the answer. It's better not to spend six months or a year in anticipation of a paid position if, in reality, your chances of getting it are minimal. Ask about the requirements for the job, and the hiring process. Will the opening be advertised within the organization before it is advertised outside? Think about whether you are willing to start as support staff (an administrative or secretarial position), and then work your way up. Find out what you can do to help prepare for the job or to assist in raising funds for the position.

**2.** If you don't have a specific organization in mind, do some research. *Good Works: A Guide to Careers in Social Change* was written to provide information on alternative careers to graduating college students. The book profiles over 800 activist groups in the United States, listing their budgets, staff size, and salaries for entry-level staff, and provides a helpful resource to anyone seeking a more fulfilling career.

Students should check to see if there is a Public Interest Research Group (PIRG), on campus. PIRGs are a national network, with chapters in over twenty-five states, which research and organize around a wide range of issues.

---

### Read the want ads

Like other professional networks, the movement has special bulletins and newsletters where jobs are listed:

*Community Jobs* lists over 200 job openings—and internships—in each monthly edition, along with profiles of non-profit organizations, resource lists, book reviews, and articles. Special regional editions list jobs in New York, New Jersey, and metropolitan Washington, D.C. *Community Jobs* is available from ACCESS, 50 Beacon St., Boston, MA 02108; 617/720-5627.

*Environmental Career Opportunities* is a newsletter that advertises about 350 positions nationwide every two weeks. *Opportunities in Public Affairs* lists 250 positions in Washington, D.C. every two weeks. Both are available from Brubach Publications, PO Box 15629, Chevy Chase, MD 20825; 301/986-5545.

*The Non-Profit Times* has numerous articles on nonprofit management and trends, with regular departments including Employment Marketplace and Resource Guide, 190 Tamarack Circle, Skillman, NJ 08558; 609/921-1251.

Check the help wanted classified listings at the back of periodicals such as: *In These Times,* 2040 Milwaukee Ave., Chicago, IL 60647; 312/772-0100; and *The Nation,* PO Box 10763, Des Moines, IA 50340; 800/333-8536.

*The Non-Profit Job Finder*, by Daniel Lauber, is designed to help your job search, listing job sources, periodicals, hotlines, and job-seeker services. Available from Planning Communication, 7215 Oak Ave, River Forest, IL 60305; 708/366-5200.

Ask around about available jobs—word travels quickly through the network of non-profit organizations and campaigns. Job announcements are routinely circulated among these groups.

---

**3.** Contract to work on a specific project as a trial to test the kind of job, as well as the specific organization. For example, you can propose that you will coordinate all aspects of an annual banquet or auction for a limited period of time, in return for a set fee.

**4.** Join the board of directors of a group you are interested in. This is a long-term strategy, in which you give significant volunteer service to the group, get to know them, and let them get to know you, before ever applying for a job. You may conceive a new project, help to raise the funds for it, and then apply for the position. You would then resign your board position in order to work on the staff.

## Become a Professional Fundraiser

Development, or professional fundraising, a field once dominated by men, is increasingly attracting large numbers of women to its ranks. 58% of the 13,500 members of the National Society of Fund Raising Executives are women, and in museums, 75% of chief development officers are women. It is a career where women can rise quickly based on their success, and still get the satisfaction of advancing a cause they strongly believe in. Channel your passion for an issue or organization into providing the money to shape needed programs.

Fundraising can also be a launching pad for a political career— Lynn Yeakel, the co-founder of Women's Way, a Philadelphia foundation, used her know-how and networks to launch her statewide campaign against United States Senator Arlen Specter in Pennsylvania.

Fundraisers may eventually find themselves working "the other side of the table," giving money away as program officers for foundations or corporations. Veteran fundraisers (those with at least five years' experience) can be certified through the National Society of Fund Raising Executives. A two-day course precedes a written certification exam. NSFRE, 1101 King St., Suite 700, Alexandria, VA 22314 703/684-0410

## Join the Staff of a Political Campaign

Political campaigns can be fun and exciting. The work is intense, the pressure can make things volatile. One thing that makes a campaign survivable is the sure knowledge that it will all be over on Election Day. Campaigns start out small and grow continuously (at least the good ones do). Local campaigns—for state legislature, for example—may never expand beyond one or two paid staff positions, while statewide campaigns may eventually have dozens of paid staff. Campaigns build momentum, and continuously add staff until the crescendo of Election Day. Dedicated volunteers who have proven their abilities on the job are usually first in line for entry-level staff openings.

Some campaign volunteers throw themselves into a congressional or gubernatorial race in the hope that they will earn the right to be considered for a paid position with the newly elected official if the campaign is successful.

State legislative and other small-scale campaigns may rely on all volunteers, a single paid campaign manager, or a combination of a campaign manager and a paid volunteer coordinator. If you are an active volunteer on a small campaign, ask if additional staff will be hired later in the campaign. This is more likely in September for November elections, or one to two months before the primary for hotly contested primary races.

Statewide or congressional campaigns may have a much larger staff, numbering from a dozen to twenty or more people. The *campaign manager* supervises the entire staff, which usually includes a *press and media team*, a *fundraising team*, and a *field staff*, responsible for all voter contact activities throughout the state or district. As a novice campaigner, you are most likely to be hired for the field staff; if you are very knowledgeable or have lots of contacts in a section of the district, that can work in your favor. Other entry-level jobs are serving as assistants to the fundraisers or press people, or driving the candidate from place to place.

Presidential primary campaigns go on the road to state after state as they follow the schedule of primaries. Like an old fashioned tent revival, they look for converts along the way. An especially active and capable volunteer in one state may be offered a job to come along and help win the primary in the next. Once a single candidate wins the nomination of each party, they build a campaign organization in every state. It is quite possible to be hired from your home state to travel extensively during a presidential campaign. Of course, you won't see much more than the inside of a lot of campaign offices, but you'll be where all the action is taking place.

### Tips for getting hired on a political campaign

■ *Work hard.* Be the person willing to stay late, drive the newspaper ad copy to the next city by daylight, and do whatever it takes. You want to distinguish yourself among the crowd of volunteers.

■ *Meet the higher-ups.* Let the field director, finance director, or press coordinator know that you are available and interested in getting a paid position with the campaign. Introduce yourself to the campaign manager briefly; don't take a lot of her time. Drop a résumé to the head of the department in which you are most interested. Campaign staffing decisions may be made quickly, and the job offered to someone on hand without much notice or formal process. You want to be known to those who do the hiring.

■ *Don't offer unsolicited advice on how to win the campaign.* Campaigns are intriguing and complex, and it's fun to think about how different strategies might have an impact on the election. But, resist the temptation to tell those running the show what they should do to win, especially if the campaign is behind at the moment. Do offer feedback from the voters, if you learn something interesting that should be passed on, such as "The voters over in Lincoln County are all upset about your position on the river protection plan."

■ *Don't threaten to quit as a volunteer if you don't get hired.* Work enthusiastically on the campaign, but don't hold people hostage with statements like, "If I don't get that field staff position, I'm going to have to quit the campaign." Do share the truth about your situation—if you're living on your savings in order to work on the campaign and will have to look for another job in a week or two, let people know that in a non-threatening way.

■ *Ask for the truth if you can handle it.* If you are hoping for a job and watching others getting hired, request a brief personal meeting with one of the supervisory staff and ask them to candidly review the possibility for you to join the staff. They may tell you that, frankly, there's no way you will get a job offer. The reasons may have something to do with you ("You just don't have the skills we are looking for.") or not ("We really need a bilingual person in that position.") In either case, you'll be aware of the situation and can make plans accordingly.

## How to Create Your Own Job

If you are highly motivated, and aren't afraid to raise money, you can create a paid position for yourself:

■ *In a political campaign.* Propose to be the liaison for a key constituency (that you have strong connections with), such as the women's or the environmental community. Write a proposal that shows how your work will bring in volunteers and votes, and include a fund-raising strategy—direct mail or house parties—that will raise enough money to pay your salary.

■ *With a statewide membership organization.* Propose that you open a branch office in another city. Study the demographics and make a realistic assessment of how many new members you could recruit there. Target a town that is politically crucial—the state senator is weak on the issue and needs pressure from his district to support a key piece of legislation next year. Fund the position through a grant from a national organization, a special mailing to members statewide, a membership drive, or a combination of those three.

■ *For an all-volunteer group.* A successful small organization may be looking to make the leap to hiring its first staffer and opening an office. Come up with a plan for how to make it work; write several grant applications for "seed money" (start-up money) and build in provisions for fundraising during the first year.

■ *Work by yourself.* If your volunteer skills are highly sought after, and you have a depth of experience to draw upon, become a freelancer who organizes fundraising events for a fee, or a consultant who facilitates meetings or trains volunteers. Be sure to talk with many prospective clients and test your ideas before you hang out your shingle and go into business.

A key to creating a new position is finding the funding for that position. Almost every nonprofit group is understaffed, and budgets are perennially tight. If you can raise the money, you can probably raise the job.

One warning—resist the temptation to start a whole new organization just so you can have a job. There are many existing organizations out there working on the issues; align yourself with one of them.

## WOMEN WHO DARE

### Tammy Greaton

I moved to Connecticut from Maine in 1980, and found a job at pillow factory. I was a sewer at the Pillowtex Corporation for six and a half years— we stuffed pillows with feathers from ducks and chickens. There were people who had worked there for ten years and were still making minimum wage. No masks were provided for people who were sweeping up the feathers—they went to the hospital for x-rays and you could see the feathers in their lungs. Someone cut off his finger because we were working double shifts all the time. And the company didn't really care, safety was not a big thing at the Pillowtex Corporation. So we decided to get a union.

I became the chief organizer at Pillowtex, even though I was making more money, and was treated better, and was not in danger, but other people were. It was when I saw how others were being treated that I became involved. We organized in two months, and brought the union in with a vote of 80 to 20. I was 21 years old at the time.

Then we went on strike for our first contract for eight months, and I got really involved in politics because the police and the city council people were against us. So I ran for my Democratic Town Committee in 1987 to change the policies of the town, and that's how I got involved with the Connecticut Citizen Action Group.

Now I work for CCAG, and I'm the Lead-Poisoning Prevention Organizer. We go door-to-door in the inner city of Hartford and identify people whose children have lead poisoning. We invite them to an educational forum and review the health risks, the dangers children are in, prevention, nutrition, and education. And then we get into political action.

We have also built a coalition in the state, with doctors, nonprofit citizen groups, and legislators who are interested in the issue. We're working very hard towards bilingual education. Thirty-two percent of the population that are affected are Spanish-speaking, and the city doesn't produce bilingual materials.

I left school in 8th grade and went to live on my own. I really don't have the book learning that most people do. I know a lot of people who have degrees. I don't, but I learned what I know from what I do. Living on my own taught me to fight for what I need.

---

## Notes

[1] "Telling the Story of a Life," Mark Garvey, ed. *1994 Writer's Market* (Cincinnati: Writers Digest Books, 1993), p. 19.

[2] Jessica Cowan, ed., *Good Works: A Guide to Careers in Social Change* (New York: Barricade Books, 1991), pp. xi–xii.

[3] David Walls, *The Activist Almanac: The Concerned Citizen's Guide to the Leading Advocacy Organizations in America* (New York, NY: Simon and Schuster, 1993), p. 31.

[4] Cowan, pp. 3–4.

CHAPTER

# 11

# Wanted: Candidates for a Change

Kitty Kimball had been a district court judge for ten years when she entered the race for Louisiana's State Supreme Court. The "good-ol'-boy" network applied pressure to keep her out. "One judge told me that it was not my turn to run," said Kimball. "My question to him was, 'When do you ever think it will be my turn?'"[1]

## NOW MORE THAN EVER

More than any other period in America's history, now is the time for women to run for political office. Behind the media-dubbed "Year of the Woman," in 1992 are decades of hard work spent building political skills and candidacies of women across America.

## SPECIAL OPPORTUNITIES FOR WOMEN CANDIDATES

Whether you'd consider running for office soon, or in the next three to ten years, be aware of the particular advantages for woman candidates.

197

Women are still seen as "outsiders" in the electoral arena, a situation which can be used to your advantage as you prepare to run.

Once women are elected to office, they may be subject to the same anti-incumbent bias as male elected officials. But first-time women candidates can defeat long-term political insiders, as Lori Lipman Brown discovered during her low-budget, person-to-person primary campaign in Las Vegas:

A local woman legislative leader made a speech that really encouraged all in attendance to consider running for office. I went home and did just that. Two senior citizens I had worked with in politics helped me decide to go for it!

First, I went to check who had filed for local offices in my area. The state senate seat was open due to the death of the incumbent. About three days before the filing deadline, I filed to run for the Nevada State Senate. One of the assemblymen who had represented one-quarter of the district in the lower house of the legislature filed as my opponent. Even though I had no money with which to run, I felt it was a good idea to get my name out there.

After filing, a group of Unitarians that I knew descended upon me to help. That was the beginning of a large troop of volunteers who were the people power behind my campaign. We were creative about garnering resources. A client of my dad's, who owed him money, paid part of it off by contributing the printing of some very plain campaign materials.

Because I had no money, I ignored the standard, slick campaign leaflets filled with rhetoric that dance around the issues. I felt I could say what I believed: I favor rent justification in mobile home parks. I am pro-choice. I told people about myself and my background. I didn't have signs and in fact printed right on my campaign brochures that the voters will not have to suffer the "political pollution" of road signs from my campaign.

I went to voter's doors and told them this was all they were going to see of me because I wouldn't be spending a lot of money on campaign materials. Many people said they always voted for the woman. And they went out and voted for the woman with no money, and no signs, who came and visited them at their doors.

We won the primary by one percentage point, by about 260 votes, against an incumbent Assemblyman who spent $38,000 and thought he had the race in the bag. We spent $1,200.

Brown was able to take advantage of these opportunities for women candidates:

## 1. The Wave of Momentum Created by Women Winning Elections

Growing numbers of women hold office at all levels, from the United States Senate to mayors of small cities. Women who serve in office provide new role models to both voters and prospective candidates. For the voters, elected women represent a change in style from the typical "old boy" politics. Studies and anecdotal reports conclude that women officials are likely to be more accessible, honest, and encouraging than many traditional male officials.[2] This style has become a priority for voters, who increasingly want politicians who make themselves available.

For future women candidates, women officeholders provide important information about how to run, win, and to avoid the pitfalls in campaigns. Because women are running and winning in so many states, you will likely find role models in your own area.

Sheryl Rivers of Windsor County, Vermont, was motivated to run for state senator when Madeline Kunin became governor of that state. "I love to arrange for school kids to visit the capitol because one of the things I do is to sit them in my chair," explains Rivers. "I tell them that they, too, can have a Senator's chair someday, because I never realized that when I was growing up."

### Read all about it

Several recent books about women and their campaign experiences provide instructive lessons for future campaigners. For full publishing information, see the bibliography at the back of this book.

- *A Woman's Place . . . The Freshmen Women Who Changed the Face of Congress,* by United States Representative Marjorie Margolies–Mezvinsky and Barbara Feinman
- *In the Running: The New Woman Candidate,* by Ruth B. Mandel
- *Storming the State House: Running for Governor with Ann Richards and Dianne Feinstein,* by Celia Morris
- *Living a Political Life,* by Madeleine Kunin
- *101 Campaign Tips for Women Candidates and Their Staff,* by Jewel Lansing
- *Running as a Woman: Gender and Power in American Politics,* by Linda Witt, Karen M. Paget, and Glenna Matthews[3]

■ *Strangers in the Senate: Politics and the New Revolution of Women in America,* by Barbara Boxer and Nicole Boxer

---

Nevada State Senator Diana Glomb had been active on many other campaigns as a leader of the Nevada Women's Political Caucus. She never considered running until people began to ask her to. Glomb's experiences on other legislative races enabled her to see that she could do it. She defeated a long-term incumbent who never even saw her coming.

We strongly encourage you to contact local women officeholders and interview them about their experiences. Women school board members, city councilors, and planning commissioners will help shed light on the specific challenges and opportunities in your local area. Be sure to speak with women who have run and lost elections, too. They offer special insights and recommendations.

Due to the much-heralded electoral victories of women, many voters are now seeking the opportunity to support women candidates. A gender gap continues to exist in most races; women voters are more likely to support a candidate or ballot measure campaign on the basis of issues of clear concern to them.

The first woman mayor of Salt Lake City, Utah, took advantage of her outsider, female status. Running as a Democrat, Deedee Corradini set up a booth at the Republican party state convention to draw support. She was targeting voters who would cross party lines to vote for a woman.

## 2. Women Activists' Experience on "Hot Button" Issues Highlights Their Qualifications to Serve in Office

So called "women's issues" are emerging as *the* issues of the 90s.

Health care, job security, and environmental quality are the issues that Americans are most concerned about. From local school boards to city councils, from state legislatures to the United States Congress, legislative bodies are grappling with these concerns. Women can win elections by using their knowledge, positions, and experience on these issues during their campaigns. While we encourage women to run for office on the basis of issues you feel strongly about, it just so happens that issues of importance to most activist women, are also priorities of the voting public.

Shirley Chisholm ran for, and served in, Congress on a commitment to principles: She voted "no" on every bill that funded the Department of Defense because she wanted to prioritize government programs that benefited "people and peace."[4]

## 3. Women Bring Practical Life Experience to Public Office

Many of us assume that the typical politician is a lawyer. Twenty years ago, lawyers comprised nearly 70% of some state legislative bodies—today that number has declined to less than 17%.[5] Voters are increasingly choosing representatives they can identify with. Women candidates are able to communicate with the average voter because they *are* more like the average voter—former Governors Barbara Roberts of Oregon and Ann Richards of Texas were both single mothers prior to their political careers. Congresswoman Maxine Waters of California began her career as a volunteer in the early childhood education program, Head Start.

Voters clearly want change—change in the way that government is run and in the way that government responds to their concerns. Women office holders represent that change, partly because they come to the job from occupations that are outside the usual. Business leaders are another group of outsiders that voters hope will seize the reins of government, and Democratic consultant Maura Bruegger notes that "Women business leaders are incredible sources of new talent."[6] In fact, some corporations are setting up special programs to groom women executives for public office.

While women may have less elective experience than men (a bonus to some voters), they are much more likely to have held an appointed government position by serving on a board, commission, or task force. In addition, women candidates are more likely to have worked on campaigns for other candidates or as staff members for an elected official before running for office.[7] Both experiences are extremely helpful to a campaign. Appointments provide specific achievements for a candidate's resumé, and prior campaign experience is critical to a successful electoral effort.

## 4. Women's Organizations Help Women Candidates

Two decades of research at The Center for the American Woman and Politics shows that women's organizations and networks provide a

vital base of support for women candidates. Volunteer support and financial contributions from members of local and national women's organizations can boost any woman's campaign.

First, there are the women's organizations especially devoted to politics. In addition to the PAC's outlined in Chapter 7, there are a wide
range of membership groups whose chief aim is to advance the roles
and issues of women in the political arena. If you haven't already, join
or get involved with one or more of these groups: The National
Women's Political Caucus, The National Organization for Women, The
National Abortion and Reproductive Rights Action League, domestic
violence organizations, the National Association of Women in Chambers of Commerce, Women for Racial and Economic Equality, the
League of Women Voters, or the Women's Economic Rights Project.

Second, women can enlist those they know through community organizations. The PTA, a garden club, the Girl Scouts, the Junior League,
children's art programs—women have been the backbones of these
groups for decades. As Molly Ivins points out, "Pretty soon these ladies
from the Junior League know an awful lot about how to raise money,
organize, build coalitions, and get publicity. Friends, they're in politics."[8] Women candidates can tap into these networks of women activists.

## 5. Pro-Choice Candidates Enjoy Solid Voter Support and Significant Assistance from Pro-Choice Groups

With a solid 65% of Americans supporting the right of women to
a safe and legal abortion, pro-choice candidates have some specific
advantages over anti-choice candidates, or those who seek to avoid
the issue.

Several organizations carry out voter identification programs to systematically locate voters who will only support pro-choice candidates,
even if it means crossing party lines. The groups communicate that
information to candidates, who work to ensure that pro-choice voters
cast their ballot on election day.

A 1992 survey of Ada County, Idaho (which includes the city of
Boise), found that 73% of voters would cast a vote based on how each
particular candidate stood on abortion. Of those surveyed, just 1.5%
said abortion was the single biggest problem facing the nation.[9] In
other words, people are willing to cast their vote on the basis of choice,
even though it is not their highest priority issue.

## 6. Term Limits Open the Doors for Political Outsiders

In 1992, fourteen states passed laws which set limits for the number of years that many officials can serve in public office. Others states are likely to follow soon. Voters are rejecting career politicians who don't appear to be loyal or responsive to their constituencies. Even in states where formal legislation was not passed, voters are turning out incumbents in large numbers, and polls indicate that trend will continue.

Because women comprise between 4 and 39% of state-level elected officials (depending on the state and level of office), we now stand to gain more electoral slots than we will lose through term limits. Women's organizations would do well to create a multi-year plan to systematically prepare women to run for office and then replace each other. For example, one woman might agree to run soon and serve for the six to ten-year limit, while another is preparing to run as her successor.

Since running for office is only one of the tactics women should pursue in their life of activism, veterans can return to the ranks of issue, community, and trade union organizations to help build power and win change in other ways, as well as recruit and mentor more potential women candidates.

## 7. Women Stand Out from the Crowd

As long as women candidates are the exception, rather than the rule, they benefit from added attention from the media and the voting public. When a woman candidate competes against several men, she is considered to have a decided advantage.

*"One red dress in a sea of blue suits, provides a ready-made bias among women voters, a hook for free press, and a message and contrast that could attract attention."* [10]

In 1992, there were twenty-three Democratic primaries that included at least one woman, no incumbent, and had at least four names on the ballot (usually one woman and three men). Statistically, women's odds should have been no better than about one in four; in fact, women won eleven of the twenty-three races.

## YOUR OWN ELECTORAL FUTURE—RUNNING
## FOR OFFICE

*"Women must set aside their petty reluctances and run for office"*
—SHIRLEY CHISHOLM

*"From a woman in office to those who are considering taking the plunge, I encourage you to study your options, then seize the opportunity and choose to be involved. It is our responsibility to do so, not only for ourselves, but for the future."* [11]

—FRANKIE SUE DEL PAPA,
ATTORNEY GENERAL AND
FORMER SECRETARY OF STATE OF
NEVADA. [11]

Right now, just for a few minutes, explore the idea of one day becoming a candidate for political office. Perhaps someone in your community has already suggested the idea. Or, maybe it's something you've thought about in private, and never shared.

Even if your first reaction is "Who me? Couldn't be!" don't run from the thought just yet. Every candidate for political office probably had the same response the first time they considered running.

Patty Murray, the mother of two children, learned that the preschool program in her local school district was going to be cut by the Washington State legislature. She organized a group of parents to travel to the state capitol at Olympia, to lobby against the cuts. During that visit, a state senator told her, "You can't make a difference here, you're just a mom in tennis shoes." [12]

Patty laced up those tennis shoes and walked door-to-door in her neighborhood, first getting elected to the local school board, then moving on to the state senate in 1988. In 1992, Patty bought a new pair of tennis shoes for every member of her family, and announced her candidacy for the United States Senate. After a grassroots campaign in which she faced tough opposition in both the primary and the general election, the voters decided to send "the mom in tennis shoes" to the United States Senate to fight for children and families.

If you, like Patty Murray, are a person who cares about your community, are motivated to take action on one or more issues, are interested in the process of government and wants to serve the public, then explore the idea of running for office sometime in the near future.

In 1992, unprecedented numbers of women campaigned for political office, including a record 2,373 women who ran for seats in state legislatures.[13] This wave of female candidates attracted a 500% increase in campaign contributions from women.[14] In 1994, women vied for lieutenant-governor posts in a whopping 77% of the races. In 1995, 19 women serve as lieutenant governors, a significant advance over the previous record of 11.[15]

## WHO ARE ELECTED OFFICIALS ANYWAY?

The closer you get to the political process, and the more time you spend watching public officials in action, the more evidence you will find to underscore a startling truth—elected officials are people just like you. Some are smarter than others, some dress more fashionably, some are impulsive, while others study intently before making decisions. Some are excellent public speakers, while others rely on thousands of personal contacts to motivate voters.

If you're curious about elective office, take some time to observe public officials in action. One day soon, attend one or more public sessions of your city, town, or county council or state legislature. Don't look for a dramatic session with media coverage and big crowds, just drop in on an everyday meeting of government at work. After observing an elective body for a while, you may find yourself thinking, "Well, I could certainly do at least a good a job as they are doing." The truth is, you probably can. The biggest difference between you and some elected officials is that they dared to run, while you haven't.

Bella Abzug was a political activist who, over the years, helped many men attain public office. Finally, Mayor John Lindsay of New York City suggested that she herself consider running. "It was like a light switch being turned on in my brain—I realized that if I had strong beliefs and ideals about how our country should be run, I could best work for them right up front, out in the open, in my own way." While reflecting on some of the men she had campaigned for over the years, she decided they "weren't any more qualified or able than I, and in some cases they were less so."[16]

Public officials are not all professionals with advanced degrees. The legislative process works best when people of diverse backgrounds come together to solve problems. Local elected officials come from virtually all walks of life. Women in public office include: Representative

Louise Townsend, a horse farmer in her fifties from Cornville, Maine, Representative Wende Barker, a former welfare mother in her forties, who works a paper route and runs a 4H extension program in Laramie, Wyoming, former Representative Leanna Lasuen, who was a 30-year-old home day care provider with three young children when elected to the Idaho House of Representatives, Senator Margarita Prentice, a nurse in her sixties from Washington state.

Barbara Roberts, a single mother of an autistic child, was shocked to find out that her son did not have the right to a public education. In order to change the law, Roberts went to the state capitol. She learned how to get the legislation drafted, but was told it would take several years to get enough votes to make it pass. Employed as a bookkeeper for a construction firm, she rearranged her schedule so she could lobby the legislature one day each week. She personally visited each member of the legislature to promote the bill. That same year, the bill passed and became the first law in the United States mandating education for handicapped children. Roberts went on to run for the school board, became a state representative and the first woman Democratic majority leader of the Oregon House of Representatives. She served as secretary of state, until she became the first woman elected governor of Oregon in 1990.

Congresswoman Maxine Waters started out working for Head Start in South Central Los Angeles. Waters was an assistant teacher, who went on to become director of parent-training programs. Her advocacy of continued funding for the program brought her into contact with politicians. "Head Start made a significant difference in my life. It helped me see how I could help people, and it helped steer me into politics." she said.

United States Senator Barbara Mikulski was a social worker and neighborhood activist before she ran for public office. Harriet Woods got involved in politics through a neighborhood issue—traffic noise which disrupted her children's naps. Woods served for eight years on the Council Bluffs, Missouri City Council, eight years as a state senator and two years as state transportation commissioner.[17]

## WHAT MAKES A GOOD CANDIDATE?

The best candidates do not just wake up one morning and decide to run for political office. Instead, they view political candidacy as an advanced level of community activism. Holding political office is a commitment of time and energy to public service, to seriously address the issues. It is not about personal power or becoming famous.

If you feel strongly about issues, and have a history of working to build your community or create change, you may feel a calling to participate in the process of government. An effective candidate knows the problems and issues facing the district and has clear goals.

The skills needed for an elected official are not necessarily the same skills required of a winning campaigner. We believe that if a woman approaches running for political office with methods she's learned as an organizer and activist, she can win her election and serve in a meaningful way. The elements which are critical to a winning campaign that assist in one's elective service are:

■ *A base of support* The most effective candidates and legislators are those who have a history of working on an issue or representing a constituency—the kind of person with a large Rolodex or card file, and is well known within their area of expertise. Once in a while, a millionaire can buy an election, or a member of a well-known family can waltz into a seat. The rest of us need a solid base of support to help reach out to the general public before and after we are elected to office.

■ *A willingness to work hard and a desire to win* You must be passionate about wanting to win, because running for office will test your physical and emotional endurance beyond anything you can imagine. Frankly, the salary alone isn't enough to make it worthwhile—you must have other reasons for wanting to serve.

■ *A history of working and caring for the community* Why should people support you? What have you done to show you care? What difference have you made in the livability of the community? Those who want to serve the public should be able to demonstrate a track record of results which appeals to voters, and proves your ability to be effective.

■ *Self-confidence in public* Whatever your qualifications for elective office, you can't get there unless you feel comfortable talking to individuals, small groups, and in large forums. These skills can be learned and practiced.

■ *Support from family, close friends, and key contacts* Everyone on your home team should be rooting for you 100%, because their lives may have to change dramatically to accommodate the campaign.

■ *The legal qualifications for serving* Every candidate for office in the United States must be a U.S. citizen at the time of filing, and must meet age and residency requirements as set out by law. Generally, candidates for public office at the federal level must be at least 25 years old to run for Congress and 35 years old to serve as president. States vary on the ages and minimum length of residency required to run for office. Check with your local government, registrar of voters, or secretary of state for requirements where you live or would consider running.

## POLITICAL CONSIDERATIONS FOR WOMEN CANDIDATES

### What Seat or Position Are You Interested In?

Every voter is represented at several layers of government. Which level of office would you seek? Who represents the district now? Is there any chance the incumbent might vacate the seat? When? Be thoughtful about what type of office you'd like to hold, what level of government office makes sense to seek, and when the optimum time is to go after a particular position.

Some political offices are *legislative*, requiring that elected officials deal with long-term planning and problem solving through the making of laws and policies. City councilors, school board members, state legislators, and members of Congress debate the issues, review policies, and write budgets. Executive offices are *managerial*, and require that officials control and direct the process and the players who make the jurisdiction function. Mayors, governors, and county executives provide visionary leadership and appoint agency heads who oversee public employees. Carefully consider the job description of the offices you might consider seeking. While the campaigning process is virtually the same no matter what office, the tasks you'll engage in while serving depend distinctly upon the position.

Next, research the district from which you would run. Could you win a race in the district? Determine the number of registered voters by party in the district you are considering—is your party in the minority or majority? Look at voter demographics—how do you match the age, race, and gender profile of the voters? How does the incumbent? What is the history of voter behavior? How does past voter behavior in the district inform future campaigns?

Talk to others, especially leaders of local organizations, and learn their perspectives. Read the local newspaper, keep track of poll results as reported in the news, and listen to talk radio shows to discover the concerns of the voting public. What local, statewide, and national issues are on the minds of the voters?

Be on the lookout for possible shifts in the political landscape—if a member of Congress files to run for the Senate, several candidates may vacate state legislative seats to run for the open congressional seat, resulting in more vacancies all the way down the line. As mandatory term limits become law in many states, start tracking those whose term will be up and by what date. Read the newspaper for clues, or join your political party or other political organizations to get the inside scoop on who's planning to run for office.

## Why Are You Running?

A candidate must be able to define clearly *why* she is running for public office. What do you stand for? What experience do you bring to public service? What successes can you point to that directly benefit people? What policies will you pursue? In short, why are *you* the person who can solve the problems that concern voters? Friends, voters, and the media will ask this question throughout the course of your campaign. Your response will be the centerpiece of your message—be thoughtful and genuine in creating it.

## How Much Will It Cost to Run?

The costs of campaigning go up faster than billboards before election day. The best way to estimate the cost of your campaign is to write a plan and approximate how much it will cost to execute. At the same time, you will hear political veterans predict how much it will cost for you to win, based on their knowledge of recent elections.

Next, try to project how much money you can raise personally. How much may be available from other campaign sources? How much support do likely opponents have on hand? Money can be the most intimidating aspect of a campaign; most first-time women candidates underestimate the amount of financial support they will receive.

## PERSONAL CONSIDERATIONS FOR WOMEN CANDIDATES

Running for public office means voluntarily placing yourself before the voters' scrutiny. As demonstrated by some highly visible candidates for national and state office, any aspect of your personal life may be raised as a point of public debate.

An anonymous tip to the press revealed that Nydia Velazquez, a candidate for Congress in the 12th district of New York City, had once attempted suicide. "When the newspaper accounts came out, I felt like I'd been raped." Velazquez said. "There are human beings that don't care about human pain when they have a political goal. But they didn't expect me to come on so strong. It backfired on them." Backfired, indeed. Velazquez became the first Puerto Rican woman in Congress, she won with 77% of the vote.[18]

### Are You Ready for Public Scrutiny?

Are you prepared to discuss or defend everything you've ever done? Are you unmarried, but living with a partner? Do you have secrets that would damage you or your family if they emerged? Is there any detail of your family, professional, or personal background that you would not want to defend in public?

What about your spouse, partner, or family members? This is of particular concern to women candidates. Since negative campaign attacks usually create sympathy for women candidates, opponents have learned to focus their attacks on husbands, partners, and family members.

The amount of public exposure your private life will receive increases in high level and more hotly contested races. Candidates for local office may not have reporters assigned to dig through your garbage, but your opponents could always choose to do so.

### Can You Withstand the Financial Impact of Running for Public Office?

Campaigns can be expensive. Your committee will raise contributions from the public, but you may have to spend some of your own funds. Although we discourage this practice, you may need to make a loan to your campaign early on, to set up a structure that can attract voters and contributors.

The time demands of political campaigns force many candidates to quit their jobs or work reduced hours. If necessary, do you have personal resources to provide daily living expenses during the campaign?

In addition, your personal living expenses can increase dramatically at campaign time—meals are eaten out because there's no time to cook, you may hire someone to clean your house, do laundry, or other chores for which you will no longer have time. Funds raised for official campaign expenses, such as telephone bills, cannot be spent for the personal needs of the candidate or family.

## Can Your Personal Life Absorb the Pressure of the Campaign?

Is your spouse or partner supportive? Do they want to be involved with the campaign? Even partners who are 100% behind your bid for office will find their patience tested many times before election day. Can the relationship sustain the pressure of taking a back seat to campaign needs? Do you have children at home? Can others step in and help care for them? Will they understand and support your decision to run for office? These critical questions must be resolved before you file for public office.

## PREPARING TO RUN

Once you've surveyed the landscape and decided that you might, one day, stand for election, you should develop a long-term plan to prepare yourself. If you are still unsure about running, pursue these activities to raise your political awareness, explore other possibilities in the public arena, and decide whether running for office is right for you.

## The Five-Year Plan—for Those with Little or No Political Experience or Contacts

*Get involved locally.* Attend and participate in meetings at your most immediate level of representation—your neighborhood or community association, town or local government.

*Work on issues and get results.* Join, or continue working with, one or two organizations focused on issues of concern to you. Volunteer for tasks and serve on committees. Look for groups that focus on the level of government you are interested in—groups who lobby City Hall or the state legislature.

***Participate actively during election season.*** Make sure you are registered to vote. Attend debates or forums at election time, and take positions on issues. Convince others to vote, and offer your analysis of the candidates and issues on the ballot. Join or attend local chapter meetings of the League of Women Voters or the American Association of University Women.

***Volunteer on political campaigns.*** Sign on to one or more campaigns for women candidates. Join your local political party or club, or attend party events. Find out how campaigns relate to these organizations.

***Get others active in campaigns.*** Professional associations, garden clubs, and bowling leagues are all fertile ground for sprouting political activists. Motivate your group to work on a campaign of interest. Invite campaign staff to talk about opportunities, and provide training for people on how to be effective campaign volunteers.

***Sign up for training.*** Attend sessions on campaigning, public speaking, or other skills you may need. Check the list of campaign schools detailed in the next chapter of this book.

Sign up for summer school with the Center for Popular Economics, and learn what's behind urban economic crises or international trade. Located at the University of Massachusetts at Amherst, CPE also offers institutes in several cities. Contact: The Center for Popular Economics, Box 785, Amherst, MA 01004; 413/545-0743.

***Find a mentor.*** As you pursue other activities mentioned in this book, look for a role model or mentor who is willing to informally train or encourage you in the process of becoming a candidate. Your mentor doesn't have to be a highly visible public official—you can learn a great deal from a politically savvy woman who knows her way around campaigns.

### Keep in mind as you work on your Five-Year Plan:

■ No matter what issues you pursue, be sure you are getting practice in skills relevant to running for, and serving in, public office, such as meeting facilitation, public speaking skills, or policy analysis.

■ Take on new involvements one at a time, and don't overextend yourself. In all arenas, you want to demonstrate that you are a person who follows through on commitments.

■ Keep names, addresses, and phone numbers of those you meet and build relationships with. Start a card file, a Rolodex, or create a mailing list with the names. Keep notes on how and where you met each person.

## The Three-Year-Plan—For Those Who Have Done Most or All of the Above.

*Become a leader and build your following.* Take a leadership role in one or two key organizations or campaigns. Join the board of directors or chair a committee for a group you have a true commitment to. As a leader, spend part-time on the organization's issue, and part-time identifying other activists who can take leadership when your term is over. Grooming others for leadership is a way of building your base and, of course, contributes to the future pool of potential political candidates.

*Learn how to deal with the press.* Get involved with press response or a media campaign—learn everything from how to draft press releases to how to organize press conferences. Speak at a press conference. Provide radio "actualities" (live radio responses) on an issue.

*Build fundraising experience and contacts.* Join a fundraising committee that offers training or an opportunity to work with experienced professionals. Help with presentations to large donors as a way of building contacts. Volunteer to help with large fundraising events.

*Educate yourself on the issues and take stands.* Clip newspaper articles on issues of interest to you; write letters to the editor stating your opinion. Keep track of others who respond to your letters in a positive way. Locate opportunities to testify to public bodies about your opinions. Neighborhood association meetings, city council hearings, and individual women's organization meetings present just some of the opportunities available for you to gather more input on issues and publicly communicate your own positions.

### Keep in mind as you work on your Three-Year Plan:

■ Build your leadership and that of others; mentor someone less experienced than yourself.
■ Increase media and fundraising skills.
■ Continue to expand and keep track of your network of contacts.

## One-Year Plan—Final Steps for the Year Before You Declare Your Candidacy

*Get a personal tune-up.* Ask your most trusted advisors for feedback on your personal presentation. Does your wardrobe, grooming, or personal style detract in any way from your ability to communicate with others? What adjustments need to be made? Get complete medical and dental exams for yourself and your family.

*Clear your agenda.* Finish home repairs and other large projects. Start stepping back from major personal and organizational commitments. Take a vacation, you won't get another one for a while.

*Test the waters.* Start meeting individually with key political and area leaders; find out about their political plans; ask for feedback on yours.

*Build an infrastructure.* Get a computer, and learn how to use it. Keep a list of those with access to other resources you may need when you start up your campaign.

*Build your campaign.* Start working on your campaign plan, with a timeline for the full year before election day. Collect early commitments; let your high degree of organization intimidate half-hearted opponents.

### Get Training

Many national organizations offer training to encourage women to run for public office, and train their staffs. The Center for the American Woman and Politics has compiled this list of campaign resources:

*Democratic National Committee (DNC):* Although the DNC does not offer training programs designed specifically for women, available materials and training programs should be of interest to women candidates and their staffs. The DNC will send materials to any qualified Democratic candidate; they also maintain a data base of campaign staffers. Contact: Democratic National Committee, 430 S. Capitol Street SE, Washington, DC 20003; 202/863-8000.

*National Federation of Republican Women's (NFRW) Campaign Management Schools:* In addition to providing ongoing technical assistance to candidates, the NFRW offers one- and two-day workshops with an emphasis on state and local campaigns. A comprehensive campaign manual is included with the registration fee. Contact: NFRW, CMS; 124 North Alfred Street, Alexandria, VA 22314; 703/548-9688.

*National Women's Political Caucus (NWPC) Campaign Skills Trainings for Women:* NWPC, in conjunction with its state and local affiliates, trains more than two thousand women candidates and senior campaign workers during each campaign cycle. The weekend long sessions are designed to educate participants on all aspects of running a winning campaign at the local or state legislative level. Materials include NWPC's campaign manual, *Political Campaigning—A New Decade: The NWPC Guide to Winning in the 90s* and supplementary handouts. Contact: NWPC, 1275 K Street NW, Suite 750, Washington, DC 20005; 202/898-1100.

*Republican National Committee (RNC)—Women Who Win:* Administered by the co-chair of the RNC, Women Who Win is a full-day training for Republican women leaders who want to be more confident and effective communicators. The training program covers: communications, press relations, public speaking, fundraising, and campaign organization. Contact: Office of the Co-Chair; Republican National Committee, 310 First Street SE, Washington, DC 20003; 202/863-8545.

*Women in the Senate and House (The WISH List):* The WISH List is a donor network that provides financial support and training to pro-choice Republican women candidates for governor, Congress, and key mayoral races. The WISH List candidate training sessions include workshops on: communications, general campaign strategy, coalition building, issues, fundraising, and PAC solicitations. A training manual is provided to all participants. Contact: The WISH List, 210 West Front St., Red Bank, NJ 07001-9819; 800/756-9474.

*Women's Campaign Fund (WCF):* The Women's Campaign Fund is a bipartisan political action committee which supports pro-choice women candidates running for public office at all levels of government. The Women's Campaign Research Fund, WCF's nonprofit leadership and training arm, convenes a biennial candidate training program entitled "Leadership 2000: Managing Our Future." The training program is designed to help women move up the political ladder. Fifty women leaders from across the country are selected to participate in the trainings. The program focuses on key policy issues, political strategies, and campaign tactics. Contact: Women's Campaign Fund, 120 Maryland Avenue NE, Washington, DC 20002; 202/544-4484.

**YWCA Institute for Public Leadership (IPL):** The YWCA Institute for Public Leadership is designed to train women for political leadership, whether running for office, managing a campaign, or advancing women's issues. This program was developed to reach women of all backgrounds in pursuit of the YWCA mission to empower women and eliminate racism. The hands-on workshop helps potential candidates assess their chances to win, practice presentation skills, and wrestle with tough issues. Managers weigh strategy decisions, role-play personnel problems, and create campaign materials. All participants receive a copy of the YWCA's *Campaign Sourcebook*. Contact: YWCA Institute for Public Leadership; YWCA Leadership Development Center, 9440 North 25th Avenue, Phoenix, AZ 85021; 602/944-0569.

## ■■■■■■■■■■ WOMEN WHO DARE 🔲⎯⎯⎯⎯⎯⎯⎯⎯⎯⎯⎯⎯

### Lisa Jo Brown

I'm now a state legislator, as well as an economics professor at Eastern Washington University in Spokane. Over the last 15 years, I've been an activist in the women's movement, the anti-nuclear power movement and the Central America Solidarity movement.

As a high school student in southern Illinois, I read a lot about the civil rights movement but didn't get involved. Then in college, I had a partial involvement in the women's movement. I was the kind who said, "I'm not a feminist but I believe that women should be paid the same as men." Eventually I got involved in a women's crisis hotline and found out about more issues.

Economics is pretty theoretical, and I became interested in how it plays out in my own state and community politics. So I started to do a lot of public speaking around Spokane on policy issues, like women's work issues, and people would say to me, "You should run for the legislature one day."

Then someone from the Washington State Labor Council sat down and talked with me about running for office, and he actually drew up a plan of action. Frankly, I didn't take the plan very seriously. I thought it was a great idea, but I couldn't see how to integrate the things on the plan with the rest of my life—I was already a full-time professor, a political activist and a single mom.

Then an opportunity opened up after redistricting—I ended up in a district that tended to vote Democratic and I'm a Democrat, and it was an open seat. I knew that was the opportunity for me to run for the legislature, and I was approached again about running.

So I sat down one weekend and called about 100 people that I knew in Spokane, and said, "This is what's going on, what do you think I should do?" A lot of them thought it was a good idea and said they would be willing to work for me. In fact, several people said, "I've got my checkbook out, let's go!" That support was really important.

Also, as a single parent, the fact that I had a really close network of people helped. I'm part of a women's group that's been together for eight years. Knowing that I had their support, and that of very close friends, and members of my family . . . I wouldn't counsel anyone to be a candidate who isn't real secure about her own personal, support network. During the campaign, three families that lived near my house invited me to drop in with my son and eat and relax, and I didn't have to do the dishes. I just knew that I could always call on them, no matter what. For me, that was key.

There are times when you're really going to question yourself, like if you get negative press. For me, it's really hard to get criticism but you can't go into politics without facing it. So far I've only served one year, and I'm still really learning. I guess I rather naively expected I'd come in and we would just vote on things, but of course there are a lot of procedures and processes and the committee chairs and the leadership have a lot of power, and so I feel like I'm still learning the process.

I've tried to develop a focus on human service issues, particularly child care, housing, and revenue. Taxes are not a popular issue for any elected official, but I felt like I had something to contribute there because of my economics background. So I've gotten on committees that reflect those interests.

Socially and economically, women have been in different places than men. Women have done more child-raising, more foster-parenting. The more diversity we have in the legislature, the more occupations, the better. In the health care reform debate, we need not just doctors, but nurses too!

In terms of process, women are more open. Generally, my experience is that women are more eager to share the power and are more interested in the outcome than in their own personal power. Maybe they weren't expecting to go into politics, and so they don't stake their entire image on this.

I've always had a sense that some people before me have made certain things possible, have opened up avenues that weren't there before. And so I draw inspiration from them and then try to pass some of that on. There's a historical highway out there, and I really encourage people to figure out how they can feel a part of that.

## Notes

[1] Elizabeth Gleick, "Eyes on the Prize," *People*, November 30, 1992, p. 88.

[2] Kathleen Casey, "Women State Legislators, Who Are They?" *Center for the American Woman and Politics News & Notes*, Fall 1992, p. 26.

[3] Linda Witt, Karen M. Paget, and Glenna Matthews, *Running as a Woman: Gender and Power in American Politics* (New York: The Free Press, 1994).

[4] Nancy Sylvester, "Women and Public Office: Creating Alternative Approaches," *The Catholic World*, vol. 234, no. 1404, November-December 1991, p. 266.

[5] Otis White, "Making Law Is No Job for Lawyers These Days," *Governing*, June 1994, p. 27.

[6] Richard S. Dunham, "A Different Kind of Launch for McDonnell," *Business Week*, August 2, 1993, p. 66.

[7] Susan J. Carroll, "Taking the Lead," *The Journal of State Government*, vol. 64, no. 2, April-June, 1991, p. 43.

[8] Molly Ivins, "The Women Who Run Texas," *McCall's*, vol. 117, no. 2, August 1990, p. 100.

[9] *Majority Rules!*, July 1992, vol. 1, no. 1, p. 13.

[10] Jennifer Sosin, *Political Woman*, vol. 1, no. 2, p. 4.

[11] Frankie Sue Del Papa, "Taking the Risk to Run for Public Office," *Journal of State Government*, vol. 64, April-June 1991, p. 55.

[12] Jennifer Sosin, "Women and the House Races" *Political Woman*, vol. 1 no. 2, December 1992, p. 4.

[13] "Women Candidates: Past Records for Major Party Nominees," *CAWP News & Notes*, Summer, 1994, p. 2.

[14] Ibid., p. 4.

[15] CAWP Fact Sheet, *Election Results: 1994*, p. 1.

[16] Witt, et al, *Running as a Woman*, p. 101.

[17] Ibid., p. 137.

[18] Elizabeth Gleick, "Eyes on the Prize," *People*, November 30, 1992, p. 91.

# Running a Winning Campaign

For a week or two around election day, many of us feel inundated with political television and radio ads, brochures, and mailings from candidates. In fact, candidates and campaign activists have been working behind the scenes for months to get their message to the voters during that crucial "window of time." The process of getting elected begins a year or more before election day, even though the voters may only become aware of the race during the final hectic push to the finish line.

What goes on behind the scenes of a political campaign? How does a first-time candidate decide what to do in order to run? Before you purchase a hefty campaign manual, hire a consultant, or attend an intensive campaign school, read this overview of the process of running a campaign. No matter which office you are seeking, these steps will be virtually the same:

## PART I:

### Preparing the Basics

### 1. Analyze your base of support

Sit down with four sheets of paper and label them "Core Group," "Team Leaders," "Supporters," and "Donors." Now think about all the people you know from your neighborhood, organizations you've been involved with, your congregation, school activities, political contacts, even your family and friends. Dig deeply—consider former college roommates, co-workers from previous jobs, or neighbors from your former residence. Go through your address book or Rolodex and your holiday card list, and enter as many names as you can under the appropriate heading.

*Core group* includes people who will: go to great lengths to help you win, give significant amounts of money and/or 10 to 20 hours per week, show up in rain and snow, start earlier and stay later, and do whatever is necessary to help you get elected. Especially high on this list are people who have access to, or can swing the votes of, at least 15 to 20 others.

*Team leaders* will commit to taking on key tasks (such as activating their own networks on your behalf), or coordinating groups of other volunteers, and will devote 5 to 10 hours per week to the campaign, and probably more as election day draws near.

*Supporters* will do something active to help the campaign; they will show up one to four times to volunteer, and will make a financial contribution.

*Donors* will give money, but not volunteer time. Assume that everyone in all the above categories is a donor as well. This category should include all of your out-of-town supporters and those unable to volunteer.

Once you've run out of names to add to your lists, take a look at what you've written. Do you have at least three to five names in your Core Group? Eight to ten Key leaders? Fifty to two hundred supporters? If so, you probably have enough of a base of support to run for a local political office. If not, turn back to the previous chapter, and work on developing a long-term plan to build your base of support for a future campaign.

The final step in analyzing your base of support is to start talking to people. Arrange personal meetings with everyone you listed as Core Group and Key Leaders, and tell them you are thinking about running for election. Solicit their opinions and advice, and ask if they would be willing to help you in your campaign. Adjust your list, moving names from category to category as necessary. After concluding these meetings, do you still have enough support to go on?

## 2. Analyze the race

What office are you interested in running for? Are you prepared to challenge an incumbent or will you wait for an *open seat*—a position with no incumbent running for re-election? What is a typical campaign budget for that type of race? Are there limits on how many terms an incumbent can serve? Has anyone else announced an intention to run for the position?

After determining the answers to these questions, gather a small group of trusted advisors to help you evaluate whether you have a reasonable chance of winning. Some may advise you to run without much hope of winning in order to "get your name out." Unless you plan to win, it's rarely worthwhile to run.

At some point, depending on the level of the office you are seeking, you may need to commission research—such as polling or focus groups—to test the win potential of your campaign, or the vulnerability of opponents. A *poll* asks voters specific questions, usually over the telephone, in order to tally feedback from a large number of respondents. A *focus group* is an in-depth discussion with a smaller, representative sample of registered voters, usually those who are undecided in your race, with whom you can test your potential to win. Focus groups are actually more useful later in the campaign, when you want to test the effectiveness of your media messages.

## 3. Secure the nomination

Once you've completed your homework, you're ready to take the first official step in getting elected—to secure the nomination as a candidate. In most *partisan* races, the candidate of each political party will be chosen in a preliminary, or *primary* election. A primary election can occur anywhere from two to nine months before the general election, and usually only the members of a political party can vote in that party's primary. In some states, caucuses, or meetings, are held in place of primaries. Candidates for president of the United States, however, are chosen at a national party meeting, or convention, which resolves the different results of primaries in many states.

Primary elections have their own sets of governing rules. In some states, you can simply file petition signatures and/or a filing fee to place your name on the ballot. In other states, especially in the eastern United States where party politics are more complex and entrenched, candidates must run in town-wide elections just to get their names placed on the primary ballot. Research your situation to prepare for gaining access to your local primary ballot.

Local governments tend to have more *non-partisan* leaders. In non-partisan races, candidates represent themselves, not a political party. Non-partisan candidates must seek the direct nomination of voters in the jurisdiction, either by gathering the signatures of registered voters on a nominating petition, or by running in a primary election where voters of any party are eligible to vote.

Depending on your local situation, securing the nomination can be very simple, or a difficult campaign, requiring its own plan and strategy. Open seats tend to attract more candidates, and a partisan primary can be more crucial than the general election in a district dominated by voters of one party.

In some areas, a political party *machine* seeks to control nominations by bringing its own members up through the party ranks. Candidates may run as part of a *slate*, or group of candidates who link their names and campaigns in order to run together.

### 4. Write a campaign plan

Simply put, political campaigns are the process of gathering and using three resources: the candidate, money, and volunteer time. Every campaign must have a *written* plan. Ideally, it lays out the most efficient, effective road map for gathering and expending those resources, given the specific lay of the land in your district. Devising a plan to allocate resources is the job of the candidate, campaign manager, and strategic advisors.

The plan analyzes the race, the strengths, and weaknesses, of the candidate as well as the opposition, and develops a strategy to garner enough votes to win. The strategy will include the use of tactics such as door-to-door contact with the voters, community meetings, fundraising events, coffees, yard signs, bumper stickers, and candidate forums. Each tactic should be analyzed in terms of what is needed to win this particular race—does it produce votes or money? Don't adopt tactics just because they're familiar, or because they worked for someone else.

A campaign that attempts to use too many different tactics can lose its focus, and the race.

The campaign plan includes a full budget for all campaign activities.

### 5. Assemble your campaign team

Key elements of the team are: the candidate, the campaign manager (who is usually paid), and a committed group of volunteers who will help implement the campaign plan. Larger campaigns will have more paid staffers, with the campaign manager responsible for hiring and supervising the rest of the staff.

Don't rush to set up a campaign committee or steering committee to run your campaign. We believe that campaign committees are largely a waste of time because they instigate lengthy meetings which just distract the campaign from it's main tasks—getting votes and raising money. Managing the campaign should be the job of one person, not a committee.

People anxious to serve on a committee can be recruited to serve the fundraising committee. Such committees set the goal of money to be raised, and carry out the events or activities to raise funds. Committee projects might include a fundraising auction, or monthly pledge system. Other groups of supporters might assemble as ad hoc working groups to meet several times and plan the logistics of your lawn sign or phone bank campaigns. Your most committed supporter's time should be spent on getting the work done, not attending meetings.

### 6. Develop your theme and a message

The *theme* of your campaign should be a one-paragraph statement that explains why you're running, and what you hope to focus on in a context that differentiates you from your opponent(s). For example:

*Lisa Jo Brown will bring hard work and a fresh perspective to state government. As a single mother, she knows the challenges of keeping a family together; as an economist, she knows the problems facing our region.*

The message of the campaign can be a simple slogan, but we suggest you develop a broader statement that supports several slogans. In this vein, your campaign message is an umbrella statement under which many sub-messages and slogans will fit.

The theme should be written within the context of the current **political climate.** The political climate is the general feeling of the voters,

and is affected by many events. Like taking the temperature of the
general public, campaign managers try to measure the political climate
by commissioning public opinion polls. The political climate is also
reflected in the questions that voters ask the candidates.

Sometimes, the political climate is less about the candidate, and
more about a general feeling toward politicians. For example, after a
year marked by corruption and scandal, the political climate will often
be anti-incumbent. In such a climate, even honest politicians may lose
their positions to a newcomer. In 1994, every Democratic woman—
and man—found their race a referendum on the administration of President Bill Clinton. The result was a giant sweep for Republicans nationwide.

Once the theme and message have been developed, the visual presentation of the campaign must be designed. Campaign logos should
be bold, with simple bright colors that prominently feature the name of
the candidate. Campaign slogans should reinforce the message, and be
employed consistently in order to build candidate recognition.

Typical campaign slogans may work well or appear hackneyed, depending on the district, location, and political climate in which you
run:

*"Experienced leadership"*

*"Time for a change"*

*"Honest and effective"*

While these slogans could hit or miss at any given time, we believe
the best campaign slogan is the one you most want the voters to remember on Election Day:

*Vote for Ann Richards for Governor*

*Vote for Cynthia McKenney for Congress*

*Vote for Doreen DelBianco for State Representative*

One way to maximize your issue experience is to "steal the rainbow"
from your opponent. All polls, those of your campaign and those of
your opponent, will likely reveal the same issue priorities of voters in
your district. If you have a track record of working on issues that are
a high priority to your voters, it is important to "get out front" early. If
you can be the first candidate to highlight the school funding issue,
and you back up your assertions with first-hand experience from your
work with the PTA or the teacher's union, then you effectively steal

the rainbow from your opponent. In responding to the issue, he/she appears to be jumping on the bandwagon after you've already set the tone and the parameters of debate. In this same way, it is important to predict the issues on which your opponent will initially focus, because you don't want to have the rainbow stolen from you.

### 7. Calculate the number of votes you need to win

Every campaign must have a numerical goal—how many votes do you need to win? You can figure out the magic number by using this formula:

---

◆

---

### Calculating votes needed to win: an example

| | |
|---|---|
| Number of Registered Voters | 32,000 |
| Multiply × Expected Turnout | × .65 |
| = Votes to Seek | 20,800 |
| × 50%, | × .50 |
| | 10,400 |
| add 1 | + 1 |
| = Votes to Win | 10,401 |

In this example, Sally Candidate only needs 10,401 votes to win a district of 32,000 voters. If the expected voter turnout is less, the number of votes she needs to win becomes smaller.

---

First, call your elections office to find out the current *number of registered voters* in the jurisdiction where the vote will take place— city, county, or state.

Multiply that number by the *expected voter turnout* for the upcoming election. Note that voter turnout varies widely from election to election—the highest turnout is traditionally in November of presidential election years, with mid-term November elections being significantly lower, and primary elections lower still.

You can get an estimate of turnout from elections officials in your state or local area. Check the number with local political experts, and watch to see how other issues on the ballot may boost turnout—controversial ballot measures or candidates, and tax increase proposals can all serve to increase turnout.

Your first calculation yields the number of *votes to seek*. That is the total number of people who are expected to vote in the upcoming election.

Of course, to win the race you don't need every vote, you just need a bit more than 50%. So next *divide Votes to Seek by 50% and add 1* (or a bit more for a more comfortable margin of safety).

Once you have determined the number of votes you need to win, you must think about where you will get those votes. You can do some *geographic* targeting (cities and towns), *constituency* targeting (labor union members, students, ethnic communities), or *demographic* targeting (women between the ages of thirty-five and fifty). At the end of this process, you should be able to break down the total votes you need to win into a realistic outline of the number of votes you hope to get from each group or area. Multiply the number of voters in each subgroup by the percentages you hope to gain from each group or area. This process may lead you to certain conclusions, such as "We really need the senior vote," or, "We're going to have to at least break even in the southern part of the district."

### 8.  Write a voter contact plan

In local campaigns, nothing can replace individualized, *personal contact* in which the candidate goes door to door to meet and greet the voters. In a congressional campaign, or races with other large districts, it becomes very difficult for the candidate to meet each voter personally. Candidates may send family members or other volunteers to broaden the amount of one-on-one contact with the voters. Candidates also rely on media contact—using mail, television, or radio to get their name and message to the voters.

The Voter Contact Plan (often called the Field Plan), represents person-to-person campaign activities in which the candidate and her representatives (family members and volunteers) engage the voters and seek their support. The Voter Contact Plan has three specific phases:

- Voter Identification (Voter ID)
- Persuasion
- Get Out the Vote

Voter ID determines each voter's current position on the race. If the election were held today, which candidate would they support? The most efficient way to contact voters is from a voter list which can be obtained from the elections office or from a private list vendor.

### Why buy a voter list from a list vendor?

This computer generated list contains the voter's name, address, phone number, and party affiliation. Lists purchased from a vendor (at an affordable price) can give you a great deal more information, such as the voter's gender, date of registration, and how many of the last seven to eight elections they've voted in. This information is printed out in a legible format of your choice, separated by household, and organized alphabetically by street within precincts. Lists can be ordered in a walking format (used for door-to-door canvassing) or as phone bank lists.

Vendor lists have up to 85% of the phone numbers for voters, while lists available from public agencies tend to have fewer.

---

*Phone banks* provide an effective, if slightly less personal, contact with voters. Phoning is efficient, and provides a safe opportunity for volunteers to perform valuable campaign services. Although it would be ideal to ID all the voters in a given election, that goal is usually only possible in a local, state legislative race. A very brief phone script is used by volunteers. At the end of each call the voter is recorded as being a supporter, an opponent, or undecided.

Once the voters are identified, each group is treated somewhat differently. Those who already support the candidate will receive minimal attention. The key group to contact for *persuasion* are the undecided voters. They have heard information from both sides of the campaign, are confused or still want to be convinced to support one of the two. These voters need a direct, personal contact from the campaign.

An ideal format for that contact is *door-to-door canvassing*. The candidate or a team of well-trained campaign volunteers should visit undecided voters, answer their concerns, and solicit their votes. If canvassing is impossible due to the terrain (houses are too spread out, apartment houses are impossible to enter), the voters can be called again, this time engaging them in a longer conversation which answers their concerns, and attempts to persuade them. Clear, honest responses should always be given to the voter, even when it is obvious that the answer might alienate the voter. In other words, never lie.

It's important to keep track of supporters whose votes you can count on—each vote is like money in the bank. As each individual voter is asked for his or her vote, the response should be coded. If they are a supporter, you need to make sure they cast a ballot on election day. If they are undecided, they need to be revisited with a persuasive message. In order to measure how close you are to the number of votes you need to win the election, keep a daily tally of the number of supporters you have identified. Ideally, you should schedule backwards from election day to determine how many supporters you need to ID each week from the beginning of the campaign. Further, each night's phone bank can be tallied like a poll—it provides up-to-date information on the efficacy of your campaign messages.

If both your supporters and the undecideds you persuade aren't adding up to enough votes, you have two choices—either try to turn around the opposition, or continue to ID and persuade additional voters. Hardcore opposition, of course, is the hardest to convince. This is why candidates sometimes choose to attack their opponents; they see it as their only hope for getting enough votes.

*Get Out the Vote* (GOTV) is the third crucial phase of your voter contact effort. The reason you've been keeping track of these supporters is to make sure they get to the polls on election day! Several different options exist for GOTV efforts—most combine some form of *poll watching* with either door-knocking or telephone-banking to track who has voted and remind those who haven't.

Your entire ID—Persuasion—GOTV effort requires good record-keeping and a great attention to detail. By election day, you will need a well-organized, easy to read list of all your supporters. Sophisticated data management systems include computers and light wands which read bar codes; lower cost systems use marking pen highlighters, and volunteers to code and prepare the lists. Don't use a high-tech system if you don't have the money and volunteer expertise to support it.

### 9. Recruit and coordinate volunteers

The voter contact activities described above require a huge network of highly organized volunteers to carry them out. Every campaign should have a volunteer recruitment plan, and one or more people assigned to coordinate volunteers. A system must be created to track and schedule volunteers and assign them to key tasks.

An early phase of the campaign should focus on recruiting and training enough volunteers to contact the voters during the final weeks of the campaign. Volunteers can be recruited creatively, from a number of sources: your initial list of supporters and members of organizations you've worked with or are endorsed by. Include any names from the voter list that are known to you; they should be contacted by your campaign and offered the opportunity to volunteer.

Volunteers are important to the campaign, and should be treated with respect and appreciation. Their work should always be well prepared—volunteers who are kept waiting or sent home for lack of work will quickly assume that they are not needed. Volunteers need to be trained properly, fed generously, and thanked repeatedly. We need to help develop the political skills of volunteers in the same way that we hope to build our own campaign skills.

### 10. Write a budget

The budget is the financial expression of the plan and timeline; *everything* in the plan should be reflected in the budget.

During the initial phases of a campaign, you may need to ask some campaign veterans to help you project the amount and type of expenditures necessary to carry the campaign to completion. Early campaign budget projections should always include three scenarios—high, medium, and low.

The mid-level scenario should reflect your basic plan. Add your dream plans to create your high budget scenario. Strip down to barebones activities—those which must be carried out under all circumstances—for the low budget plan.

The expenditure side of the budget should estimate costs for all campaign activities, leaving a healthy margin for unexpected expenses. The income side should at least equal expenditures, and match the fundraising plan developed by the finance committee. Remember that the expenditure side of the budget reflects what is in your campaign plan, and *not* how much you think you can raise.

### Campaign budget items

Staff—campaign manager, volunteer coordinator, organizers

Office—rent, phone installation and monthly charges, furniture, computers, copy machine, supplies, and miscellaneous equipment

Fundraising—direct-mail, house party kits, event costs

Mailings to Voters—five to ten mailings, printing, graphic artist, postage

Volunteers—Food, mailings to volunteers

General Expenses—voter lists, volunteer cards, walking piece, brochures, press packets, visibility items (buttons, bumper stickers, signs), victory party

Paid Media—production costs, consultant, advertising time

Research—polling, focus groups

Cash flow is critical to campaigns. Printing bills and television and radio ads must be paid "up front," not after the big fund-raiser next week. Every campaign budget should include a cash flow analysis and projections.

## 11. Raise money

Campaigns run on money. One way that campaign fundraising differs from raising money for nonprofit organizations or charities, is that complex and unique events may not be necessary to raise money. Supporters often feel a strong sense of urgency, and will donate money if asked appropriately. The candidate is always the best person to do the asking because she will get the most positive response.

Therefore, the candidate's time (a finite resource), should be organized wisely by the campaign manager to include several hours of fundraising each day. Contributors who can give in the range of $100 or more should be targeted for contact by the candidate. Lower-level contributors should be asked by others in the campaign, perhaps by a member of the candidate's family.

A finance committee should develop a fundraising plan that includes soliciting contributions at every level of giving—the $1 contributors and the $1,000 contributors all have their part in the campaign. The fundraising plan should include direct mail appeals, fundraising events, high dollar fundraising, as well as appeals to PACs. Fundraising should be incorporated into every activity of the campaign, and not treated as distinct from all other efforts. Special attention should be paid to local and national women's PACs. Everyone on the campaign should raise money, not just the fundraising committee.

### 12. Create a media presence

What kind of media will be used to get the message out? How much will the campaign rely on literature, television, radio, print ads, and other media? Basic brochures and small signs may be augmented by specialized mailings, billboards, radio or television ads. What target groups of voters will each form of media seek to reach? How does the presentation of the media match the campaign message? A bare-bones, no nonsense candidate's message would be undermined by glossy brochures and fancy ads.

The media plan includes *earned media* (free coverage you generate through news stories) as well as *paid media* (ads purchased on radio, television or cable programs). The media budget should include several spending options, based on the success of campaign fundraising efforts. The candidate or campaign should seek donated services for production of media wherever possible. As with your overall campaign budget, a core media plan should be supplemented with options for additional buys if fundraising is successful.

### 13. Consider campaign consultants

Consultants will want to conduct polls, write your campaign plan, produce television or radio ads, and give you advice, *all for a fee*.

Do you need one or more campaign consultants in order to win? That depends on whether you and your campaign team have the know-how and experience to do what's necessary to win. For a reasonable price, one consultant may fine-tune your campaign plan, providing the margin you need to get over the top. Another may charge huge fees, convince you to go into debt for a massive media campaign, and leave you holding the bills, as well as a loss, after election day.

Many campaigns flourish without a consultant. Let common sense prevail as you interview campaign consultants. They may be experts in their fields, but you are the best judge of what will work for you. Interview several consultants, and ask experienced campaigners to help you choose between them. Find someone you feel comfortable with, someone you can trust. As the candidate, you are the customer; ultimately you must determine the tone and content of your message to the voters of the district.

## What Makes a Winning Campaign?

Every political campaign is unique, but a winning campaign always has certain qualities:

### It makes the most effective use of its resources

The candidate with the most money does not always win. That is why campaign volunteers are a crucial resource of any campaign. Used strategically, the combined effort of many well-organized volunteers can overcome a better financed opponent.

### It presents clear, consistent messages

One overarching general theme should incorporate several sub-themes. Messages should be consistent in tone and visual presentation. The colors and logos of the campaign should be distinctive, and repeated in everything the campaign puts out.

Resist the temptation to respond to your opponents—maintain a clear communication with the voters.

### It answers the questions in the minds of the voters, and speaks in a language that voters can understand

You can invest in research—like polling or focus groups—to find out the concerns of the voters. Another simple form of research is for the candidate to take notice of frequently asked questions at the doorstep, or in public appearances. The campaign should speak to those concerns, in the most direct and personal way possible—through one-on-one interactions with the voters.

### It undermines the arguments of the opposition

Well-placed arguments from your side can put your opposition on the defensive. That's just where you want them to be. A winning campaign forces its opponents to backtrack and explain their position.

### It dominates the dominant mode of communication

Whether it's on television or radio, on the doorsteps or at neighborhood meetings, you've got to overwhelm your opposition at every level of communication. This requires a strong combination of media and grassroots activity.

### It involves large numbers of well-organized people

It takes lots of personal contacts to educate people, to build up name recognition, and support. Volunteer time should be prioritized into voter contact activities. Anyone can buy television ads, it takes someone special to motivate volunteers to go door-to-door on a rainy weekend.

Volunteers should be treated like the tremendously valuable resource they are. Volunteers will show up the first time because they believe in the candidate. They'll come back if their time was well used, and if they had a positive experience with the campaign. We've only got one chance to treat people right.

### It builds momentum

Nearly all winning campaigns have a strong sense of momentum—the public gets the distinct impression that more and more voters are coming over to one side. Momentum doesn't just happen—it has to be created, and factored into the plan at all levels.

Momentum is the difference between announcing a list of 12 endorsers on a single afternoon and announcing one, two, or three endorsements each day over a two-week period late in the campaign. Undecided voters will be swept along by momentum at the end of the campaign.

The campaign also has to be prepared for the heavy demands of momentum—you've got to set up a structure that will constantly incorporate more and more people.

### It follows a plan and prioritizes activities

Most campaigns look and sound chaotic. There is a constant surge of visitors and phone calls, each one requiring action.

The difference between a winning and a losing campaign may be found in how it creates order out of chaos on a daily basis. The winning campaign has a plan, and every supporter should be invited to participate in that plan, with an appropriate role to play.

All activities are prioritized. Invitations for the candidate and staff should be evaluated with a simple question. "Does this activity lead to votes, volunteers, or money for the campaign?"

Ideas and developments that require significant changes of the plan should be evaluated carefully. The plan should be a living document—neither rigidly adhered to, nor too easily scrapped.

A winning campaign analyzes the resources at hand, measures the political climate, crafts a plan or strategy to contact the voters with the most effective message possible, and works tirelessly to accomplish all that is necessary to win.

## PART II:
---
### Overcoming Potential Obstacles

It would be unrealistic to suggest that women candidates don't face serious obstacles in the course of running for office. Some obstacles can easily be offset, while others will be overcome only as we undo the systemic unfairness women face.

### 1. Private lives have priority

Some women are prohibited from undertaking electoral efforts due to busy personal lives. Raising young children, elder care, and other family obligations create insurmountable time commitments which may preclude running for office. Recognize these barriers before you file for office. There is no sense in running for office unless you're going to win, and can serve as required. Perhaps a run for the United States

Senate will not fit into your life at this point, while a bid for a lower level office, with a lesser time commitment, may indeed work. Seek an appointment to an advisory board or commission, and gain experience that will greatly benefit your later run for higher office.

Wait until the time is right. Research shows that women tend to enter politics later than men. For example, women in state legislatures are older (only 31% were below age 49) than the men (42% were below age 49). These studies demonstrate that women are more likely to enter politics as a second career after completing their childraising career.[1]

### 2. Lack of access to big money

The fact that the average contribution to United States Senator Barbara Boxer's 1992 campaign was $28 says more about her lack of access to big money than about anything else. Most women candidates report lower average campaign contributions than their male counterparts.

The reasons for this include: (1) More men have more money, give larger political contributions and are more likely to contribute to male candidates; (2) Women candidates don't ask for contributions as large as men do; and (3) Women don't know as many large givers as male candidates do. Here are some ways to overcome this considerable disadvantage:

■ *Plan ahead.* Make a fundraising plan early, that designates gift ranges; expect to achieve a certain number of gifts in each range:

### Gift range chart

| Gift Amount | Number of Gifts Needed | Prospect/ Donor Ratio | Number of Prospects Needed |
|---|---|---|---|
| $1500 | 3 | 5:1 | 15 |
| $1000 | 6 | 4:1 | 24 |
| $ 500 | 12 | 4:1 | 48 |
| $ 100 | 100 | 2:1 | 200 |
| $ 50 | 120 | 2:1 | 240 |
| Total $32,500 | 241 | | |

In this sample fundraising plan, Clara Candidate will raise $32,500. She expects that $50 donations will be easier to get—one of every two people she asks (the Prospect:Donor Ratio) will say yes. On the other hand, she may have to ask five people to give $1500 in order to find the one who will make the contribution. If Clara spends part of her three-year electoral plan developing contacts with those potential large givers, she is more likely to be successful than if she starts from scratch just six or twelve months from election day.

***Make specific requests.*** You can't count on someone's vote if you don't ask for it. Likewise, you can't get a campaign contribution for a specific amount without asking. Get training on fundraising for major gifts. Practice, and practice some more. Videotape your phone calls or try some in-person role-playing while asking for $500 or $1,000.

***Build a comprehensive fundraising team.*** People are most likely to give money if they are asked by someone they know and respect. If you don't know 100 people who will each give you $500 or more, then find ten of your friends or supporters who each know ten potential large donors. Ask supporters either to get the contribution or help you get it.

Many women candidates have won elections even though they were greatly outspent by their male opponents. Judy Billings, Washington's Superintendent of Public Instruction, spent about $120,000 to win her seat, compared with almost $400,000 spent by her male opponent. Karen Vialle, former Mayor of Tacoma, won her race despite being outspent three to one. None of the political pundits thought Lorri Lippman Brown could win her state senate primary race in Las Vegas, Nevada, because she only spent $1,200. But her effective, door-to-door campaign provided early retirement for an over-confident, big-spending incumbent. Knowing they were outspent, these women candidates did everything they could to maximize fundraising and grass-roots efforts.

The only way to offset the disadvantage of being the financial underdog is with the power of organized numbers of people. While entrenched opponents might have access to unlimited money for campaign mailings, well-organized women's campaigns can offset that perceived advantage with volunteers who personally deliver brochures, and make personal contact with voters. Likewise, efficient use of the candidate's time to prioritize door-to-door or phone contact with voters is inexpensive, and likely to yield more votes than a campaign that merely aims costly mailings at the voters within three weeks of the election.

### Women for women

One woman candidate formed a powerful fundraising team to secure funds for herself and other Democratic women legislative candidates. A group of 20 activist women organized a series of three "Women for Women Breakfasts" at which attendees heard speeches by local women political leaders. The committee of twenty brainstormed the names of 1500 women activists they knew in the city and sent an invitation to each one. The twenty leaders each took a task—one designed the invitations, one confirmed the three speakers, and one supervised the mailing. The breakfasts did not have an admission fee, but included a fundraising pitch after each speaker: they raised over $10,000.

### 3. Incumbency

American voters no longer want to support career, or long-term politicians. In fact, the California ballot includes a line labeled, "None of the Above." Incumbency can hurt women seeking re-election as much as it hurts men. Incumbents are now retiring more and more frequently: in 1992, 110 incumbent members of Congress decided not to run for re-election. In 1994, 90 more reached the same decision.

Neither women nor men should run for office in order to secure a permanent career. As emphasized earlier, holding public office is only one tactic for women activists to win power, and effect change. With this in mind, ways to avoid the negative aspects of incumbency, and falling early victim to the voters' axe are to:

- State from the outset your intention to serve for one or two terms.
- Campaign on specific issues and positions, so that in future campaigns you can report on the results achieved.
- Get elected by meeting the voters of your district, and re-elected by staying in touch with them. Always attend to this crucial base-building process by sending out regular updates and newsletters, and scheduling months to doorknock and phone your constituents when the legislative body is not in session. Your payoff is both staying tuned in to community needs, and identifying prospective candidates to take your place when you retire.

### 4. Double standards

It's no secret that women have to be twice as good as men to get half the credit. Ann Richards observed, "Ginger Rogers did everything Fred Astaire did. She just did it backwards and in high heels."

*Nobody ever says to men, how can you be a Congressman and a father?*
                    —CONGRESSWOMAN PATRICIA SCHROEDER

From the special scrutiny of women's child care arrangements, to the lack of women's bathrooms in the United States Senate building, to criticism of elected women who wear jeans to the supermarket, women continue to fall victim to a double standard of judgment—one not applied to men.

Numerous examples of the special or sexist treatment of female leaders include:

- Continual media references to the apparel, haircut, or physical size of women
- Use of the terms "aggressive," "feisty," and "pushy" to describe behavior in women that would be called "tough" and "decisive" in men
- Assumptions that women's expertise and interests lie solely in the emotional concerns about education and health care, instead of recognizing their fiscal skills and financial concerns

Only a full-court press against systematic sexism will eliminate these stubborn practices. As obvious as it seems, the more women step forward to run, the more likely it is that voters will concentrate on their qualifications to serve in office.

### 5. Catch 23?

*"More women than men hope for a woman President (young women are especially intent on this), but more men than women believe they'll see it happen."*[2]

                    —LIFE MAGAZINE

Women can indeed be self-defeating. We can view ourselves having a great deal of potential power or hold ourselves back by conceding the halls of political, corporate, and media power to others.

### 6. False barriers to women candidates

Myths persist which are meant to discourage females from seeking public leadership positions. "You can't serve in office and be a good mother." "Women don't have enough experience on the issues to get elected." "She's too emotional to withstand a tough, contentious campaign."

Women bring special perspectives to the issues society is grappling with on a daily basis. Voters want help in confronting these serious challenges and are willing to select representatives who are more like them; are more likely to understand, and sympathize with their daily struggles. Mothers make the cut.

All these challenges can be, and have been, dealt with by preceding women leaders. Given the very real barriers women face to getting elected, don't create your own just to keep yourself from trying.

A recent survey of local women officeholders (primarily mayors and city councilors), revealed that 70% thought *the greatest barrier* to women winning office was the lack of women candidates.[3]

## Special Considerations for Single Women Candidates

According to the Center for the American Woman and Politics, women legislators are twice as likely as men to be unmarried; three times as many women as men are divorced or widowed.[4]

Single women who run for office need a strong network to take the place of support functions family members often play for other candidates. Multnomah County, Oregon, Chair Beverly Stein recommends:

If you're thinking of running and preparing yourself to run, you should also be thinking about developing your support network. Hopefully you'd invested in those relationships for years ahead of time, because now you're going to ask people to give a lot during a time when you're not going to be able to give very much to them.

I don't like to ask volunteers or staff to pick up my dry cleaning, or do other personal chores, because I just don't believe in that. For that kind of support, I tend to rely on my friends, people who understand this is not just for my convenience, it's a matter of allocation of a precious amount of time.

And so my friends took on very practical aspects of my daily life. During my first campaign, we had people who would drop food off for us on a regular basis. One friend did my yard work, others picked up the dry cleaning. During my last campaign, two women friends came over and helped organize my closet with outfits that were appropriate for campaigning, because you can't even waste time getting dressed in the morning.

Now I make a point, in between elections, of trying to nurture my relationships. I bring people little gifts, remembering what they gave to me during the campaign.

Other candidates report that voters may assume that women without children don't know or care about education and other family issues. You may want to speak out on these issues early in your campaign.

## Special Considerations for Lesbian Candidates

Lesbian candidates for office must confront homophobia, either in the form of attitudes in the minds of the voters, or as outright gay-baiting by an opponent, or other segments of the community.

Dale McCormick, a 47-year-old carpenter from Maine, found ways to break down the fear and misunderstanding that voters may have about lesbian candidates:

> Because I'm a lesbian, we presumed there might be some discomfort with me; so my campaign committee decided that meeting people was the best way to overcome that. My door to door campaign was a central part of my race for state senate.
>
> Starting in April, for the June primary elections, I went door to door from three or four in the afternoon until it got dark. After we won the primary and cleaned up our voter lists, I went out from July to November, every single day. I didn't miss a day, including Sundays. I figure I visited 5,000 houses, and I saw about 6,000 people all together.
>
> Only four towns out of twelve in the district were good for walking. In the rural towns I'd ride my bike because it was too far to walk between houses but too close to drive. People really liked it, and they got the impression that if I was saving gas, maybe I wouldn't waste their money either.
>
> As the president of the statewide Lesbian and Gay Political Alliance, I was very out, for years. I included it in my announcement speech, and I never backed away when asked. But I didn't bring up the lesbian issue directly at the doorstep, and we didn't put it on our literature. My opponent was gay-baiting me, sending out literature about Sodom and Gomorrah, and I just kept sticking to the issues of concern to the voters—health care and property tax reform.
>
> My opponents wanted to type cast me, and people didn't go for it. The fact that I had personally met so many voters really undermined their ability to do that to me. Eventually, when I walked up to houses people would say, "You're Dale McCormick, aren't you?" before I'd even open my mouth. They'd say "I'm so glad you stopped, and by the way, I don't care if you are a lesbian."

Dale and other lesbian candidates nationwide concur that it's best to be open about your identity from the beginning of the campaign. However, the candidate should always address issues of concern to the voters. Excellent training is available to lesbian and gay candidates through the Gay and Lesbian Victory Fund, Candidate Training Institute, 1012 14th St. NW, #707, Washington, DC 20005; 202/VICTORY (202/842-8679).

## Special Considerations for Minority Women

Minority women who run for office must confront racism as well as sexism.

*When asked why she was running for office, Sherrelynn Marshall, of Stillwater, Oklahoma, said her campaign would focus on attacking racism. She told a poignant story about her husband, who she described as 'a big black man' walking toward the checkout counter of a menswear department. A white customer had left his wallet on the counter as he gathered up his packages. When he looked up and saw Marshall's husband, he dropped his purchases and grabbed his wallet. . . . This sort of thing goes on all the time in our community . . . I want to make a difference.[5]*

Since women of color have to jump twice as many hurdles as white women to prove their worth, they should take advantage of all support networks that may be available to them:

Women of color have unique contacts with civil rights groups and church groups that most white women do not have. David Bositis of the Joint Center for Political Studies in Washington, D.C. points out that black women, as a group, have had to bear more responsibility for family caregiving than either their male counterparts, or white women. As a result, black women have developed stronger community, social, and spiritual bonds than these groups. "When minority women use these contacts and these bonds, they have a support base for politics that is hard to match."[6]

Cynthia McKinney, the first African-American woman elected to Congress from Georgia, was strategic about the use of race in her campaign. Capitalizing on her years of activism and leadership within the black community, McKinney was successful in branding her opponents—a white, male state senator and an African-American male state representative—as, "Too closely aligned to the state's dominant power structure and unresponsive to Georgia's black voters."[7]

A significant number of minority women electeds now serve as mayors of small towns, particularly in the southeastern United States. These communities are closely knit and enjoy well-organized, connected minority institutions such as churches and community associations. These small town mayors provide special motivation and models for women of color in other parts of the country.

National, state, and local level women's organizations are establishing women of color and diversity committees, whose goal is to encourage more political leadership within communities of color. As Loretta

Ross, formerly of the NOW women-of-color program, points out, "Women of color . . . have to do their homework on the inner politics of the organization, to learn how to get power and how to use it. Women of color have to give up the notion that white women can do something for us. The task is to build a constituency."[8] Women of color are forming their own groups. The Women of Color Leadership Council in Washington, D.C. is helping minority women build their political futures.

*Women and minorities, when they are elected to office, are constantly torn between how to represent their constituency at large and how to represent the group from which they come. There's a constant pressure on them from both of these constituencies. The group from which they come will extend far beyond their district even if they are governors.*[9]

—POLLY BACA

Martha Choe, of Seattle, Washington, points out the need for minority women to build coalition campaigns:

In 1991, I was elected to the city council of Seattle, Washington, becoming the first Korean-American elected official in the United States. In thinking about running, my big fear was "What if I lose; can I stand the humiliation?" Then I thought of my father, who immigrated to this country in 1948; he was 41 years old, with $200 to his name, and he didn't know anyone here. I thought of his courage, and I realized that this race was not so much of a risk, compared to what he had done. With the support of my friends and family, I knew that it would be a positive experience, even if I didn't win.

I won with 70% of the vote, through a terrific combination of support from people of color, women, nonprofits, business, educators—everyone I knew through my years of grassroots involvement. I was taken totally by surprise by the groundswell of support, both in terms of money and volunteers, from the Korean community. One clear lesson to me, as a woman and a woman of color is that you cannot make it unless and until you build coalitions.

Women who challenge cultural and ethnic limitations understand the importance of making themselves available to mentor other women to follow in their footsteps. State Representative Lynda Morgan Lovejoy, of New Mexico, tells her story:

I grew up surrounded by family members who were involved in tribal politics in the Navajo Nation. I got involved locally, serving as secretary of our local chapter of the Navajo Government.

I enjoyed working with people, and felt that somehow this kind of work was meant for me. Then a few local men suggested that I run for State Representative in New Mexico. They said, "We've elected male after male, and they haven't done much for our people. We're looking for someone who can work with our people, communicate with our people, and we think you're that person."

At that time, I was very afraid—I didn't have the confidence to run. I went to visit my grandmother, and an aunt, and another older woman I look up to, and they were very encouraging. Those visits got me motivated to go forward and run.

Still, there was a strong belief among many older people that a woman is not prepared for the pressure, the hard work and long hours of public office. In my first campaign, I didn't have the kind of support that I expected from the Navajo women.

I was first elected in 1989, the first Indian woman elected to the New Mexico House of Representatives. I've found strength in my inner self—mentally, emotionally, and spiritually—that this is my destiny.

For me it's been very rewarding, because I can tell other women my experiences, and lay the groundwork for them. Now I consider myself a role model for women who are thinking about running and are fearful about stepping forward. I encourage them to get a good education, get some experience in local politics, to gradually work their way up and be open to all the choices they may have in the political field.

## WOMEN WHO DARE

### Beverly Stein

Especially if you're a woman, you don't immediately leap toward the idea of running for office. You sort of slowly get it into your head that you can do this. I had hit a point in my life where I either had to run for office or take on some other big challenge. I first filed as a candidate for State Representative in 1988, two to three years after I seriously started to think about it. By then, I knew it was time—you've got to know in your heart that you're ready to run, or you're not going to be able to pull it off.

During the three year period before I filed, I started taking steps to position myself to run. I looked at my volunteer activities and shifted some energy into new involvements. Now, I was building on ten or fifteen years of political activism in certain sectors, so I certainly wasn't trying to lay the groundwork everywhere. I was looking for places where I didn't have such strong contacts, though.

I learned that there was potentially an opening in the Legislature—if the current representative decided to run for higher office—and paid attention to what was going on with that seat. I kept track of the electoral arena—who the players were, who was running, and what they did. I started honing in on the district, shifting my efforts from working in the broader community to the geographic area that I wanted to represent.

It became a waiting game—there was a period of about a year where I was in a holding pattern. I had to be patient and wait for the right opportunity, so I just bided my time.

Probably *the* most important thing is having a good campaign manager. That's something few candidates pay enough attention to—finding that one person that's going to be there through it all with you. That should be a person you identify two years out, too. While you're preparing yourself as a candidate, the campaign manager can start going to campaign school and learn what it's going to take. Which one of your friends, or political colleagues has the basic skills, really believes in you, and is ready to be there for you? A good campaign manager doesn't have to have run a campaign before, but they should know how to organize and have the basic skills to do it. It should be someone that you can actively trust, so you can do your part of the campaign and have the confidence that they will make everything else happen.

In some ways, no one can imagine what it's like to run for office until you've been through it. It's like a marathon—it means stretching yourself to the limit of your physical, emotional, and mental endurance, day after day. A lot of candidates don't really realize how much it's going to take—you have to want it bad enough to just keep going through exhausting stuff, boring stuff, ugly stuff, and you have to just keep going. You've really got to have that fire in the belly. By now I've run eight or ten times, in both primaries and generals. It's important to have your life in order, whatever that means to you. If you're a single person you should make sure you've got proper emotional support around you. If you're married or in a relationship, be sure that your spouse or partner is ready to take this on, and that your children are, too.

During the early part of my first campaign, I didn't give a speech that wasn't written out word for word. I wasn't comfortable unless I had my speech completely written out. I had heard too many candidates talk and not say anything, and I committed to myself that if I was going to get up and speak, that I would say something really substantive. Now I can give very good speeches, heartfelt, with substance, outlined on the back of a napkin five minutes before the speech. Public speaking is a learnable skill, and being nervous at first shouldn't inhibit anyone because it gets amazingly easier over time. I had never directly asked anyone for money before I became a candidate. Because of my activist history, I had a big base of support during my early campaigns—a lot of money just came rolling in when I announced my candidacy. We did events and mailings, and that's pretty much how we raised the budget. I don't think I really had to work hard to raise money until I ran for county chair.

It wasn't the easiest thing, but I decided that if I have to do it, that's what I'll do. And so I raised $200,000 in eleven weeks, and it came, most of it, from people I had never met before. It's not magic, it's method. I had a method worked out, and I just put the time in, making the calls and keeping track of names on little note cards.

Part of what makes it easier for me is that I know I represent a larger cause. I think of myself as a collection of causes. I'm not into this just to advance myself, that's not my history. I have ideas that I want to make happen. I want to change the world, and I don't have a hard time making the leap between asking for money and knowing that it's going to help me change the world.

---

## Notes

[1] Malcolm Jewell and Marcia Lynn Whicker, "The Feminization of Leadership in State Legislatures," *PS: Political Science & Politics*, December 1993, p. 707.

[2] Lisa Grunwald, "If Women Ran America," *Life*, June 1992, p. 40.

[3] Susan A. MacManus, "How to Get More Women in Office: The Perspectives of Local Elected Officials," *Urban Affairs Quarterly*, vol. 28, no. 1, September 1992, pp. 159–170.

[4] Kathleen Casey, "Women State Legislators: Who Are They?" *Center for the American Woman and Politics News & Notes*, Fall 1992, p. 26.

[5] Shirley Ragsdale, "A Brilliant Handbook for Women in Politics," *Muskogee Daily Phoenix*, October 20, 1993, p. 3.

[6] Teola P. Hunter, Speaker Pro Tem, Michigan House of Representatives, "A Different View of Progress—Minority Women in Politics," *The Journal of State Government*, vol. 64, no. 2, April-June 1991, p. 50.

[7] Martha Angle, "The Seats of '93 Grew From the Seeds of '65," *Congressional Quarterly*, January 16, 1993, p. 150.

[8] Helen Zia, "Women of Color in Leadership", *Social Policy*, Summer 1993, p. 51.

[9] Susan J. Carroll, ed., *Women, Black, and Hispanic State Elected Leaders: 1990 Symposium on the State of the States* (New Brunswick, N.J.: Eagleton Institute of Politics, 1991), p. 26.

CHAPTER

# 13

# Making Your Money Talk

*Money is power, not only in the marketplace at large but also in the marketplace of social change.*

—MARIANNE PHILBIN
CHICAGO FOUNDATION FOR WOMEN[1]

## CAN YOU SPARE SOME SOCIAL CHANGE?

In American society, money *is* power. Men are groomed to understand and respect the links between power and money—they join clubs, pay dues, make significant donations, sit on boards that allocate funds, write budgets, and sign checks. Americans donate $125 billion a year to universities, churches, museums, social service, political, and public interest organizations. And while 60% of donors are women, men still firmly control the institutions that dispense money to charities, civic, and social causes.

To gain *our* fair share of political power, to implement crucial programs and fund alternative organizations, women must step forward and

245

deal more directly with money. In addition to demanding equitable salaries in the workplace, we've got to improve our abilities to ask for, manage, spend, and donate money wisely. This chapter looks at women as donors and fundraisers, and examines the many ways that women are changing their relationship to money.

## TAKE CHARGE OF YOUR GIVING

Women resent being treated as political "lightweights," yet sometimes our financial response to a political request fits that description. Many are accustomed to giving hours—not dollars—to help a cause. When asked for a contribution, no matter the issue, or level of income, we write a $15 check today just as we did ten years ago.

While the majority of donors in the United States are women, most consistently give smaller contributions than men—about 30% less, in fact.[2]

> *Women substitute significant contributions of time and energy for significant contributions of money to the philanthropic causes we support. We rarely make claims of equal access to the family's resources for the purpose of philanthropy. We give relatively small amounts squeezed out of the grocery budget. Or, we make philanthropic meat loaf out of the leftovers from our own salaries.*[3]
>
> —KELLER CUSHING FREEMAN

It's time to re-examine our ideas about giving money, and to take a new look at our priorities. One easy way to do this is to take out our checkbooks and ask:

- How much did I spend for the last pair of shoes I bought?
- What was the price of my last outfit?
- How much am I willing to spend for a night out on the town?
- What were the dollar amounts of my last three contributions to political, civic, or social causes?

How do those figures compare? As your income rises, are you spending more money on shoes, clothing, and entertainment? Have your charitable, political, or civic contributions risen as well?

Now ask yourself if electing a well-qualified woman to public office, joining the fight against domestic violence, or making a contribution to save the environment is worth as much to you as some of the purchases you've listed. Does your checkbook reflect your true priorities?

Even if your income is low, don't dismiss the idea of giving some "social change." Almost everyone can afford to give something, even if it's one dollar. The amount isn't crucial—what's important is that the donation be significant to you. Even a small contribution can inspire others to give. Giving money to a cause may be one way you feel you can help change the situation for all women.

## Set Up a Giving Plan

If we do not think of ourselves as donors, we'll never prioritize or plan our donations. Some of us sort through the requests we receive in the mail, putting many of them aside because we don't know how to judge the effectiveness or trustworthiness of the groups asking. Others give money only when someone they know asks for a donation.

To maximize the effect of your giving, think and plan ahead about where you want your money to go. Try to do this at least once a year. Here are some steps you can follow to create your own Annual Giving Plan:

### 1. Analyze your past giving

Review your tax records and check register, or make a list from memory of all the contributions you made in the last two years. How much did you give, and to whom? How did you feel about the money you gave away? About the organizations receiving your donation? Do your contributions reflect your values?

Divide your total annual giving by your total income for the same year; the resulting number represents your giving *as a percentage of* your income. The Internal Revenue Service reports that most taxpayers give away approximately 2% of their income, an amount of between $400 and $1800 per year. How does your percentage compare to the 2% United States average?

### 2. Set a goal amount for your giving for next year

Will this figure be the same as last year, or will you target a higher amount? Will your contributions amount to 2% or more of your income? Members of some religious denominations follow a practice of *tithing*, or donating 10% of their annual income to make the world a better place. Could you do the same?

Whether it's 1%, 2%, 5%, or 10%, set a target amount for your donations for the year. Remember that a moderate annual increase you can actually follow through on is better than projecting a huge goal that you will be unable to carry out. If it's easier to budget on a monthly basis, try setting aside $10 per month or week. That amounts to $120 or $520 per year!

### 3. List your priorities for next year's giving

List the causes, concerns, issues, and types of groups you'd like to support. This is your personal list of how you'd like to change the world. Think about what you'd like to fund, not what you "should," or "always" fund. After making the list, set your priorities by placing number #1 beside your most important issue, #2 next to your second choice, and so on. Do you want to give a small amount to encourage every group on the list, or channel your money to the top two or three priorities? Will you contribute one lump sum, or spread donations over monthly or quarterly amounts? Do you prefer to get more for your contributions by using your money to purchase tickets to fundraising events, or by spending at an organization's annual auction?

If not already on your list, add annual "obligations" you plan to maintain, such as contributions, membership dues, and requests that you just can't turn down (like tickets to your neighbor's annual charity dance). Note the amount of each of these contributions, and take a moment to consider whether you really want to keep supporting these causes.

Rewrite your prioritized list, under the title *My Annual Giving Plan*. Even with a relatively small amount to donate, your plan will help focus your efforts, strengthen your impact, and respond to requests more systematically. Keep your plan on hand as you sort through the many funding requests that come through the mail and other sources. Each request for money during the year can be analyzed against the criteria of your giving plan. This system makes it a bit easier to turn down low-priority requests.

### 4. Research your options

If you already know which groups you want to support, set up a meeting with a member of the board or staff to find out more about their plans and programs for the year. Ask how much money goes towards fundraising expenses, and how much actually goes to fund their programs.

If you are certain about your issue priorities, but don't know which groups will make the best use of your money, ask active community or political leaders who work on the issue which groups are most effective, and why. Tell them you are considering making a contribution, and want to target your money to the group that can best utilize it.

Read fundraising appeals and newsletters, attend meetings, and network to find groups that work efficiently or use strategies that best fit your goals. For example, do you want to support a legal team, a direct action organization, or an outreach and education group?

### Organize a funding circle

If the process of developing a personal plan seems a bit daunting, or if you'd like to encourage other women to join you in becoming pro-active about their giving, invite a small group of friends to go through this process together.

1. Make a list of organizations or issues, and assign each member of the group to do research and report back. Or, invite a speaker from each of several organizations to make a brief presentation.

2. Decide whether you want to pool your money and make donations from a common fund, or share research and information, and make individual funding choices. In either case, you can magnify your impact, and learn more, by working with a group.

3. Meet regularly—monthly or quarterly—and write a check ($1, $5, $10, $25, or $100) at each meeting. With several of you in the group, you could become major donors in the course of a year!

## JOIN AND SUPPORT WOMEN'S FUNDING NETWORKS

Savvy women fundraisers are organizing networks to help raise money for women and their issues at the federal, state, and local level. Funding networks by and for women include women's funds and foundations (which give money to nonprofit organizations that help women and girls), and women's political action committees (which assist women candidates of all political parties). If you want to target your money to help women, you'll find local, and national, opportunities to give.

### Women's Funds and Foundations

Consider that:

■ 75% of the people in poverty in the United States are women and children. Yet, less than 5% of all charitable contributions in the United States go to women's organizations.[4]

■ While 60% of directors and support staff of foundations are women, more than 75% of trustees—those who make the funding decisions—are men. As long as most corporate and foundation board members are men, issues such as violence against women, or child care, will rarely emerge high on lists of funding priorities.

■ The United Way historically favors programs for men and boys over those for women and girls. In 1990, the United Way gave $39 million more to the YMCA than the YWCA, gave seven times as much money to the Boys Clubs as the Girls, Inc., and favored the Boy Scouts over the Girl Scouts by $32 million.

Women's funds and foundations organized to reverse that non-funding trend, to combat poverty among women, and support programs that promote women's health, fight domestic violence and sexual assault, and eliminate employment discrimination. In 1980 there were only four women's funds; by 1985 the total was 23 in 14 states. Currently there are over 60 funds with names like the Women's Foundation and Women's Way.

*Women raise the dollars and decide how they're spent. Grants and allocations support programs that assist women and girls in overcoming racial, economic, political, sexual and social discrimination. The benefits of women's funds are far-reaching: women are empowered, creative community institutions are built, and society is strengthened as a whole. The world gains from the full participation of women and girls.*[5]
—NATIONAL NETWORK OF WOMEN'S FUNDS

In 1992, forty-three women's funds granted more than $10 million to programs for women and girls, representing an increase of 61% over the year before. From 1985 to 1992, women in the funds contributed, and raised, $80.7 million; by 1993 the number of these funds had grown to fifty-seven.

One exciting aspect of the women's funding movement is that it nudges women towards exerting greater control over their money. "It's a feminist act to take control of my money and use it to help women," says Abigail Disney, of the entertainment clan. "In the women's funding movement, we don't call our husbands or fathers for advice. We're not doing this to get our pictures in the paper, we're doing it because we are women."[6] The funds bring together women from divergent social classes and ethnic backgrounds, and activists encourage one other to give to their fullest potential—resulting in contributions from 50 cents to more than $1 million.

In large cities and small towns across the United States, women are finding creative ways to close the gender gap in charitable giving. The Women's Foundation of San Francisco offers financial counseling programs to teach women how to manage their money, including how to think about giving some of it away. Several years ago the Women's Foundation confronted the United Way of the Bay Area with the fact that it gave $1 million more to boys than girls programs. United Way subsequently promised to narrow the gap over five years with a pledge of $850,000 to girl's programs.

Women's Way in Philadelphia helped create a trend to offer alternatives to workplace payroll deduction campaigns in private companies and government agencies traditionally controlled by the United Way. Women's Way offers a payroll deduction option for employees of the city of Philadelphia, and raises nearly $1 million annually for its fifteen member groups.[7]

### What you can do:

- Educate yourself about money and how to handle it. Take classes or find female financial advisors to increase your comfort level.

- Get involved in the women's funding movement. To find the women's foundation or fund closest to you, contact the National Network of Women's Funds; 1821 University Avenue, Suite 409N, St. Paul, MN 55104; 612/641-0742.

- Analyze United Way support for women's and girl's programs in your area.

- Because corporate giving to women and girls is even smaller than United Way donations, women who work for corporations should encourage their employers to be more responsive to women's and children's programs that request support. Get involved in the giving program of your corporation, or try to set up a Women's Advisory Committee, as Digital Corporation and others have done.

## MONEY FOR WOMEN CANDIDATES

Ellen Malcolm watched the number of women Democrats in the United States House of Representatives decline from fourteen in 1972 to twelve in 1987. Campaign after campaign, one sad truth emerged— terrific women candidates just couldn't raise big money from traditional political sources. Malcolm started EMILY's List (Early Money is Like

Yeast) in 1985, with the clear conviction that not only money, but *early* money, was the crucial element that female candidates needed. Malcolm recruited thousands of formerly apolitical women and turned them into savvy donors and campaign activists. Since then, the number of women Democrats in the Congress reached a high of 36 and EMILY's List expanded from helping to elect women to national office to support for women trying to attain positions as governors and state-wide and local positions.

The Senate Judiciary Committee's treatment of Anita Hill is credited with boosting membership and contributions to EMILY's List. In 1992, the Political Action Committee raised $6.2 million in contributions for 55 Democratic women candidates, more money than any other political action committee gave to House and Senate races that year.

Two Colorado women broke stereotypes when they hosted a political fund-raiser called Serious Women, Serious Issues, Serious Money—and charged $1,000 a head. They set a goal of raising $1 million, asking women to give ten times the amount they'd ever given before. Observers from as far as Washington, D.C. doubted they could do it, but they met their goal.

In 1992 EMILY's List spawned a sister organization, the WISH List (Women in the Senate and House) for pro-choice Republican women. There are nine national women's PACs, or donor networks, and 37 state PACs or donor networks (in 22 states) organized to give money to women.

---

### What you can do:

- Find out if there is a Women's PAC in your state or city. For a list of federal and state women's PACs (including the eleven in California) contact: The Center for the American Woman and Politics, Eagleton Institute of Politics, Rutgers University, New Brunswick, NJ 08901; 908/828-2210. Contact elected women officials in your state.

- Join the fundraising committee for a woman candidate in your area.

- Join EMILY's List or the WISH List.

---

## RAISE MONEY FOR YOUR FAVORITE CANDIDATE OR CAUSE

If you can't give away more of your own money, find ways to raise more. Become a fundraiser for your favorite cause, and multiply your impact as a donor. Demonstrate your support, leadership qualities, and enthusiasm to an organization by doing some freelance fundraising on your own. Be sure to let the group know who you plan to approach, to avoid duplicating other fundraising efforts already under way.

If you're a potential future candidate who hopes that like-minded people or organizations will want to support you later on, be sure to pitch in and help them *now*. If you want to prove your mettle to an organization to secure a leadership role or a staff position, fundraising can open many doors.

Simply put, the only way to raise money is to ask for it. Every fundraising event, raffle, bake sale, or charity ball is simply a forum to make it easier for fundraisers to ask for support. Most organizations combine a variety of methods to raise money—grassroots events, direct mail, telephone solicitation, grant writing, and high-dollar solicitation of major donors. The simplest way to raise money is direct solicitation—someone asks someone else for a donation.

Kim Klein, author of *Fundraising for Social Change*, and a fundraising consultant works with nonprofit organizations, explains that when asked *why they gave money* to a cause, people most often responded:

1. They liked or trusted the person asking and wanted to encourage or support them.
2. They supported the cause.
3. They gave because they were asked.

## What's So Scary about Fundraising?

Anyone can raise money. All it takes is a bit of training and a little practice. Yet many people are terrified of asking for money. When you really think about it, what's the worst that can happen? Most nightmare scenarios revolve around the simple fact that someone might say "no."

In fact, if the approach is made correctly, with a request that is reasonable for the donor, quite often the answer will be "yes." A third category of responses may sound like "no," but actually mean "maybe." They include answers like, "not right now" (but maybe later?) "not $500" (but maybe $250?), "not a donation" (but maybe a pledge to donate later?).

Any answer that includes a "maybe" is an opportunity for gentle and respectful negotiation.

Many times we assume our friends won't want to, or can't, give because of our own fear of asking. Let them make those decisions. Don't think of the situation as asking a favor or presuming on a friendship; give them the benefit of information you have gathered, and offer them an opportunity to join in supporting a worthwhile cause. Experienced fundraisers say that if you never get "no" for an answer, you aren't asking for enough money, or approaching enough people.

If you're still intimidated, try to remember the last time you were approached for a contribution. What was your response? Is that a response that you should fear from others?

## Ten Ways to Raise $100, $500, or $1000

1. Invite some friends over for lunch or dessert.

   An effective way to begin your development career is to organize a small fundraising lunch or dessert party. Invite two, three, or four of your closest friends, and ask them to bring their checkbooks along. Explain that you want to discuss an issue of importance to you, and that you are going to ask for their support as well.

   On the day of the event, be prepared to talk for five or ten minutes about the issue, and why it is so crucial. Tell your friends that you are giving money to the cause, and that you have set a goal of raising $_____ (name the specific amount). Then, ask them to make a specific donation, to help you reach your goal. You may also want to let them know if this is your first attempt at raising money; whether or not they give money, they are sure to be sympathetic.

2. Write a letter to your friends.

3. Sell tickets to an event.

4. Provide names for others to call, in addition to your own calls.

5. Sell an item or service that you can provide—a quilt, a car tune-up—and donate the proceeds.

6. Host a spaghetti dinner or talent show, alone or with others, and charge an entrance fee.

7. Organize a yard, book, or bake sale, or, combine all three.

8. Ask that birthday, wedding, or anniversary gifts be in the form of donations to your favorite cause.

9. Make a presentation to a church or other appropriate group to which you belong, requesting funds for an issue or organization.

10. Host a house party or invite your friends to hear a speaker from your favorite organization. At the end of the talk, make a "pitch" for funds.

# CHECKBOOK ACTIVISM

Much has been written about socially responsible investing and consuming, and about how our daily spending decisions can affect or change the world. Make connections between what you read in the newspaper and how you spend your money. Support women-owned businesses and women in the professions. Target your consumer spending to help people and organizations you believe in.

Refer to *Shopping for a Better World* to find out the brand names of supermarket and other products that are made by businesses you want to support.[8] The book rates companies on their contributions to charity, advancement of women and minorities to top management and board positions, their impact on the environment, contributions to the community, and workplace and family benefit issues. The *Better World Investment Guide* provides guidelines for ethical investing and compares 50 of the largest held companies with 50 top companies recommended by experts on ethical investment. A third book, *Rating America's Corporate Conscience*, profiles 125 major American companies, with enough in-depth information to let you create your own list of heroes and villains.

Working Assets, a socially responsible money market fund, offers credit card services that benefit peace, anti-hunger, and other progressive organizations. When you sign up $2 goes into the fund. Each time you use the credit card, five cents is added. To date, credit card customers have generated over $2.3 million for hundreds of groups, including Oxfam America, The Sierra Club, The Children's Defense Fund, The Hispanic Health Council, The Rainforest Action Network, and the AIDS Action Council. Working Assets Money Fund, 230 California St., San Francisco, CA 94111; 800/933-5764.

Working Assets Long Distance Phone Service diverts 1% of its revenue to nonprofit groups such as Planned Parenthood, Greenpeace, and Amnesty International. Every month, the phone bill outlines a particular political issue needing citizen action; subscribers are invited to make a free phone call any Monday to voice their opinion to decision-makers on the topic. Call 800/788-8588 for details.

## For More Information

*The Grass Roots Fundraising Book: How to Raise Money in Your Community*, by Joan Flanagan.[9]

*The Successful Volunteer Organization: Getting Started and Getting Results in Nonprofit, Charitable, Grassroots, and Community Groups,* by Joan Flanagan.[10]

*Fundraising for Social Change,* by Kim Klein.[11] A comprehensive guide to the methods and mechanics of fundraising for nonprofit groups.

*The Thirteen Most Common Fundraising Mistakes,* by Paul Schneiter and Donald Nelson.[12]

*Responsible Philanthropy* is a quarterly journal covering trends in philanthropic support for racial, ethnic, women's, and low income movements. For a complimentary copy write National Committee for Responsive Philanthropy, 2001 S St. NW, #620, Washington, DC 20009; 202/387-9177.

*Investing from the Heart,* by Jack Brill and Allan Reder, offers essentials of personal money management, and the preparation of a personal financial plan. It provides a list of companies sorted by various social investment concerns.

*Chronicle of Philanthropy: The Newspaper of the Non-Profit World* is published bi-weekly with regular departments on fundraising and managing nonprofits. 1255 Twenty-Third St. NW, Washington, DC 20037.

*The Grassroots Fundraising Journal* is an excellent journal published six times a year. PO Box 11607, Berkeley, CA 94701; 510/704-8714.

## ■■■■■ WOMEN WHO DARE ▭▭▭▭▭

### Nita Brueggeman

I became political because I was a member of the labor movement, and because my folks talked about politics at home. The first time I ever joined a union I was fourteen years old, working at a food processing plant during the summer in California.

After I got married, I worked at a garment factory in Washington State. I started working with women's issues, and saw that the labor movement, even with all of its problems, does provide a better vehicle for women to advance to leadership positions than most other organizational structures. After two or three years of really hard work, I was considered a leader in the labor movement in Washington State.

I became very involved in politics, and started volunteering on campaigns. I got hooked on politics—I think it's the most exciting and fun thing that I do. I've been appointed to three separate boards by three different governors, but I've never had the desire to be an elected official, because I think getting people there is a lot more important than being there myself. I really like helping people put together a viable campaign and then making them stick to some of those campaign promises—I feel that's the most important part of my political work.

I can remember working actively on one political campaign, and yet when they were asking for money, no one ever asked me. Some people think that women never donate money, but that's a lie. Before, there was no expectation of women giving money, but that's changing quickly.

I've learned to start giving 'till it hurts. During the political season, I don't buy new clothes, I don't go out to dinner. I make major commitments to women candidates because I know how important it is.

I think EMILY's List is right on target. They're convincing women to give, to give more, and give consistently. They pick really solid candidates that meet their basic criteria, so you can trust their choices. When I see a candidate is backed by EMILY's List, I'm willing to put money into the campaign.

I used to write a check for $25, because it was easy. Now that same $25 check is always $100, and that's not so easy, but that's almost become a minimum for me. Not because I have so much more to give, but because it's so very important. I'm willing to do it because I know there's another woman who wants to and can't. And we've got to show that women can be a credible group of donors.

I've been in EMILY's List for several years, and I send the annual membership and contribute to three or four campaigns per year. I start at home first, with local races, and then I read the information they send and write checks to women in other states.

I supported Patty Murray, Jolene Unsoeld, I gave money to Carole Moseley-Braun and to Lynn Yeakel. I met Barbara Boxer a number of times and gave her money. I don't just support candidates from my own state because the issues are bigger than any one state. And getting women elected in more and more races helps us all.

I know that nearly $200,000 came into my state alone from women all around the country. So I would be really negligent if I didn't send checks out, too. In order to make the whole thing work, we have to send money out around the country.

My standard donation in a Congressional race is $1,000 in the primary and $1,000 in the general election. I know it sounds crazy, but this year I will give away about 15% of my income. It's a lot, but I feel I'm not really making a sacrifice if it doesn't mean anything to me. Sometimes I write checks, and then say, boy, I hope I can make all my other commitments.

There are times I drag myself out to one of these perfunctory political events, and once I get there I think, you know I really like these people!

These are good, hard working, moral people and I'm glad they're out there doing things. It takes you beyond your own little circle of friends and family, into a broader community. These are people who give of their time freely because they care. They don't even know you, but they care about you and your kids. They're working to make your life a bit better. These are the kind of people I like to know.

## Notes
[1] Ruth Richman, "Special Gifts: Women Put Their Money Where It Really Counts," *Chicago Tribune*, December 13, 1992, p. 1.
[2] Ibid., p. 1. According to research by the Gallup Organization, in 1991 women reported giving 30% less than men did for the same year.
[3] F. Keller Cushing Freeman, "For Women, A Time to Close Philanthropy's Gender Gap," *Chronicle of Philanthropy*, June 2, 1992, p. 6.
[4] The Foundation Center in New York reports only 4.8% of giving was targeted at women's issues in 1991.
[5] National Network of Women's Funds brochure, St. Paul, Minn., 1994, p. 2.
[6] Claudia Dreifus, "Sisters Act," *Town and Country*, May 1, 1994, p. 104.
[7] Alternative funds that offer diverse options for workplace giving include Black United Funds (14 local funds), environmental funds (16 now exist), arts funds (25 are organized), federations of health agencies, and social action funds.
[8] *Shopping for a Better World* (New York, N.Y.: Council on Economic Priorities, 1990).
[9] Joan Flanagan, *The Grass Roots Fundraising Book: How to Raise Money in Your Community* (Chicago: Contemporary Books, 1992).
[10] Joan Flanagan, *The Successful Volunteer Organization: Getting Started and Getting Results in Nonprofit, Charitable, Grassroots and Community Groups* (Chicago: Contemporary Books, 1981).
[11] Kim Klein, *Fundraising for Social Change*, 2nd ed., (Inverness, Calif.: Chardon Press, 1988).
[12] Paul Schneiter and Donald Nelson, *The Thirteen Most Common Fundraising Mistakes* (Washington, D.C.: Taft Corporation, 1982).

# Appendix: Directory
# of Organizations

*Association of Community Organizations for Reform Now (ACORN),* 739 8th Street SE, Washington, DC 20003; 202/547-2500.

*American Federation of State, County, and Municipal Employees (AFSCME),* 1625 L Street NW, Washington, DC 20036; 202/429-1000.

*American Federation of Labor–Congress of Industrial Organizations (AFL–CIO)* Organizing Institute, 1444 Eye Street NW, Washington, DC 20005; 800/848-3021.

*AIDS Action Council,* 1875 Connecticut Avenue NW, Suite 700, Washington, DC 20009; 202/986-1300.

*American Nurses Association Political Action Committee,* 600 Maryland Avenue SW, Suite 100 West, Washington, DC 20024; 202/554-4444.

*America Online,* Suite 200, 8619 Westwood Center Drive, Vienna, VA 22182; 800/827-6364.

*American Association of University Women,* 1111 16th Street NW, Washington, DC 20036; 202/785-7700.

*American Society of Training and Development,* 1640 King Street, Box 1443, Alexandria, VA 22313; 703/683-8100.

*Catholics for a Free Choice,* 1436 U Street NW, Suite 301, Washington, DC 20009; 202/986-6093.

*Center for the American Woman and Politics,* Eagleton Institute of Politics, Rutgers University, New Brunswick, NJ 08901; 908/828-2210.

*Center for Policy Alternatives,* 1875 Connecticut Ave. NW, Suite 710, Washington, DC 20095; 202/387-6030.

*Center for Responsive Governance,* 1000 16th Street NW, Suite 500, Washington, DC 20036; 202/857-0044.

Center for Responsive Politics, 1320 19th Street NW, 7th Floor, Washington, DC 20036; 202/857-0044.

*Center for Women Policy Studies,* 2000 P Street NW, Suite 508, Washington, DC 20036; 202/872-1770.

*Children's Defense Fund,* 25 E Street NW, Washington, DC 20001; 202/628-8787.

*Coalition of Labor Union Women (CLUW),* 1126 16th Street NW, Washington, DC 20036; 202/466-4610.

*Communication Workers of America (CWA),* 501 3rd Street NW, Washington, DC 20001; 202/434-1100.

*Compuserve,* 5000 Arlington Center Blvd., PO Box 20212, Columbus, OH 43220; 800/848-8199.

*Data Center,* 464 19th Street, Oakland, CA 94612; 510/835-4692.

*Democratic National Committee (DNC),* 430 S. Capitol Street SE, Washington, DC 20003; 202/863-8000.

*Essential Information,* PO Box 19405, Washington, DC 20036; 202/387-8030.

*Fairness and Accuracy in Reporting (FAIR),* 130 West 25th Street, New York, NY 10001; 212/633-6700.

*Family Violence Prevention Fund,* 383 Rhode Island Street, Suite 304, San Francisco, CA 94103; 415/252-8900.

*The Fund Raising School,* Indiana University Center on Philanthropy, 550 West North Street, Suite 301, Indianapolis, IN 46202; 800/962-6692.

*Gay and Lesbian Victory Fund,* Candidate Training Institute, 1012 14th Street NW, #707, Washington, DC 20005; 202/VICTORY.

*The Giraffe Project,* PO Box 759, Langley, WA 98260; 206/221-7989.

*Girl Scouts,* 420 5th Avenue, New York, NY 10018; 212/940-7500.

*Grantsmanship Center,* PO Box 17220, Los Angeles, CA 90017; 213/482-9860.

*Gulf Coast Tenants Leadership Development Project,* 533 France Street, Baton Rouge, LA; 504/387-2305.

*Highlander Research and Education Center,* 1959 Highlander Way, New Market, TN 37820; 615/933-3443.

*Interfaith Center on Corporate Responsibility,* 475 Riverside Drive, New York, NY 10115; 212/870-2293.

*Junior League,* 660 First Avenue, New York, NY 10016; 212/683-1515.

*Susan G. Komen Foundation,* 5005 LBJ Freeway, Suite 370, Dallas, TX 75244; 800/IM-AWARE (462-9273).

*League of Women Voters,* 1730 M Street NW, Suite 1000, Washington, DC 20036; 202/429-1965.

*Midwest Academy,* 225 West Ohio Street, Suite 250, Chicago, IL 60610; 312/ 645-6010.

*Ms. Foundation for Women,* 120 Wall Street, 33rd Floor, New York, NY 10005; 212/742-2300.

*National Abortion and Reproductive Rights Action League (NARAL),* 1156 15th Street NW, Suite 700, Washington, DC 20005; 202/973-3000.

*National Association for the Advancement of Colored People (NAACP),* 4805 Mt. Hope Drive, Baltimore, MD 21215; 410/358-8900.

*National Association of Meal Programs,* 206 E Street NE, Washington, DC 20002; 202/547-6157.

*National Association of Social Workers (NASW),* 750 First Street NE, Suite 700, Washington, DC 20002; 202/408-8600.

*National Association of Women in Chambers of Commerce,* PO Box 4552, Grand Junction, CO 81502; 303/242-0075.

*National Black Women's Health Project,* 1237 Ralph David Abernathy Blvd SW, Atlanta, GA 30310; 404/758-9590.

*National Breast Cancer Coalition,* 1707 L Street NW, Suite 1060, Washington, DC 20036; 202/296-7477.

*National Coalition of 100 Black Women,* 300 Park Ave., Suite 200, New York, NY 10022; 212/974-6140.

*National Coalition Against Domestic Violence;* PO Box 18749, Denver, CO 80218; 303/839-1852.

*National Coalition for Nursing Home Reform,* 1224 M Street NW, Suite 301, Washington, DC 20005; 202/393-2018.

*National Committee on Pay Equity,* 1126 16th Street NW, Suite 411, Washington, DC 20036; 202/331-7343.

*National Committee for Responsive Philanthropy,* 2001 S Street NW, Suite 620, Washington, DC 20009; 202/387-9177.

*National Council of La Raza,* 810 1st Street NE, Suite 300, Washington, DC 20002; 202/289-1380.

*National Federation of Republican Women's (NFRW), Campaign Management Schools,* 124 North Alfred Street, Alexandria, VA 22314; 703/548-9688.

*National Gay and Lesbian Task Force (NGLTF),* 2320 17th Street NW, Washington, DC 20009; 202/332-6483.

*National Network of Women's Funds,* 1821 University Avenue, Suite 409N, St. Paul, MN 55104; 612/641-0742.

*National Organization for Women, (NOW),* 1000 16th Street NW, Suite #700, Washington, DC 20036; 202/331-0066.

*National Rainbow Coalition,* 1700 K Street NW, Suite 800, Washington, DC 20006; 202/728-1180.

*National Society of Fund Raising Executives (NSFRE)*, 1101 King Street, Suite 700, Alexandria, VA 22314; 703/684-0410.

*National Training and Information Center*, 810 N. Milwaukee Avenue, Chicago, IL 60622; 312/243-3094.

*National Urban League*, 500 East 62nd Street, New York, NY 10021; 212/310-9000.

*National Wildlife Federation*, 1400 16th Street NW, Washington, DC 20036; 202/797-6800.

*National Women's Political Caucus (NWPC)*, 1275 K Street NW, Suite 750, Washington, DC 20009; 800/729-6972.

*New School for Social Research*, 66 West 12th Street, New York, NY 10011; 212/229-5630.

*Nine to Five, National Association of Working Women*, 614 Superior Ave NW, Cleveland, OH 44113; 216/566-9308.

*Oxfam America*, 26 West Street, Boston, MA 02111; 617/482-1211.

*Parents and Friends of Lesbians and Gays*, PO Box 96519, Washington, DC 20090; 202/638-4200.

*Rainforest Action Network*, 450 Sansome Street, Suite 700, San Francisco, CA 94111; 415/398-4404.

*Republican National Committee (RNC)*, 310 First Street SE, Washington, DC 20003; 202/863-8545.

*Sierra Club*, 730 Polk Street, San Francisco, CA 94109; 415/776-2211.

*The Third Wave*, 185 Franklin Street, New York, NY 10013; 212/925-3400.

*Toastmasters International*, PO Box 9052, Mission Viejo, CA 92690; 714/858-8255.

*U.S. PIRG*, 215 Pennsylvania Avenue SE, Washington, DC 20003; 202/546-9707.

*Women for Racial and Economic Equality*, 198 Broadway, Room 606, New York, NY 10038; 212/385-1103.

*Women in the Senate and House (WISH List)*, 210 West Front Street, Red Bank, NJ 07701; 800/756-9474.

*Women's Action for New Directions (WAND)*, 691 Massachusetts Ave., Arlington, MA 02174; 617/643-6740.

*Women's Campaign Fund (WCF)*, 120 Maryland Avenue NE, Washington, DC 20002; 202/544-4484.

*Women's Community Cancer Project*, c/o The Women's Center, 46 Pleasant Street, Cambridge, MA 02139 Boston; 617/354-9888.

*The Women's Project*, 2224 Main Street, Little Rock, AR 72206; 501/372-5113.

*Working Assets Money Fund*, 230 California Street, San Francisco, CA 94111; 800/933-5764.

*YWCA Institute for Public Leadership (IPL)*, 726 Broadway, New York, NY 10003; 212/614-2779.

# Selected Bibliography

Although some of these titles are out-of-print (OP), they are noteworthy and may be found in libraries.

Aburdene, Patricia and John Naisbitt. *Megatrends for Women*. New York: Villard Books, 1992. Survey of future trends, how women are shaping and benefiting from them.

Alinsky, Saul. *Reveille for Radicals*. New York: Vintage Books, 1969.

————. *Rules for Radicals*. New York: Random House, 1972. The primers on community organizing goals and techniques.

Allen, Cathy. *Political Campaigning—A New Decade: The National Women's Political Caucus Guide to Winning in the 90s*. San Francisco: Packard Press Pacific, 1990. Concise primer on how to run campaigns.

Arrendondo, Lani. *How to Present Like a Pro: Getting People to See Things Your Way*. New York: McGraw Hill, 1991. Useful tips to hone public speaking skills.

Bagdikian, Ben. *The Media Monopoly*, 4th ed. Boston: Beacon Press, 1992. Analysis of the true corporate nature of America's media.

Barnard, Sandie. *Rise Up: A New Guide to Public Speaking*. Englewood Cliffs, N.J.: Prentice-Hall, 1993. A good beginner's resource.

Barnet, Richard J. and Ronald E. Muller. *Global Reach: The Power of Multi-national Corporations*. New York: Simon and Schuster, 1973. The tried and true presentation of corporate America and how this empire overlaps government and media.

Boxer, Barbara and Nicole Boxer. *Strangers in the Senate: Politics and the New Revolution of Women in America.* Washington, D.C.: National Press Books, 1994. An insider's guide to one woman's experiences in the United States Senate.

Boyte, Harry C. *The Backyard Revolution.* Philadelphia: Temple University Press, 1980. Anecdotal accounts of a wide variety of citizen organizations across the country—who they are, and what they do.

Brill, Jack and Allan Reder. *Investing from the Heart: The Guide to Socially Responsible Investments and Money Management.* New York: Crown Publishers, 1992. Essentials of personal money management and the preparation of a personal financial plan. Provides lists of companies by social investment concerns.

Carroll, Susan J., ed. *Women, Black, and Hispanic State Elected Leaders: 1990 Symposium on the State of the States.* New Brunswick, N.J.: Eagleton Institute of Politics, 1991. An honest discussion of challenges facing each group.

Center for Policy Alternatives. *Women's Resource Directory.* Washington, D.C., 1993.

Chomsky, Noam and Edward S. Herman. *Manufacturing Consent: The Political Economy of the Mass Media.* New York: Pantheon Books, 1988. An in-depth and fascinating analysis of the media machine, and how it churns out continued support for United States government policy.

Cohen, Jeff and Norman Solomon. *Adventures in Medialand: Behind the News, Beyond the Pundits.* Monroe, Maine: Common Courage Press, 1994. Press, politics, and government in the United States.

Coss, Claire. *Progressive Activist, Lillian Wald.* New York: Feminist Press, 1989. A fine biography of the woman who founded public health nursing in America.

Council on Economic Priorities. *Shopping for a Better World: A Quick and Easy Guide to Socially Responsible Supermarket Shopping.* New York: Ballantine Books, 1992. A handy reference for checkbook activists.

Cowan, Jessica, ed. *Good Works: A Guide to Careers in Social Change.* New York: Barricade Books, 1991. Wonderful catalog of the range of citizen groups across the United States, who they hire, and how to contact them.

del Kieffer, Donald E. *How to Lobby Congress: A Guide for the Citizen Lobbyist.* New York: Dodd, Mead and Co., 1981. Helpful and concise.

Earth Works Group. *50 Simple Things Kids Can Do to Save the Earth.* Kansas City: Andrews and McMeel, 1990. Explains how using resources affects the world, and how young people can protect the environment.

——— *Kid Heroes of the Environment: Simple Things Real Kids Are Doing to Save the Earth.* Berkeley, Calif.: Earthworks Press, 1991. Inspiring to young people and adults.

EMILY's List. *Thinking of Running for Congress? A Guide for Democratic Women.* Washington, D.C.: EMILY's List, 1991. Designed to help potential women candidates evaluate the political feasibility of the race and make the sound early decisions necessary for a winning campaign.

Evans, S. M. *Born for Liberty: A History of Women in America.* New York: Free Press, 1989. Helpful background to understanding current struggles.

Faludi, Susan. *Backlash: The Undeclared War Against American Women.* New York: Crown, 1991. Finally, a serious writer who reveals the emperor's new clothes. Documented, chronological study of the reprisals women continue to experience by standing up for their rights.

Flanagan, Joan. *The Grass Roots Fundraising Book: How to Raise Money in Your Community.* Chicago: Contemporary Books, 1992. Excellent guide for perfecting organizational fundraising skills.

————. *The Successful Volunteer Organization: Getting Started and Getting Results in Nonprofit, Charitable, Grassroots and Community Groups.* Chicago: Contemporary Books, 1981. The title says it all.

Freedman, Marc. *The Kindness of Strangers: Adult Mentors, Urban Youth, and the New Voluntarism.* San Francisco: Jossey-Bass, 1993. Mentoring as a rewarding volunteer activity.

Garland, Anne Witte. *Women Activists: Challenging the Abuse of Power.* New York: The Feminist Press, 1988. Well-written, moving portrayal of several women who took on the power holders, and what they achieved.

Garvey, Mark, ed. *1994 Writer's Market.* Cincinnati: Writer's Digest Books, 1993. A guide to getting published; where and how to sell what you write.

Gastil, John. *Democracy in Small Groups: Participation, Decision-Making and Communication.* Philadelphia: New Society Publishers, 1993. Alternative, non-hierarchical ways to run meetings and organizations.

Graebler, Ted and David Osborne. *Reinventing Government.* Reading, Mass.: Addison Publishing Co., 1992. Analyzes specific new approaches to running various components of government. Concrete, easy-to-read. Useful in considering ways of running a government or an organization.

Greever, Barry. "The Tactical Investigations for People's Struggles." Reprinted in *Organizing for Social Change: A Manual for Activists in the 1990s.* Bobo, Kim, Jackie Kendall, and Steve Max. Arlington, Va.: Seven Locks Press, 1990. An activists guide, originally published as a pamphlet, to conducting research to assist in organizing.

Greider, William. *Who Will Tell the People?* New York: Simon and Schuster, 1992. Frank, provocative analysis of the political system in America. Who the power players are and how they operate, be it for or against the people.

hooks, bell. *Ain't I a Woman: Black Women and Feminism.* Boston: South End Press, 1981. An enlightening volume by Gloria Watkins.

Horwitt, Sanford D. *Let Them Call Me Rebel: Saul Alinsky, His Life and Legacy.* New York: Knopf, 1989. Subjects covered: radicals in the United

States, the biography of Alinsky, and the history of community organizations in America.

Isaac, Katherine. *Civics for Democracy: A Journey for Teachers and Students.* Washington, D.C.: Essential Books, 1992. Excellent, usable text for high school social studies teachers who understand the importance of teaching citizen activism and empowerment.

Kaminer, Wendy. *Women Volunteering: The Pleasure, Pain and Politics of Unpaid Work from 1830 to the Present.* Garden City, N.Y.: Anchor Press, 1984. An excellent summary of the history of women's volunteer movements in the United States.

Klein, Kim. *Fundraising for Social Change,* 2d ed. Inverness, Calif.: Chardon Press, 1988. A comprehensive guide to the methods and mechanics of fundraising for nonprofit groups.

Kokopeli, Bruce and George Lakey. *Leadership for Change: Toward a Feminist Model.* Philadelphia: New Society Publishers, 1984. Alternative, non-hierarchical leadership models.

Kunin, Madeline. *Living a Political Life.* New York: Knopf, 1994. Reflections by the former governor of Vermont, one of our country's strongest progressive woman role models.

Lansing, Jewel. *101 Campaign Tips for Women Candidates and Their Staff.* Saratoga, Calif.: R & E Publishers, 1991. Universally helpful hints for current or prospective women candidates.

Lauber, Daniel. *The Non-Profit Job Finder.* River Forest, Ill.: Planning/Communications, 1992. Explains how to find the 80% of nonprofit jobs that never get advertised.

Levering, Robert. *The 100 Best Companies to Work for in America.* New York: Currency/Doubleday, 1993. A guide to help you seek employment in a place that is "acceptable" in its treatment of workers, in responsibility to the community, as well as in the product or service it offers the consumer.

Lidenberg, Steven et al. and the Council on Economic Priorities. *Rating America's Corporate Conscience: A Provocative Guide to the Companies Behind the Products You Buy Every Day.* Reading, Mass.: Addison-Wesley, 1986. This book may change your buying habits.

Lorde, Audre. *Cancer Journals.* San Francisco: Spinsters Press, 1980. A collection of poems and prose written during Lourde's struggle with breast cancer.

Lustberg, Arch. *Testifying with Impact.* Washington, D.C.: United States Chamber of Commerce, 1983. A specialized guide to effective speaking at public hearings.

Mandel, Ruth B. *In the Running: The New Woman Candidate.* New Haven: Ticknor and Fields, 1981. First person accounts of women who have campaigned for office, and the difficulties they face.

Margolies-Mezvinsky, Marjorie and Barbara Feinman. *A Woman's Place . . . The Freshmen Women Who Changed the Face of Congress.* New York:

Crown Publishers, 1994. Focuses on what 24 congresswomen faced in their first eight months in office.

Mattison, Georgia and Sandra Storey. *Women in Citizen Advocacy: Stories of 28 Shapers of Public Policy.* Jefferson, N.C.: McFarland and Co., 1992. Illustrates the process as well as the people who create policy.

Morris, Celia. *Storming the Statehouse: Running for Governor with Ann Richards and Dianne Feinstein.* New York: Charles Scribner's Sons, 1992. The inside story of two campaigns.

Nadler, Leonard and Zeace Nadler. *A Comprehensive Guide to Successful Conferences and Meetings: Detailed Instructions and Step-by-Step Checklists.* San Francisco: Jossey-Bass, 1988. A helpful guide for event planners.

National Association of Towns and Townships. *Survival Guide for Elected Leaders.* Washington, D.C., 1994. Geared specifically to public officials serving at the local level. Since these are usually volunteer's jobs, it is helpful to read what others have done, to be able to approach the task better informed.

Nelson, Joyce. *Sultans of Sleaze: Public Relations and the Media.* Monroe, Maine: Common Courage Press, 1993. Describes the behind the scenes maneuvers of the American press—newspapers, television, and radio stations—and the corporations that own them.

Rajoppi, Joanne. *Women in Office: Getting There and Staying There.* New York: Bergin and Garvey, 1993. Useful remarks by one woman who has run for and held office.

Roiphe, Katie. *The Morning After: Sex, Fear and Feminism on Campus.* Boston: Little Brown, 1993. Controversial perspective on acquaintance rape and young women.

Robert, Henry M. *Robert's Rules of Order.* Modern edition completely revised by Darwin Patnode. Nashville: T. Nelson, 1989. Traditional tool for running meetings.

Rosso, Henry A., and Associates. *Achieving Excellence in Fundraising: A Comprehensive Guide to Principles, Strategies, and Methods.* San Francisco: Jossey-Bass, 1991. An excellent guide for serious fundraisers.

Ryan, Charlotte. *Prime Time Activism: Media Strategies for Grassroots Organizing.* Boston: South End Press, 1991. Public relations and politics; political aspects of the mass media. A complete, wonderfully functional manual.

Schneiter, Paul and Donald Nelson. *The Thirteen Most Common Fundraising Mistakes.* Washington, D.C.: Taft Corporation, 1982. It's better to read this book than learn from your own mistakes.

Smucker, Bob. *The Non-Profit Lobbying Guide: Advocating Your Cause and Getting Results.* San Francisco: Jossey-Bass, 1991. Clear and concise tips for first-time lobbyists.

Surbeck, Linda. *Creating Special Events: The Ultimate Guide to Producing Successful Events.* Louisville, Ky.: Master Publications, 1991. Covers promotion and planning of special events.

von Schlegel, Abbie and Dr. Joan M. Fisher, eds. *Women as Donors, Women as Philanthropists.* San Francisco: Jossey-Bass, 1994. An important analysis of the connection between women and money.

Walls, David. *The Activist's Almanac: The Concerned Citizen's Guide to the Leading Advocacy Organizations in America.* New York: Simon and Schuster, 1993. Handy reference manual.

Witt, Linda, Karen M. Paget, and Glenna Matthews. *Running as a Woman: Gender and Power in American Politics.* New York: The Free Press, 1994. In-depth analysis of the underpinnings of women's candidacies; focuses on women who have run for high-level office.

Wolf, Naomi. *Fire with Fire.* New York: Random House, 1993. A must-read for all feminists in the 1990s. Uplifting analysis of how far women have come, and how much further we can go, using political power.

Zinn, Howard. *A People's History of the United States.* New York: Harper and Row, 1980. A comprehensive history text that we should have had access to in high school. America's history told from the perspective of the people rather than merely its leaders. A must for all budding and veteran activists.

## Periodicals

*Chronicle of Philanthropy: The Newspaper of the Non-Profit World,* 1255 23rd St. NW, Washington, DC 20037. Published bi-weekly with regular departments on fundraising and management of nonprofits.

*Community Jobs, The National Employment Newspaper for the Non-Profit Sector,* ACCESS, 50 Beacon Street, Boston, Mass. 02108; 617/720-5627.

*Environmental Career Opportunities.* PO Box 15629, Chevy Chase, Md. 20825; 301/986-5545. A bi-weekly newsletter advertising jobs in the environmental movement.

*Governing,* Times Publishing Co., 2300 N St. NW, Washington, DC 20037; 202/887-6261. Once you are elected, this is a useful monthly for comparing what you're doing with others serving at similar levels of government office.

*The Grassroots Fundraising Journal,* PO Box 11607, Berkeley, Calif. 94701; 510/704-8714. An excellent journal, published six times a year.

*In These Times,* 2040 Milwaukee Ave., Chicago, Ill. 60647; 312/772-0100.

*Multinational Monitor.* Washington, DC: Essential Information, Inc. 202/387-8030. Provides an update on the questionable practices of American corporations at home and abroad. Published monthly.

*The Nation,* PO Box 10763, Des Moines, Iowa, 50340; 800/333-8536.

*Non-Profit Times,* 190 Tamarack Circle, Skillman, N.J. 08558; 609/921-1251. Articles on nonprofit management and trends with regular departments, including Employment Marketplace and Resource Guide.

*Responsible Philanthropy.* Quarterly journal of the National Committee for Responsive Philanthropy, 2001 S St. NW, #620, Washington, D.C. 20009;

202/387-9177. Covers trends in philanthropic support for racial, ethnic, women's, and low-income movements. Write for a complimentary copy.

*Sound Opportunities.* The Northwest's Nonprofit Employment Newsletter, 2708 Elliott Ave. Seattle, Wash. 98121; 206/441-8280.

*Z.* Boston, Mass. Published monthly by the Institute for Social and Cultural Communications. An independent political magazine of critical thinking about political, cultural, social, and economic life in the United States. Subscriptions: 617/787-4531.

# Index

Boldface page numbers indicate main essays.
The letter *q* following a page number indicates a quotation.